CLIMATE LYRICISM

MIN HYOUNG SONG

CLIMATE LYRICISM

DUKE UNIVERSITY PRESS
Durham and London 2022

Printed in the United States of America on acid-free paper ∞
Project editor: Lisa Lawley
Designed by Aimee C. Harrison
Typeset in Garamond Premier Pro and Trade Gothic
by Westchester Publishing Services

Library of Congress Cataloging-in-Publication Data
Names: Song, Min, [date]- author.
Title: Climate lyricism / Min Hyoung Song.
Description: Durham : Duke University Press, 2022. | Includes
bibliographical references and index.
Identifiers: LCCN 2021018231 (print)
LCCN 2021018232 (ebook)
ISBN 9781478015116 (hardcover)
ISBN 9781478017738 (paperback)
ISBN 9781478022350 (ebook)
ISBN 9781478091806 (ebook other)
Subjects: LCSH: Climatic changes in literature. | Literature,
Modern—20th century—History and criticism. | BISAC: LITERARY
CRITICISM / Modern / 21st Century | SOCIAL SCIENCE / Ethnic
Studies / General
Classification: LCC PN56.c612 s664 2022 (print) | LCC PN56.c612
(ebook) | DDC 809/.9336—dc23
LC record available at https://lccn.loc.gov/2021018231
LC ebook record available at https://lccn.loc.gov/2021018232

Cover art: Ed Hawkins (University of Reading), *Warming Stripes for
GLOBE from 1850–2019*. From #showyourstripes (Creative Commons 4.0
license), https://showyourstripes.info/.

This title is freely available in an open access edition made possible by
generous support from Boston College.

FOR JAMES A. WU

CONTENTS

PART III. **URGENCY**

INTRODUCTION

The Practice of Sustaining Attention to Climate Change

WHENEVER I THINK ABOUT CLIMATE CHANGE, which is often, I struggle to make sense of its enormity. So much seems to be at stake. Maybe everything. And there's not a lot of time to try to blunt its most destructive impacts. Yet I don't know if anything I do matters. I feel powerless. I run through the routine of my days, scurrying from one activity to the next while one thought gives way to another in an unrelated jumble, and this is all that my existence seems to amount to, a blur of mere busyness in the shadow of a colossus remaking shorelines, altering the seasons, transforming planetary hydrologic cycles, ending the evolutionary pathways of billions of living beings, and changing the very quality of the air and water. I don't want to dwell on the topic of climate change. I want to focus on the tasks right before me and the easily graspable texture of my immediate surroundings. These seem so much more manageable. It's not that I don't care. I do very much. I just don't know what good thinking about it all the time will do.

Maybe you feel this way too. Maybe, like me, you too want to retreat into the everyday as a kind of refuge. If so, why do you and I feel this way? So much of it comes down to the fact that you and I lack strong models of a *shared agency*. Your ability to act in ways that have the intended effects is in doubt. You don't know how to connect with others and find ways to expand what you can do alone, so that together you can act in a way that makes a difference. Every such act would embolden you more, putting you in a loop. You can feel a power growing as you connect with more and more people and as ideas gain a solidity that you find irresistible. Others feel their pull too. More and more people line up alongside you, as you line up alongside them, to keep pushing to make those ideas real. They are not just full of potential, nor have they entered the realm of the possible. They exist as something more tangible, and you will not be satisfied until they are fully realized.

I want to find ways to democratize agency that break the spell of powerlessness, so that thinking about climate change emboldens rather than leads to a shrinking back. The models of shared agency I am after focus on collective approaches to problem solving. They are mindful of constraints and limitations, because they must be. They are aware that any one form of agency is not the only source of action in the world, and they work actively against notions of a preordained progress and mastery. They decide their own goals and test them out constantly to see if these are the destinations they want. And they keep pushing toward these goals and hopefully in the process become more effective. What I am calling *climate lyricism* refers to this self-conscious working through. It is the striving for a practice that insists, as the philosopher and activist Grace Lee Boggs insisted, that thinking should not be separated from doing.[1] Thinking is itself a form of doing, and doing is a form of thinking. Unfortunately, the two separate easily from one another, as in an idyllic thinking or a mindless doing, and so what is needed in response is a consciously created routine that makes each partner to the other.

Such a practice has to be *sustaining* because momentum needs feeding to keep an activity going. *Attention* itself has to be cultivated again and again, not merely given to an object in a moment of abrupt realization. The practice of sustaining attention to climate change that climate lyricism seeks to build up thus refers to a perpetual project of making yourself and others aware of the changes occurring in the physical world in its myriad manifestations. In the process, you and others together physically and mentally work out how to survive, and even flourish ?, in the midst of such changes.

Climate lyricism begins by turning anthropocentric habits of expression (especially the kind developed alongside the growth of European settler colonialism) back on themselves, so that the nonhuman is given human characteristics and asserts the kinds of powers that humans are traditionally thought to be the only ones capable of possessing. In this way, the distinction between human and nonhuman becomes fuzzy and challenges the usual hierarchy of value that always privileges the well-being of the human over the nonhuman and that overrepresents some humans at the expense of others. Climate lyricism is also an attention to expression itself, to consider how innovations in speech, address, image, sound, and movement call forth shifting ways of apprehending a phenomenon that eludes familiar scales of comprehension. It is finally—a criterion that I hadn't thought of when I first used the phrase but that has since become essential for me—a demand for a response. Whatever knowledge any reading might produce is engaged in a practice that requires collective engagement and a commitment to what is shared. For this last reason, I want to focus on the idea of human agency as needing nurturing. While it is obviously dangerous to overestimate the power of human agency, there is also grave danger in underestimating it.

As I have tried to develop this concept, my ambitions for it have grown. Much is known about climate change, but much more remains a mystery that everyone has a role in figuring out. Even in the presence of such a mystery, mitigation and adaptation are required, both actions that are as much about making meaning as they are about making dramatic social, political, economic, and infrastructural transformations. Paying attention and sharing what has been observed are actions, just as much as scientific research, activism, and the Hydra-like task of reorganizing how human societies operate. *Climate lyricism* thus names both an active mode of making (trying to write literature that is relevant to an understanding of the environmental troubles plaguing the present) and an active mode of attending (making sense of how literature, regardless of its manifest content, might have something relevant to say about these troubles).

I am thus claiming for the study of literature a prominent role in developing a practice of sustaining attention. Climate change operates in a temporality that is not synchronous with human habits of thinking about time and in a space that is not commensurate with human inhabitation. It is occurring everywhere and nowhere in particular and in both short durations and impossibly long expanses of time. Also, many powerful bad actors are poisoning what is said and can be said about the subject. They deny it is happening, impugn those who want to call attention to it, and work against the solutions that are most likely to address its many challenges. These factors gum up familiar strategies for maintaining attention, many of which are associated with the art of fiction and as a result require creativity, experimentation, and a deliberate willingness to wrestle with existing forms in order to imagine new ones.

At the risk of sounding reductive but with the advantage of providing clarity, the strategies for holding attention associated with fiction can be described as including the following steps:

- Create a handful of compelling characters.
- Put them in a unique situation, and place before them a challenging dilemma.
- Differentiate between characters who are driven to overcome this dilemma and characters who (or situations that) exacerbate that dilemma or pose new dilemmas.
- Allow conflict to play itself out in patterns of defeat and triumph, betrayal and collaboration, despair and hope.
- Hold out the promise that some final resolution is coming.

The promise of resolution, in particular, is important, because no matter what the dilemma, there is always an attainable goal toward which the characters can work. As pleasurable and as compelling as these narrative elements are (especially in the surprise breaking of these conventions), these strategies are difficult to maintain when protagonists and antagonists are mixed up, and the divide between them is hard to perceive; when the situation is diffused and involves billions of unique individuals; and when no actions so far have succeeded in dramatically lowering greenhouse gas emissions and keeping them trending in that direction.

In the scrambling of such habituated attention, concerns about economic precarity and feelings of cultural dislocation dominate, with little incentive to consider how they might be connected to worsening ecological processes. Anger is thus directed elsewhere, and there is no shortage of others who can—more easily than wealthy and well-connected executives—be made the villains of present-day morality plays, such as undocumented immigrants or Black criminals or Muslim foreigners. If everything feels as if it is unraveling, and life for many is becoming impossible to live, it must be the fault of some menacing, shadowy racial Other. This is the shout of the demagogues to willing ears.

In opposition to such lines of thought, I single out the lyric because it is a mode of literary attentiveness with special properties—such as compression of expression, a heavy investment in apostrophe, the careful observation of what is observable in language, a probing of what comprises the human—that many writers are taking advantage of, and remaking, in productive ways. I focus especially on what I call a *revived lyric* (inspired by Hoa Nguyen's poem "Up Nursing"), which is not concerned with the spotlighting of an individual "I" or the exploration of a profound psychic interior, with which the lyric is often associated, but focuses instead on the space between a first-person speaker and a second-person addressee.[2]

Cathy Park Hong touches on this notion of the revived lyric in her book of personal essays on being an Asian American and a poet when she observes, "The lyric, to me, is a stage, a pedestal from which I throw my voice to point out what I'm not (the curse of anyone nonwhite is that you are so busy arguing what you're not that you never arrive at what you are)."[3] While this might sound like the exploration of psychic interiority, especially in the parenthetical "what you are," the emphasis is emphatically on the apostrophe: "I throw my voice." This leads to a difficult exchange, often one sided, because the apostrophe isn't always answered, and often irresolvable, because so much work is required to fend off characterizations of the self that are meant to demean. Nevertheless, the "I" and the unspoken "you" to whom the voice is thrown are in a relationship. The "I" and the "you" seek to discover what they have in common, what forms this commonality can take, what aspirations they want to work toward and even fight for together, and what kinds of shared agency are possible. The lyric, moreover, stages such explorations with a focus on wreckage. It recognizes loss and absence as constitutive rather than aberrant. As Hong writes when she returns to the topic of the lyric, "The lyric as ruin is an optimal form to explore the racial condition, because our unspeakable losses can be captured through the silences built into the lyric fragment."[4]

The development of a revived lyric has been led by poets and fiction writers who are *minor* in some way—characterized, that is, by what Sianne Ngai describes as a "deficit of power."[5] Their works aren't always the obvious choices for a discussion on literature and climate change, because more often than not they are focused on the topic of race and related subjects. For me, what makes them interesting for a study on literature and climate change is that they demand attunement to the everyday in original, and often-estranging, ways that made me, when I read them, more aware of the extraordinary that is all around me. Too often, climate change is imagined as happening somewhere far away and in an always deferrable future, and as a result it is difficult to grasp the ways in which it is occurring in the here and now.

For instance, the Pulitzer Prize–winning journalist Elizabeth Kolbert's thoughtful book on the science of climate change, first published in 2006, begins with the observation, "Such is the impact of global warming that I could have gone to hundreds if not thousands of other places—from Siberia to the Austrian Alps to the Great Barrier Reefs to the South African fynbos— to document its effects. These alternate choices would have resulted in an account very different in its details, but not in its conclusions."[6] She leaves out the possibility that she could have just stayed at home. The effects of global warming (which is what climate change in the present is) are everywhere, and no one has to go far to find them, much like the effects of racism, and yet the choices Kolbert offers for where she might have gone to report on her story are many far-flung places, which—no doubt unintentionally—reinforces the idea that this phenomenon is largely happening elsewhere, distant from a largely U.S.-based readership.[7]

The distant and the close-by are imagined anew in the many works I discuss in this book, and the past is never just past. These works are multitudinous, multiracial, and multimodal, and operate as an archive for thinking with climate lyricism on what is shared and the power that can come from sharing. This archive includes poets like Claudia Rankine, Craig Santos Perez, Sally Wen Mao, Ilya Kaminsky, Tommy Pico, Ed Roberson, Aimee Nezhukumatathil, M. NourbeSe Philip, Layli Long Soldier, Li-Young Lee, Frank O'Hara, Bernadette Mayer, Ada Límon, Solmaz Sharif, and many more; novelists like Amitav Ghosh, Richard Powers, Kazuo Ishiguro, Teju Cole, Kim Stanley Robinson, N. K. Jemisin, Jeff VanderMeer, Jenni Fagan, Jenny Offill, Pitchaya Sudbanthad, George Saunders, J. M Coetzee, Han Kang, Khaled Khalifa, and, again, many more; and David Bowie.

Reading their poetry and fiction (and listening to their songs) *for* climate change can act as a powerful mnemonic for attention. This mnemonic—a way of fixing in memory what I should always be on the lookout for—grows more powerful by closely attending to specific works and examining large numbers of them, each reinforcing the other and adding to an ever louder claim on thought. This is why I make it a point to name so many authors here and to refer to many more in what follows. Their multitude offers occasion after occasion for readers who are purposefully attuned to the topic of climate change to reflect on what is happening to the physical world around them and how these changes affect the very fabric of their everyday experiences. They help create a hum that pierces perception, intertwines with daily activities, and makes living with climate change not only perceptible but a matter of what Kandice Chuh, following Immanuel Kant's lead, calls a "sensus communis."[8] This living is built into the very act of breathing and moving through space and social interaction. It depends on what Ronak Kapadia describes as making "sensuous what has been ghosted by U.S. technologies of abstraction."[9]

I make it a point as well to move back and forth across racial, ethnic, and national divides in my readings. I do so *not* because I believe such divides are insignificant. They reflect long histories of struggle, unrest, and abuse that tie the present and the future to the past in ways that can't be ignored—in ways that make the past alive now and in the time to come. I want to think with these divides, to consider how they yield surprising moments of contact, occasions for collaboration, recognitions of likenesses. This doesn't mean that such alliances come easily. It does mean that conditions exist for some form of conviviality to be nurtured, with *conviviality* naming a lowered bar of experiencing social togetherness and working alongside one another that enhances the power I can exercise alone.[10]

Julie Sze's *Environmental Justice in a Moment of Danger* dramatizes how this can happen. It links Native American–led activists protesting the Dakota Access Pipeline in the name of water protection with the residents of Flint, Michigan, afflicted by a lead-poisoned water supply. Next, Sze considers the parallels between the majority African American population in Flint and the largely Latinx residents of California's agricultural Central Valley, both struggling for the right to clean water, greater political control over their local communities, and corporate press coverage, which is needed but can be fickle and simplifying. And then she considers how the state responded to the devastation caused by Hurricane Katrina and Hurricane Maria. The former, Sze observes, "set the template for how race and class sharpen the negative impacts of environmental disasters, both in disaster planning and in the racialized aftermath of privatized 'recovery.'" As a result, Katrina "opens the era" of devastating Atlantic storms made worse by negligent housing and retail development, destruction of wetlands, and environmental racism, while "Maria mirrors and exemplifies it."[11] As these examples suggest, divisions don't just divide. They also make solidarities possible. They make the distant and the close-by look contiguous on a map. They enable recognition of a shared struggle in ways that at first might not be apparent.

Just as important, the literary works I discuss in this book, especially those written from minor perspectives, lead me to consider how attention to the everyday itself is not possible without recognition of the legacies of conquest, racism, exploitation, and extraction that are everywhere. The phenomenon of climate change does not exist in isolation from these histories but is very much an inextricable product of them. Reading for climate change, then, continues work in race and ethnic studies and in particular in Asian American studies, which are the academic fields I have long been a part of and have learned the most from.

Consider the work of Mel Chen, for instance, which foregrounds how humans are curtailed by the animacy of objects that scramble the assumed hierarchies of human language. The *human* does not name a simple category; humans are set off from one another in fundamental ways: "Animacy hierarchies slip and give, but they do not do so willy-nilly; I have suggested that they slip in particular privileged terms of sexuality, race, and ability."[12] The centrality of these issues resists a flattening of ontology.

Consider as well the work of Dean Itsuji Saranillio, who, in a carefully researched account of how Hawai'i became a state, is keenly aware of how his understanding of history haunts dominant accounts of the human in narratives of progress: "Extreme weather patterns, rising sea levels, the warming of the planet, and nonhuman extinctions all tell us that the fail-forward pattern of settler colonialism and capitalism has hit a limit.... This calls for a critical engagement with the past and present as a means to produce alternative futures to the settler state. It means to understand economic crises as an abstraction that makes the primacy of the ecological crises seemingly secondary."[13] This analysis gestures toward the need both to prioritize environmental concerns *and* to understand how they trouble powerful forms of narrative that are constantly trying to organize history as the chronicle of an unavoidable movement from a primitive past to an ever more civilized future (with *civilized* defined in very narrow prescriptive and proscriptive terms). Such narratives of progress rob people of their sense of agency, for they insist that the flow of historical events follows a fixed path that cannot be altered by those in that path. That some, like the Kānaka 'Ōiwi, or native Hawaiians, are trampled by such progress becomes, then, sad but unavoidable. Against this kind of narrative arc, Saranillio's approach seeks to find in the past alternatives to the world as it is now. Such alternatives speak to a potential that remains active. They refuse foreclosure and claims of inevitability and carve out opportunities for more groups of people to have more influence on the shape of their lives.

At stake in such a narrative is the image of "Man" as both the main protagonist and the destination of a narrative of progress. Chuh describes this propensity as accepting "the sovereignty and autochthony of the human even as—or precisely because—it justifies the conquest and dispossession, enslavement and eradication that constitute the course of liberalism in its intimate partnership with capitalism."[14] If so, what ideas of the human emancipated from "liberalism's grasp" and not defined by Man are possible? Aimee Bahng focuses on members of the "undercommons" who "refuse to participate in, and are denied access to, the ladder of corporate productivity and take comfort instead in forms of kinship and occupation that survive alongside and below the radar of freewheeling global entrepreneurialism."[15] All of this is to say that, as LeiLani Nishime and Kim D. Hester Williams insist, "race is inextricable from our understanding of ecology, and vice versa."[16]

I worry, however, that the notion of the undercommons does not do much to build up a sense of shared agency. I am fascinated by the idea that those who are disenfranchised can find ways to extract back from institutions that hoard resources the means necessary for their survival, but *how* can the disenfranchised do this? And how can they share and maintain such resources so that more people can benefit and become more empowered? It seems to me that for the idea of an undercommons to find material shape, it needs purposeful exertion, and so I find it noteworthy that Stefano Harney and Fred Moten, who first coined the term, do not have much to say about agency, nor do they seem to have a high opinion of the idea: "What the beyond of teaching is really about is not finishing oneself, not passing, not completing; it's about allowing subjectivity to be unlawfully overcome by others, a radical passion and passivity such that one becomes unfit for subjection, because one does not possess the kind of agency that can hold the regulatory forces of subjecthood, and one cannot initiate the auto-interpellative torque that biopower subjection requires and rewards."[17] Some subjects certainly have access to agency in a way that other subjects do not. But the recognition of such dramatic inequality seems to lead to a prizing of passivity and a suspicion of all agency. The undercommons, then, names a desire to disengage from existing institutions.

Maybe these institutions are beyond repair (there is a lot of convincing evidence), but what is the vision for what will replace them if they must be dismantled? In the preface to Harney and Moten's book, Jack Halberstam claims, "We cannot say what new structures will replace the ones we live with yet, because once we have torn shit down, we will inevitably see more and see differently and feel a new sense of wanting and being and becoming."[18] I have no faith that an ideal set of social relations will magically be imaginable only after the existing institutions have been taken down. A surer path, it seems to me, is to work to build the structures you want and to see where these structures lead you. I am inspired by the work of the community organizer Mariame Kaba, who describes her efforts toward the abolition of the prison-industrial complex to be profoundly creative. Such efforts, she writes, constitute "a positive project that focuses, in part, on building a society where it is possible to address harm without relying on structural forms of oppression or the violent systems that increase it." The question that guides this work, then, is, as Kaba continues, "What can we imagine for ourselves, and the world?"[19]

The skepticism that surrounds this kind of positivity is where race and ethnic studies (alongside queer studies) might find too much overlap with prominent scholarly and literary work on the human as inextricably entangled with the nonhuman. Elsewhere I describe the *new materialisms* as a "loose confederation of intellectual trends" that grow out of "frustration, if not hostility, toward arguments about a reality that is merely a consequence of our linguistic and cultural mediations."[20] This loose confederation addresses what Diana Coole and Samantha Frost describe as "fundamental questions about the nature of matter and the place of embodied humans within a material world."[21] Led by figures like Donna Haraway, Bruno Latour, Jane Bennett, Timothy Morton, and Stacy Alaimo, who represent significant differences in foci and a wide range of disciplinary backgrounds, the intellectual movements of the new materialisms have emphasized the existence of a physical world separate from human perceptions of it and in the process have questioned the power of human agency.

Things are understood to exert their own kind of agentic power. The human, as a result, has to be humbled, so as not to be the sole source of mastery and dominion—which is why, perhaps clumsily on my part, these two sentences have been written in the passive voice. Humans are kin to a dazzling variety of living forms (Haraway); are constrained by the small power of multitudinous actants (Latour); are enmeshed in networks of distributed agency that confound attempts to lay blame (Bennett); are caught in hyperobjects that are so unfathomable in scale they can barely be apprehended, if at all (Morton); and are dissolved into their surroundings in ways that defy mapping (Alaimo).[22] The variety of these arguments is tremendous, but they trend toward a way of thinking that returns the human to a world of animistic possibilities, of limited control, and of a will—usually alienated from itself—that must constantly negotiate with a complex being for what it needs and wants.

Arguments like these have gained substantial prominence. Consider *The Great Derangement: Climate Change and the Unthinkable*, a widely cited book on climate change, literature, history, and politics by the celebrated author Amitav Ghosh. "Who can forget those moments," he asks on the first page, "when something that seems inanimate turns out to be vitally, even dangerously alive?"[23] Such moments lead people to glimpse a world where human action occurs in intimate collaboration with the objects and things around them. This world also tempers claims of human mastery with the realization that these objects and things have an animacy that constrains, redirects, and exerts force over action of any kind.

This is the very world that the narrator of Ghosh's novel *Gun Island*, which was published after *The Great Derangement*, is plunged into. Deen is a dealer of antique books who is somehow asked to track down the origins of an obscure Bengali folktale; the tale focuses on a seventeenth-century trader who was forced from his home in the Sundarbans by environmental calamities (explicitly associated with the Little Ice Age) and who traveled the northern regions of the Indian Ocean and the eastern regions of the Mediterranean in search of refuge.[24] Several people help Deen in his quest to make sense of the origins of this tale, but none so much as Cinta, a famous retired Italian historian of Venice.

Cinta gets the most important lines in the novel, as she connects the old folktale to what's happening in the present. The novel is not shy about chronicling some of these effects. Climate change makes extreme weather events—like Cyclone Amphan, which occurred just a year after the publication of the novel—more commonplace, renders the Sundarbans an ever more precarious place to live, sets afloat an increasing number of migrants, and expands the range of dangerous animals and insects. She says to Deen:

> Everybody knows what must be done if the world is to continue to be a livable place, if our homes are not to be invaded by the sea, or by creatures like that spider, and yet we are powerless, even the most powerful among us. We go about our daily business through habit, as though we were in the grip of forces that have overwhelmed our will; we see shocking and monstrous things happening all around us and we avert our eyes; we surrender ourselves willingly to whatever it is that has us in its power.[25]

This passage makes explicit the kind of thinking that seems to be gaining ground in literary discussions about climate change and resonating beyond its disciplinary borders, as if the study of literature is an amplifier of such ideas. Humans ramble through their days, stuck in patterns they can barely perceive through a somnolent gaze, aware at best that they are witnessing one extraordinary event after another but unable ultimately to integrate this knowledge into their daily lives and, worse, unable to intervene in any way. The extraordinary and the daily are incompatible. They lack control even over their own lives.

Gun Island imagines the glimpsing of this state of being as a violent experience. Cinta again explains, "That is why whatever is happening to you is not a 'possession.' Rather I would say that it is a *risveglio*, a kind of awakening. It may be dangerous of course, but that is because you are waking up to things that you had never imagined or sensed before."[26] This idea of an awakening is old, already ancient when Henry David Thoreau invoked it in *Walden* ("To be awake is to be alive. I have never yet met a man who was quite awake. How could I have looked him in the face?"), and remains integral to the view of the world that the new materialisms offer.[27] Eyes must be opened, and it is the work of literature in particular to make such an opening possible so that readers may comprehend more clearly what there is to be comprehended rather than the illusions that ordinarily occupy their senses.[28]

I've learned a lot from these arguments, some more than others, but I am deeply concerned about the political implications of a way of thinking that depends so much on the turn away from human agency. This way of thinking tends to assume humans have too inflated an idea of their power, which leads them to make reckless decisions and enact changes to their environment with a careless disregard for consequences. For those who have made most of the decisions that have led to the current moment of environmental danger, a humbling would be beneficial for the environment. Ironically, this same humbling can be highly reassuring for the same people. Agency itself is so complex that responsibility becomes impossible to adjudicate. Thus, if humans lack agency, they can't be responsible for the outcome of their decisions and actions.

One result of this attitude toward human agency is, as Heather Houser puts it, a decoupling of "responsibility and agency."[29] Eva Haifa Giraud makes a similar point when she reasons, "Though it might be important to recognize the nuances of a given situation, this can also make it difficult to determine where culpability for particular situations really lies, let alone offer a sense of how to meet any ethical responsibilities emerging from these situations."[30] For the vast majority of humans, then, many of whom have fought ferociously for the basic right to be called human and have questioned what this right might mean, an inflated idea of their power is not a problem they must overcome. The idea that, as Houser again puts it, "some actors are more accountable than others" is also an important prerequisite for political struggle as humans seek to understand why the world is the way it is and who has helped to create and uphold its inequalities.[31] Similarly, the insistence on a weak human agency leads to the very compelling question, What's the point of knowing if what needs to be done can't be done?

From the latter, much more populous vantage point, the attitude toward human agency that Anna Kornbluh dubs "anarcho-vitalism" does not seem very appealing. This attitude treats formlessness as "the ideal uniting a variety of theories, from the mosh of the multitude to the localization of microstruggle and microaggression, from the voluntarist assembly of actors and networks to the flow of affects untethered from constructs, from the deification of irony and incompletion to the culminating conviction that life springs forth without form and thrives in form's absence."[32] For Kornbluh, what is most troubling about this exaltation of formlessness is its implicit idealization of powerlessness. This exaltation encourages people to take on the role Ghosh's novel assigns to Deen. As mostly spectators, they do not participate in the making of the scenes that are unfolding around them, of which they are inextricably a part, for attempts to make seem to lead to unforeseeable human-inspired destructive consequences. Human agency is wielded in one way, available to specific classes of persons, and is as a result suspect. The only ethical role for anyone, then, is a sad witnessing of events as they unfold—if, that is, they are even lucky enough to attain such a level of awareness—and, at most, a tearing down of everything.

The belief that drives this prizing of powerlessness grants nature, or some idea like nature, the ability to repair what humans have damaged. In Richard Powers's acclaimed novel *The Overstory*, the much-respected scientist and widely read author Patricia Westerford, a character who seems modeled after Rachel Carson, tells an audience, "The 'environment' is alive—a fluid, changing web of purposeful lives dependent on each other."[33] Nonhuman life maintains itself, and so what is the human role in helping this life regain a health that human activities have damaged? Westerford writes in one of her books, "The best and easiest way to get a forest to return to any plot of cleared land is to do nothing—nothing at all, and do it for less time than you might think."[34] Near the end of the novel, as if following this way of thinking to its logical conclusion, Westerford gives a talk about the "single best thing you can do for the world." As a finale, she plans to kill herself.[35]

Against the idea that, to address the environmental crises human activity has wrought, humans should "do nothing" and maybe even cease to exist, Kornbluh proposes a different approach, one that gives literary studies a significant role:

> We live in destructive times, on an incinerating planet, over institutional embers, around prodigious redundancy between the plunder of the commons and the compulsive echolalia "Burn it all down." Theory must prepare to build things up, and literature models that building. . . . Our skills of understanding the composition of made things must be turned to the work of celebrating making. Humanists, too, are makers, equipped for the task of constructing new togetherness, new compositions, new orders, and to sustaining those formations in time and space.[36]

It's weird for me to observe this, given my focus on feelings of powerlessness, but it should be obvious. Humans collectively wield an enormous—though not absolute—agency. This agency, derived from the highly complex organization of human labor (its purposeful form), has transformed the physical world again and again and is now transforming it in a way that might make large parts of the planet uninhabitable for humans and many other life-forms because it serves the single-minded pursuit of generating profit. The signs are everywhere of the power of this agency, and of its abuse, so much so that the very claim that there is a wilderness that exists somehow beyond the reach of human intervention should seem ideologically suspect.

And yet for many people—if not most people—agency *is* weak; the ability to direct this agency, like capital, has itself been concentrated among a small number of powerful individuals and institutions. While some have more agency than others, contingent on factors like race, class, nationality, region, gender and gender identity, and sexuality, most people's power is much weaker than the power commanded by a few. It's also possible that much greater exertions of a collective human agency are required as environmental damage increases and the climate is thrown more wildly out of balance, so no matter how powerful human agency is in the aggregate, it may not be powerful enough to respond to the forces it has unleashed.

To realize that collective human agency is strong, if increasingly hindered, while personal human agency is often very weak and distributed in a heavily lopsided manner, and to strategize ways of redistributing an overly concentrated human agency so as to democratize it does not require a startling risveglio, as Cinta insists in *Gun Island*. Rather, it requires a practice of doing and thinking, which together "build things up," to borrow Kornbluh's phrase. The practice of sustaining attention to climate change that I want to *build up*, then, seeks to found habits of thought and action that together contribute to a strengthening of shared agency.

In the chapters that follow, I court overfamiliarity and prescription by addressing the reader as "you," *as if* you are here before me, across a table, preferably in a pleasant room or even in an outside café on a sunny cool day, possibly drinking some coffee or "having a Coke," to borrow a phrase from the title of Frank O'Hara's famous poem.[37] It's also *as if* you and I are chatting with each other, and I am saying, perhaps obnoxiously, ruining the moment, making it a lot less fun: Look at this novel or this poem, consider how it relates to your experience of the everyday, feel how fucked up the everyday has become, even more so than before; of course, the everyday has been this way for a long time, the very mention of a Coke should remind you of this, but climate change is making everything worse; don't shy away from how bad this makes you feel, stay with it, stay with the full range of all of your emotions, live your life as if all of this matters, linger over how marvelous the experience of living is, and try to find others to share this experience, so that you can take some comfort in not being alone, so that together you and others can find ways to make a difference.

I write in the second person because I am asking, alongside the lyric, what you and I have in common. This commonality is forged in recognition of a shared struggle and not in trying to ignore entrenched divides in the name of a universal sameness. This commonality is founded on the belief that my well-being, and maybe even my very survival, is bound up with yours. I am asking, What kinds of shared futures can you and I imagine and bring into the realm of the possible, despite a highly organized investment in business as usual? I am asking, How can you and I together make more livable worlds by making use of an agency that gets stronger the more use it gets and the more people find ways to make use of it?

These are not easy questions to address for many very compelling reasons. I avoid using the first person plural as much as possible (it's used once in the middle of the book and again at the end) in order to foreground the challenges of answering these questions and to take seriously all the impediments that exist in striving to form publics, coalitions, and sustaining bonds of solidarity explicitly around the topic of climate change. I advocate for engaging the struggle as a daily practice.

PART I

SCOPE

WHAT IS DENIAL?

Kazuo Ishiguro's *Never Let Me Go*, Teju Cole's *Open City*,
and Sally Wen Mao's "Occidentalism"

TAKE A MOMENT TO PUZZLE OVER how well written Kazuo Ishiguro's
novel *Never Let Me Go* is, not only because it's pleasurable to do so but because
it offers a vivid, if indirect, way to contemplate the everyday denial of climate
change. The novel starts slow and eases readers into a world that the narrator
takes her time describing. Partly, the patient unrolling reflects who Kathy H,
or Kath, is as a person (what the *H* stands for is never explained). She is extremely cautious about the way she speaks. She doubts herself and her authority a lot. She wants very much to be right and not say anything that might be
misleading or give the wrong impression. She is there for others, even when
they are failing her. Here's a typical passage that exemplifies these traits: "This
was all a long time ago so I might have some of it wrong; but my memory of it
is that my approaching Tommy that afternoon was part of a phase I was going
through around that time—something to do with compulsively setting myself challenges—and I'd more or less forgotten all about it when Tommy
stopped me a few days later."[1]

Notice the foregrounding of the faultiness of Kath's memory ("I might
have some of it wrong"), the insistence that her version is subjective ("my
memory of it"), the apologetic aside contextualizing what happened in
some mitigating circumstance ("a phase I was going through"), the project

to improve herself that's at once ill defined and self-pathologizing ("something to do with"), the several self-referential movements of the prose that consistently undermine her authority ("I might," "my memory," "I was," "I'd more or less"), and the ways in which she places herself in a position of innocence ("I'd more or less forgotten"). She has little memory of the incident even though, years later, she recalls it with perfect clarity. In this way, Kath, a product of the experimental British boarding school Hailsham, reflects her training in the very way she speaks to her readers, for what the instructors at the school teach their pupils is to think before they speak, to question what they think they know, and to choose every word spoken with care. Only later do the readers discover that what at first appears like precision turns out to be obfuscation.

Readers are thus brought to the truth slowly, in circles, allowing them a plausible excuse for their naivete and confusion at every turn even as they become aware of *what* these students are. Only at the end of the novel, when her former teacher, or guardian (as teachers are called at Hailsham), explains everything to them with brutal candor, are Kath and Tommy, the love of her life, forced to admit what they haven't been able to admit to themselves. There is no deferral. The rumors that Hailsham students are special because if they fall deeply and truly in love with one another, they can put off the inevitable are just that, unsubstantiated wishful thinking. Like all the other clones they know, they will soon have their organs systematically harvested until they die. Or, in the language of the novel, until they "complete." They are also told in the same crushing encounter that the art the school had collected when they were young was being exhibited to the public as proof that clones have souls.

Even after this encounter, when she is forced to confront the harsh facts of her existence, Kath seems to retreat into elegy, making the novel's end poignant. Kath tells her readers, in words that practically hum with restrained beauty and longing, "I was thinking about the rubbish, the flapping plastic in the branches, the shore-line of odd stuff caught along the fencing, and I half-closed my eyes and imagined this was the spot where everything I'd ever lost since my childhood had washed up, and I was now standing here in front of it."[2] When I read these words, I'm mystified as to whether she has fully acknowledged the brutality of the system she and her friends have been caught up in or whether she is still practicing her impressive learned obfuscation. Throughout this narrative Kath not only is immersed in a complex state of denial but also works hard to maintain herself in this state.

The following seeks to catalog the varieties of denial that are at work in *Never Let Me Go* and to consider how much denial itself is an active state. It's not just something that is done to you. Nor is it something you accept only once. It's a constant choosing, a turning away from the world as it is. To help in this task, I draw on the work of the sociologist Stanley Cohen and the anthropologist Kari Norgaard (whose work led me to Cohen). The chapter then considers Teju Cole's novel *Open City*, which demonstrates how even the most worldly and observant figure can fall into one or more of these states of denial and as a result contribute to a sense of the everyday devoid of concern for climate change. In this latter section, I am interested in the ways in which the cosmopolitan observer replicates the scientism of present-day climate change skepticism. In the name of science, the facts of climate change are put into doubt by insisting on an ultimately unscientific level of certainty. A short discussion of Sally Wen Mao's poem "Occidentalism" concludes the chapter, as it suggests a relationship to the treasures of the past that might be liberating, an alternative to clinging too hard to denial in its multiple forms.

Never Let Me Go and *Open City* were published within a few years of each other, in 2005 and 2011 respectively, at a time when scholars and activists increasingly associated the problem of denial with the political stalemate surrounding climate change.[3] Even as emissions continued to rise at an accelerating rate, attention to the problem lingered at the margins of public policy debates, especially in the United States but not only there. It makes sense, given the ways in which denial became identified as an acute problem that needed to be addressed, that these novels would reflect on this problem. Their authors may not have intended to do this, but these novels' focus on the ways in which what is known is also simultaneously not known provides insight into the ways in which climate change has been similarly constructed as a fact acknowledged and unacknowledged. The primary purpose of this chapter, then, is to provide a precise vocabulary for talking about what denial is. Denial is the problem that I am tasking the revived lyric with addressing, and so I want to explain what denial is.

LITERAL, INTERPRETIVE, IMPLICATORY

Stanley Cohen offers a helpful rubric for thinking about denial. He argues that when the focus is on the content of what is being denied ("the *what*"), there is "the dictionary definition: the assertion that something did not happen or is not true."[4] Examples of such a literal denial of facts with regard to climate change in particular abound. The Chinese made it up. There's no scientific consensus. It's a fiction scientists invented to get more funding for their research. The climate is always changing and will revert back to the norm given time. It would be arrogant to believe humans can affect something as vast as the planet's ecology. These statements are provably false and are spread with the intention to drown out claims that are widely supported by extensive scientific research.

There is never any hint in *Never Let Me Go* that Hailsham is involved in this crudest and most superficial type of denial. Hailsham does its work in subtler ways. It leans heavily on what Cohen calls "interpretive" denial: "the raw facts (something happened) are not being denied. Rather, they are given a different meaning from what seems apparent to others."[5] When the children are taught to use words like *guardian*, *donate*, *carer*, and *complete*, the facts aren't refused, but they aren't fully acknowledged either. And when the children are encouraged to discuss the great works of British literature and the activity of making art, there is a subtle acceptance of ideas of the human that exclude them. As Tommy and Kath recall years later, a guardian told a student "that things like pictures, poetry, all that kind of stuff . . . *revealed what you were like inside*. She said *they revealed your soul*."[6]

Likewise, when news reports observe that a hurricane cuts northeast across the Gulf Coast and slams into the Florida Panhandle in a way that has rarely, if ever, been observed before, as happened in the fall of 2018, they might give readers every detail about its wind speed, the tidal wave that preceded it, the amount of property damage it left behind, responses from local officials, and the path the storm continued to take after it made landfall. All the raw facts are in such stories, and yet they are silent about the probable connections such a major hurricane has to climate change.[7] Such omissions are accompanied, in both news reporting and common speech, by breathless descriptive phrases like *freak storm*, *unusual weather*, *once in a lifetime*, *once in a century*, or even *once in five hundred years*. While the intent might be to emphasize severity, the stress falls on the singularity of the event—even as the evidence suggests such an event is becoming less singular.

No wonder the guardian Miss Lucy grows agitated as Kath and her cohort reach the end of their time at Hailsham. They don't seem to be able to interpret the actual meaning of the words they use all the time. She overhears them fantasizing about what they might do with the rest of their lives, and she blurts out, "The problem, as I see it, is that you've been told and not told. You've been told, but none of you really understand, and I dare say, some people are quite happy to leave it that way. But I'm not. If you're to have decent lives, you have to know who you are and what lies ahead of you, every one of you."[8]

Miss Lucy seems willing to speak the truth unvarnished by lies or circumlocution, but in considering this passage more closely, I have come to realize she might be engaged in a third kind of denial. This time it's what Cohen calls "implicatory." The facts are acknowledged in an explicit way, but this knowledge is not integrated into everyday life: "justifications, rationalizations, evasions" become tools for abetting such failure, so as to avoid "the psychological, political or moral implications that conventionally follow."[9] If *X*, then *Y*. Follow the line of thinking to its logical conclusion. Miss Lucy seems to believe that being told so that "you really understand" will allow the students to lead more self-aware lives, which she equates with "decent" lives, and to avoid deluding themselves with errant dreams of becoming something else. Their future is immutable, and being told properly means they have learned to accept it.

Such passive acceptance, however, is not the behavior these students would necessarily engage in if the facts of their lives were more comprehensively explained to them. If *X*, then not *Y* but *Z*. If the students truly understood that they are being raised for slaughter, they would find ways to rebel against this unjust system. They would refuse to aid in their own destruction. They would try to run away or defy the system. They might even attempt to destroy it. So, of the three types of denial identified by Cohen (literal, interpretive, implicatory), it's the last that seems hardest to overcome. Jacquelyn Ardam recalls how her students, when she teaches *Never Let Me Go* in a college classroom, "get demonstrably frustrated with Kath and the other clones. They ask: where is their anger? Why don't they rebel? Why do they passively accept their deaths?"[10] Such questions never occur to Miss Lucy, who believes that if her students were told the truth about what they are in as explicit a way as possible, they would simply accept what they cannot change and learn to live their lives within their tragic confines. Such questions also never occur to anyone else in the novel, including the clones. The system, it seems, exists and has to be accepted. Readers respond to this implicit message by trying to articulate what isn't said in the text, to get beyond the implicatory denial that surrounds everything about the story Kath tells. They want to say that there is no possibility for a "decent" life for these characters so long as the system itself remains in place.

Yet the readers, too, are stuck. As Ardam continues, "I, summoning something in myself that I don't usually summon, pause and then intone: why don't you rebel? Where is your anger?"[11] Implicit in this response is the awareness that the story Ishiguro tells in *Never Let Me Go* is an allegory. He seems to be speaking about one subject, the plight of clones in a fictional world, yet, all the while, he is speaking about another, the ways in which so many people lie to themselves, are caught up in euphemisms and a willingness to go along to get along because they don't want to cause any trouble.[12] If this is correct, readers, reading allegorically, need to pull the string of this thought further, to consider how Kath's unjust world is like their own. They need to be attentive not only to what they are told and not told but also to the implications involved in recognizing these meanings.

One end result of such thinking for the contemporary reader is climate change. Although this concern is never mentioned in Ishiguro's novel, it is nevertheless the great unspoken topic—unspoken not in the sense of a literal or even an interpretive denial but rather in the inability to follow the implications of what a candid acknowledgment of the facts of climate change says about the current system of extraction, production, and distribution of goods and services that depends so much on the burning of fossil fuels. This system also depends on, and produces, inequalities of every kind and perpetuates a way of thinking that divides populations by race and other categorizations of worth. Some people are thus less human than others and as a result more disposable or even necessary to kill so others deemed more human can live. To consider such implications fully is to consider how addressing climate change requires more than the widespread adoption of renewable energy, a rapid phasing out of fossil fuel use, and the careful deployment of adaptation strategies, as important as all of these are. It requires a rebellion against a system that relies on the poisoning of the air, ground, and water to produce profit.

That many seem unable to equate knowledge with rebellion could suggest that Miss Lucy is right after all: the full implication of acknowledging the truth is, for the most part, a sad acceptance of fate. To "really understand" leads not to rebellion but to acceptance and a search to live out one's life in as "decent" a way as one can muster in the shadow of an inevitable tragedy. As a practical matter, however, if this is the case, and understanding means learning to be even more quiescent, then there would be no point for the children in *Never Let Me Go* to overcome this final layer of denial. There would be little difference between being in denial and accepting the truth.

This last point raises a difficult ethical possibility. If Miss Lucy is right, and understanding leads only to quiescence, then perhaps it is more humane to treat the clones the way Hailsham has. That is, they should be told and not told, allowed to stay in a soft state of denial that makes their existence bearable and leaves open the possibility that they might, in the time they have, be able to find happiness. Here it's useful to consider the students themselves as not-passive characters in this story. They aren't simply under the full control of the guardians, accepting whatever is given to them. They themselves work hard to maintain the soft state of denial that Hailsham promotes, even when they are pulling some of it away. A student asks, Why does the school take their artwork? And Kath recalls "feeling furious at Polly for so stupidly breaking the unwritten rule." Still, she continues, she was "terribly excited about what answer Miss Lucy might give."[13] It's easy to imagine how the anger Kath feels toward Polly will lead her and her peers to ostracize her, as they have done to other students who have violated their many unwritten rules. At the same time, Kath and her peers want to know the answer to the question. Polly is a scapegoat who can be punished for violating the rules while asking the very thing that everyone wants to ask themselves—but in a way they can't fully acknowledge to themselves.

THE SOCIAL ORGANIZATION OF DENIAL

At this moment, when Kath reveals that she and her cohort had actively participated in controlling how much they learned about a fundamental aspect of how they could live their lives, the novel gives a glimpse of a complex form of denial. It doesn't fit any of the types discussed so far, which have been primarily concerned with the ways in which the refusal of facts is imposed on a group of people. Rather, it focuses on the ways in which people may experience all three in an informal but nevertheless highly organized manner that they themselves work hard to maintain. As Kari Norgaard observes, much of the social science discussion on why so many seem unalarmed by climate change and unlikely to become active around this issue has tended—until recently—to rely on what are called "attention deficit" models. These assume that people do not know much about climate change and would act if they did.[14] Norgaard makes the very reasonable point, which has been widely adopted by others, that there is already a wealth of information about this phenomenon. It's rare, especially in educated circles, to meet people who don't understand at least the basic science and the likely consequences of continued planetary warming. What might explain, then, the relative inattention that surrounds this subject among the people she interviewed? As she continues to explain, a "social organization of denial" prescribes a "sense of knowing and not knowing, of having information but not thinking about it in their everyday lives."[15] As she later points out, drawing explicitly from

Cohen's work on denial and from a wealth of ethnographic research in a town in Norway, "How does one not think about something that is important? It takes work."[16]

A "social organization of denial" seems essential to what Cohen means by "everyday denial." This term refers to the ways in which people shield themselves from a disturbing fact by actively turning away from its implications. They don't talk about it or think about it, even though they haven't refused the factuality of what is avoided. The more a fact is shunned in this way, the less chance there is for someone to verify it. No one sees mirrored in other people's recitation and response to its enunciation the urgency that is climate change's due. Silence instills doubt, makes people wonder if they are exaggerating a fear, and leads to paralysis. Add to this the fact that often, especially in the United States, the most vocal are the ones shouting down the possibility that climate change should be taken seriously, and it's easy to understand how doubts can grow and lead not just to implicatory or interpretive denial but literal denial as well.

This is a simple point: repeat a lie enough, and it becomes difficult to refute, especially if there aren't people clamoring loudly about what is true. A structural asymmetry is at work here as well. The repetition of a lie is more often than not supported by for-profit media that thrive on controversy and sensationalism (whatever gets attention) even as they are careful not to alienate their advertisers (attention is carefully molded). Those who want to clamor loudly about what is true are at a structural disadvantage, made more disadvantageous by the bad feelings that inevitably accompany the acknowledgment of what's actually happening.

Cohen's definition of this state gets at its complexity by using language that is remarkably—maybe eerily or uncannily—similar to the language Miss Lucy uses with her students (also echoed by Norgaard): "*A statement about the world or the self (or about your knowledge of the world or your self) which is neither literally true nor a lie intended to deceive others but allows for the strange possibility of simultaneously knowing and not-knowing. The existence of what is denied must be 'somehow' known, and statements expressing this denial must be 'somehow' believed in.*"[17] The "somehow" of knowing and not knowing, or being told and not being told, or saying and not saying, is a social function. It is a "statement," which assumes an audience as well as a speaker. Not speaking is as much a statement as speaking, and both are equally active. "It takes work," as Norgaard puts it, to avoid a topic as pervasive and important as climate change. The students of Hailsham must work hard, as well, to enforce spontaneously created and largely unwritten rules regulating speech about what they are in everyday interactions because to do otherwise can lead, in a cascading and uncontrollable way, to implications they don't want to explore. In the same way, people in everyday circumstances must work hard to enforce the rules that regulate speech about climate change.

This state of denial resembles what the media scholar Marita Sturken calls an "absent presence," a recognition of an embarrassing fact that avoids discussion of it in a way that would get at its full implications.[18] Caroline Chung Simpson elaborates on this idea by turning to the mass incarceration of Japanese Americans. The "proliferation of information" that surrounded this event after World War II, Simpson insists, "ironically furthered the nation's avoidance of the deeper challenge of the role of internment in our understanding of postwar and cold war national history."[19] The facts of mass incarceration are fully acknowledged, as is the long struggle for such acknowledgment and the eventual official apology by the U.S. government for its wrongdoing, but in the process the event becomes an occasion for signaling the nation's exceptional ability to recognize such wrongdoing as well as the perseverance of Japanese Americans, who insisted on living up to the ideals of the very nation that imprisoned them. This framing doesn't allow the more disturbing aspects of the event to be explored, much less acknowledged, such as the ways in which mass incarceration is tied to how the nation has defined itself through racial exclusions. Instead, in the latter half of the twentieth century, this framing performed the ideological work of promoting, in Dean Itsuji Saranillio's words, "the idea of the United States as a racially diverse nation based on harmonious race relations," which served U.S. interests "during the Cold War."[20]

What I especially appreciate about the emphasis on the everyday in *everyday denial* is the way it conjures action. It takes effort for people to construct the memory of the mass incarceration of Japanese Americans during wartime in this way, as signaling not an abuse of power but power's virtues. The effort is habitual, something that has to be done repeatedly, like getting up, brushing your teeth, and preparing breakfast for your family. Every day, I wake up and do these things, so much so that I equate the start of a new day with these activities. It may be automatic, but it is also often the product of a mighty force of will, especially on those mornings when I want to sleep longer and curse the alarm.

These dynamics are especially familiar to me as someone who specializes in the study of Asian American literature, because they exist in the way race is often talked about in the United States. To go back to the example of Japanese American mass incarceration, the most well-known literary works focusing on this event that were written by Japanese Americans, such as Monica Sone's memoir *Nisei Daughter* or Hisaye Yamamoto's short story "Miss Sasagawara," push the event itself into the background, almost as if it were an inconvenience or a minor setback in the course of their characters' lives. As Traise Yamamoto observes about such works, they "are frustratingly *un*autobiographical, not given to personal disclosure or passages of intimate self-reflection. . . . Tonally, they are the equivalent of pleasant acquaintances."[21] In other words, a deliberate distance is maintained between subject and reader, which allows the injustices of mass incarceration to be both recognized and scrupulously avoided.

It's possible to read *Nisei Daughter* and miss its short description of the narrator's experiences in an internment camp surrounded by barbed wire and armed soldiers, which appears in half of a short chapter. The amount of effort Sone had to put into marginalizing this experience to this degree is astonishing. Likewise, "Miss Sasagawara" focuses on the young narrator's rumination about the title character's deteriorating mental stability. The latter is eventually hospitalized in a psychiatric hospital. As the story progresses and Miss Sasagawara's behavior becomes more erratic, the reader must work to keep in mind that the story is taking place in an open-air prison and that what the other characters treat as normal is in fact highly abnormal. Given these dynamics, the story seems to ask, Where's the line between reason and insanity? Who's crazy in this world?

I thus think of *everyday denial* as referring to an arduously willed state of refusal to acknowledge something that otherwise exists in plain sight. The turning away from the implications of a disturbing fact is *as active as* the turning toward this fact. The turning can't just be done once. It's an activity that has to be performed again and again, a constant and habitual and deliberate choosing not to attend to something that on other levels of cognition—the literal, the interpretive, and even the implicatory—may have already been conceded. Because of its repetition, everyday denial can be remarkably durable. It can be maintained despite overwhelming evidence to the contrary, so that my home can be washed away by a storm the likes of which have never been recorded for my region and I still insist that nothing but a familiar variability in the weather is at work. The durability of everyday denial suggests that it would be a mistake to assume that conditions will worsen enough that people will be forced to acknowledge what has happened to their climate and take collective action. No matter how bad a situation gets, people can still maintain an everyday denial that refuses, dilutes, and misdirects.

Because of its dynamic nature, however, I want to assert that every act of everyday denial is an opportunity for its undoing. There's a kind of give-and-take between everyday denial and what might be called in contrast *everyday attention*, in which people can work through the difficulty of self-consciously contemplating a fact like climate change. This task can't be done just once. It has to be repeated again and again and requires as much work as a turning away. I want to go even further, to suggest that there is no permanent state of everyday denial or everyday attention. There is only a switching between them, so that what matters most is the balance.

As Kath and her friends demonstrate in *Never Let Me Go*, however, the balance often tends to skew toward denial. They allow themselves to learn enough to follow along and function in the world they find themselves in, but they are always careful not to cross the lines that demarcate this world. This habit is what makes Kath and Tommy so unusual. They have, inadvertently perhaps, crossed one of these lines by seeking out their former guardians and having the facts fully and candidly explained to them. They can no longer easily retreat into the different kinds of denial they have known, and it's only then that Tommy, on their drive back to the medical center where they live, asks for some time alone in a field, where he can vent in anger as loudly as he can.

Tommy's rage is impotent, for he will quickly fall back into place and give up his last set of organs without further resistance, but for this one short moment, readers get a glimpse of how the scale can tip toward everyday attentiveness. It has its costs—this tipping against an active not-knowing that can make the everyday a familiar, functional, bearable state of mind to reside in even when the everyday itself is a container for systematic oppression and an enabler of catastrophe—but it may be what's necessary to break free from the spell of quiescence.

SKEPTICISM AND SCIENTISM

Teju Cole's *Open City* features an impressively erudite, cosmopolitan, and sensitive narrator. Julius, a psychiatry fellow at a New York hospital who grew up in Nigeria, spends his evenings and days off walking around the city. When he accrues enough vacation time, he travels to Brussels, where he befriends a Moroccan clerk, Farouq, who works at the internet café where Julius catches up on his emails. Farouq is friendly and well versed in Western continental philosophy. The two have heated conversations about colonialism, literature, racism, and Zionism. Throughout his walks and travels, the narrator notes not only the physical landscape but the history of that landscape. He sees a church in Harlem and recalls the building's history as a theater, "America's third largest when it was built, seating over three thousand. . . . Al Johnson had played there, as had Lucille Ball, and back then it had been surrounded by expensive restaurants and luxury goods shops."[22] Visiting the former site of the World Trade Center, he finds himself musing about what was there before the towers went up and then fell down: "There had been communities here before Columbus ever set sail, before Verrazano anchored his ships in the narrows, or the black Portuguese slave trader Esteban Gómez sailed up the Hudson; human beings had lived here, built homes, and quarreled with their neighbors."[23]

Julius thinks about his own comparatively luxurious childhood in his family's home in Nigeria and the poverty he encountered, as when getting a suit made in a poor neighborhood to wear to his father's funeral: "These children stared when my aunt and I emerged from her car because, from their point of view, we would have represented unimaginable wealth and privilege."[24] Race and its role in a history of colonial exploitation saturate these ruminations. As Stephen Sohn writes (while discussing a different novel), because such ideas about race "exhibit a kind of geographical and historical expansiveness that could be mislabeled as a postracial aesthetic, these works demand that readers attend to the relational power structures arising in colonial and postcolonial contexts."[25]

Race is something that readers have to notice deliberately in *Open City*, because nothing seems to escape Julius's perceptiveness, and his observations can blend into each other. He is keenly aware of how racism and colonial exploitation have shaped the very buildings and places he walks through—and as such he is less encumbered by the kind of protective denial that characterizes the clones in Ishiguro's novel. He is comfortable with people of every background, class, gender, and sexuality, even as he is quietly scornful of the hypocrisies of others. Just as important, his interests include bird watching, classical music, literature, philosophy, independent film, history, poetry, photography, and architecture. Everything about his character suggests that he notices race because he notices everything.

And yet, for all his sensitivity, weaknesses in his perception slowly appear.[26] He visits a detention center for undocumented migrants in Queens and hears the testimony of a Liberian man whose family was slaughtered during the civil war there and who himself narrowly escaped being conscripted as a child soldier. Julius responds, "I wondered, naturally, as Saidu told his story, whether I believed him or not, whether it wasn't more likely that he had been a soldier."[27] Later he has a chance encounter with Moji, the sister of a childhood friend, and he flatters himself that she must have had a crush on him. She invites him to a party hosted by her boyfriend. At the end of the party, she confronts him with an accusation of rape. She tells him, "Things don't go away just because you choose to forget them. You forced yourself on me eighteen years ago because you could get away with it, and I suppose you did get away with it. But not in my heart, you didn't."[28]

It's possible that Julius's skepticism about Saidu's story is well founded and even that Moji is somehow misremembering what happened between her and Julius when they were much younger. Still, both moments suggest troubling gaps in Julius's thinking. Julius's use of the word *naturally* in questioning Saidu's story suggests that any attentive listener would harbor similar doubts—I certainly wouldn't have. The novel gives no reasons readers should doubt Moji's sincerity, and Julius never refutes her claim. Rather, he withdraws from it, and the next chapter moves on to tell of something else that happens to him. Such moments shock me precisely because Julius is so aware of his surroundings and so careful to place what he sees in historical contexts stripped of self-serving narratives and erasures of atrocity. An active knowing dances around an equally active not-knowing in the play of everyday denial.

What does he fail to see despite his perceptiveness? What does he allow himself to forget? What do such gaps reveal about the extent to which an individual can make meaning of what he or she sees? In an important moment early in the novel, Julius observes, "But I was no longer the global-warming skeptic I had been some years before, even if I still couldn't tolerate the tendency some had of jumping to conclusions based on anecdotal evidence: global warming was a fact, but that did not mean it was the explanation for why a given day was warm. It was careless thinking to draw the link too easily, an invasion of fashionable politics into what should be the ironclad precincts of science."[29] At this point in the novel, readers have encountered Julius's rich thought processes but not any of the doubts about his character that are introduced later. This makes it easy to interpret these sentences as another sign of his sharp reasoning. It *is* naive to think that a single day of heat—or cold—reveals anything about a phenomenon that requires years of meticulously collected data to track. Indeed, the tendency to conflate weather and climate has been highlighted by James Hansen, one of the scientists most responsible for helping to make climate change an important public concern in the United States and beyond. As he and his coauthors write, "The greatest barrier to public recognition of human-made climate change is probably the natural variability of local climate. How can a person discern long-term climate change, given the notorious variability of local weather and climate from day to day and year to year?"[30]

At the start of *Open City*, Julius acknowledges what Hansen's article goes on to demonstrate: that the increasing volatility of the weather is due to something other than normal variability. Julius observes, "The absence of this order, the absence of cold when it ought to be cold, was something I now sensed as a sudden discomfort."[31] Hansen and his coauthors would likely respond, "The climate dice are now loaded to a degree that a perceptive person old enough to remember the climate of 1951–1980 should recognize the existence of climate change."[32] Julius, however, shakes off what his senses tell him by expressing fears of confirmation bias. He worries that he is reading into signs the meaning that he already expects: "Still, the way my thoughts returned to the fact that it was the middle of November and I hadn't yet had occasion to wear my coat made me wonder if, already, I was one of those people, the overinterpreters. This was part of my suspicion that there was a mood in the society that pushed people more toward snap judgments and unexamined opinions, an antiscientific mood."[33] Julius insists that inferences of anthropogenic climate change from personal observation are wild leaps of logic, "a more general inability to assess evidence" that fuels a political climate in which "partisanship [is] all."[34] His skepticism communicates to the reader that despite the Nigerian heritage bequeathed to him by his father (his mother is German), which he equates with ethnic ways of being that are at odds with his commitment to cosmopolitanism, he considers himself someone who can rise above ethnic-seeming superstitions and quaint ways of thinking. His skepticism is a proud badge of his high educational attainment, intellectual sophistication, social status, and knowledge of the world around him.

Julius's reasoning, and the cultural associations it might conjure, is what Wendy Hui Kyong Chun questions when she observes that the public respect for science has ironically created expectations of an impossible standard of scientific certainty: "The debate continues . . . because of the reification of science as absolute and certain; a significant number of those who have reservations regarding the existence of global climate change are not dupes, ideologues, or postmodern theorists but rather vocal supporters of science."[35] Such expectations have become so pervasive that the Fourth National Climate Assessment, a report on the state of scientific knowledge about climate change and its impacts on the United States mandated by a 1990 law, offers this observation: "Uncertainty is also a part of science. A key goal of scientific research is to increase our confidence and reduce the uncertainty in our understanding of the world around us. Even so, there is no expectation that uncertainty can be fully eliminated."[36]

The views of many climate change doubters rest on the assumption that science can indeed arrive at irrefutable truths and provide perfect understandings of how phenomena occur. Julius echoes the plea for "better" science that many doubters make, one that is founded rhetorically on a concern that political causes can cloud scientific reason. As a result, the public continues to be misled by interpretations of data that can be stretched to mean many different, and often-contradictory, things. For someone to insist that an unusually warm winter is a sure sign of climate change is, from Julius's perspective as well as the perspective of many doubters, just as irresponsible as James Inhofe, the Republican chair of the U.S. Senate's Committee on Environment and Public Works, throwing a snowball during a committee session to show that climate change is imaginary.[37] The only apparently logical position to take in the face of such extremes would then be the one Julius takes: to treat both sides of the argument with skepticism and refuse to commit to either.

In the rest of the novel, the author works to unravel this simple stance. Cole does so first by revealing that Julius is not to be completely trusted. Despite his sensitivity, his thinking fails him at key moments, most notably in his relationship to Moji. What he initially mistakes as sexual interest is actually revulsion. Moji, meanwhile, speaks with an earnest passion that calls into question Julius's habitually skeptical stance: "On our way into the park, Moji had said to me that she was more worried than ever about the environment. Her tone was serious. When I responded that I supposed we all were, she corrected me, shaking her head. What I mean is that I actively worry about it, she said, I don't think that's generally true of other people."[38] Moji becomes in this moment an example of someone who ruins the mood of a social gathering by bringing up something too serious. As a result, she challenges Julius's glib remark and its complicity with implicatory denial. While everyone may pay lip service to environmental concerns, she takes them seriously in a way that Julius simply does not. Perhaps she is being parochial, and even ethnic (in a way that Julius seems to associate with the not scientific), in being so earnest, but such concerns do not seem to matter to her. Her stance contrasts notably with Julius's habit of distancing himself from ethnic particularity by embracing a cool and discerning cosmopolitanism.

The rightness of this kind of earnest concern about the environment is buttressed throughout the novel by observations Julius makes about the weather he has been experiencing. At the start of the second half of the book, alluding to Wallace Stevens's poem "The Snow Man," he undercuts the tone of the poem by noting what the weather has actually been like:

> I made an effort to develop a mind of winter. Late last year, I actually said to myself audibly, as I do when I swear these oaths, that I would have to embrace winter as part of the natural cycles of seasons. . . . But it was to be a year without a real winter. The blizzards for which I braced never came. There were a few days of cold rain, and one or two cold snaps, but heavy snow stayed away. We had a series of sunny days in the middle of December, and I was unnerved by that mildness, and when the season's first snow did eventually fall, it was while I was in Brussels, getting drenched by the rain there. The snow was in any case short-lived, melted away by the time I returned to New York in mid-January, and thus did the impression of unseasonal, somewhat uncanny, warm weather persist in my mind, keeping the world, as I experienced it, on edge.[39]

An exceptionally mild winter can be explained as an anomaly. When successive winters are noticeably warmer than usual—or so extremely cold and snowy that hundred-year-old records are broken repeatedly—it becomes harder to argue that nothing is happening. Words like *usual* or *natural* lose their meaning, and a sense of unease begins to dominate, growing into an inchoate sense of dread, foiled expectations, and uncanniness. The recognition of such emotions may not lead to an aesthetic practice that can connect climate change to the everyday, but it points to the gap between the two. To say that anomalous weather is happening because of climate change is at once true and too obvious a statement. Climate change may seem like such a large topic that others respond with a shudder and a shrug. The unease is what lingers, and it needs compounding to prevent the weirdness of what is happening to the weather from receding into the background.

Unease mounts throughout the rest of *Open City*, culminating in an anecdote about how the Statue of Liberty, until 1902, used to be a working lighthouse. "The birds," Julius tells readers, "many of which were clever enough to dodge the cluster of skyscrapers in the city, somehow lost their bearings when faced with a single monumental flame."[40] For years, Colonel Tassin, "who had military command of the island," kept a detailed record of the birds who died in this way. Before his arrival on the island, other officials had sold the carcasses to hatmakers and other merchants in the city. Afterward, the dead birds were donated to museums. The narrative concludes, "The average,

Colonel Tassin estimated, was about twenty birds per night, although the weather and the direction of the wind had a great deal to do with the resulting harvest. Nevertheless, the sense persisted that something more troubling was at work. On the morning of October 13, for example, 173 wrens had been gathered in, all dead of impact, although the night just past hadn't been particularly windy or dark."[41] From the obvious allegorical nature of concluding the novel with a story about the Statue of Liberty, which inevitably connects this story to a larger national context and its guiding mythologies, to the use of a word like *harvest* to refer to the number of dead birds, this ending seeks to conjure for the reader a heightened mood of foreboding.

Several implicit and unanswered questions contribute to this unease. In the absence of obvious causes, what brought about the birds' death? Why couldn't the birds steer clear of a single spotlight after having successfully navigated past the much brighter lights of the city? Why does Tassin record so meticulously the gruesome details of the number and species of the birds that died and their time of death? The reader is left with haunting mysteries, an uncertainty that partially unravels the standard of scientific certainty that Julius conjures in his skepticism about global warming. The more diligently Colonel Tassin documents what has happened, the greater the reader's sense that something is evading such record keeping. There is a strange, perhaps occult, force at work. Science itself becomes an imperfect instrument, less the search for certainty and more, as Chun argues, a start toward building "habits" that shape responses to the challenges ahead.[42] The unease generated by this final anecdote reminds the reader simultaneously of a history of colonial expansion and nation building, the crashing of planes into the Twin Towers and the wars that followed, and something else even more difficult to put into words.

In death, the birds are made into things—objects of trade and scientific curiosity. They might remind the reader of the way racism can make humans into things that occupy the space between the living and the dead. Slavery, for instance, was a form of social death, making slave bodies into objects that could be traded or studied. The birds might also remind the reader that all humans are subject to forces beyond their understanding that can lure them into danger and suddenly end their existence. The mystery of death conjured in the final pages of Cole's novel thwarts ruling-class claims of mastery, cognitive superiority, and exceptionalism. People are like birds, a part of the world rather than some entity that can stand fully apart from it. Because of history and group differences and greater vulnerability, some are more aware than others of these similarities, even as they struggle to assert their agency—humbled as it might be—in such a world.

WHAT IS CLIMATE DENIAL?

Denial of climate change is more than just the literal refusal to accept well-documented facts. It's a refusal to admit these facts candidly and to think through their implications as far as they will go. It gains its strength in the everyday turning away from these same facts, a turning away that is active and maintained with great difficulty. It is also a turning to science as an absolute arbiter of facts, asking in the process for an unreasonable level of proof that breeds skepticism despite the ready availability of evidence. It is an elevation of a certain way of being in the world that mistakes skepticism for worldliness and mistakes a rising above ethnic or minor concerns for sophistication. It flourishes in conditions of heightened individualism, where the atomism of the person builds barriers to communal awareness and circumvents the possibility of much-needed collective action. It is written into books, and artifacts more generally, so that belief is informed by a ruling set of ideas, a hegemony, that not only dominates in the past and the present but can be passed down to future generations. It is finally a simplification, a promise that easy solutions can be found by the use of brute force and a return to a past way of being in the world, which seems to so many to be what Kath calls in *Never Let Me Go* a "golden time," despite the fact that she was being raised to have her organs surgically removed and given to someone deemed more human and therefore worthier of life.[43]

In thinking about this definition, I find myself returning to a poem by Sally Wen Mao. "Occidentalism" is worried about the past and the written and made legacies it has left behind. The speaker of the poem wants to talk back to these legacies,

> make Sharpie lines, deface
> its text like it defaces me.

She admires the world-famous artist Ai Weiwei for the time in 1995 when he filmed himself dropping a rare Han dynasty urn, smashing it on the ground. Mao writes:

> If only recovering the silenced history
>
> is as simple as smashing its container: book,
> bowl, celadon spoon. Such objects cross
>
> borders the way our bodies never could.

Unfortunately, Mao continues:

> That bowl is unbreakable. All its ghosts
> still shudder through us like small breaths.
>
> The tome of hegemony lives on, circulates
> in our libraries, in our bloodstreams. One day,
>
> a girl like me may come across it on a shelf,
> pick it up, read about all the ways her body
>
> is a thing.[44]

While symbolic acts of defiance are possible, it's more difficult to work against the force of a consecrated past that continues to shape the ruling ideas of the present. Indeed, this past is preserved in the present's very idea of what is most worth preserving—like the Han vase. Value adheres to things and bodies, creating hierarchies within and between them regarding what qualities should be prized, allowed to travel freely, and emulated again and again and what qualities are dismissed as worthless.

This way of apprehending the world can nurture denial in its many varieties, just as the guardians at Hailsham steep their pupils in attitudes toward literature and art that pose the very existence of their souls as needing proof. Or this legacy can guide the thinking of a figure like Julius, so highly educated and well read, invested in culture and refined discernment, but still unable to recognize how the texture of his surroundings is changing as winter becomes something else. I admire how Mao's poem can state such concerns directly to the reader without the preoccupation of character, plot, or world building. Her poem, an example of what I call in the next chapter a *revived lyric*, is not a work of fiction, nor is it interested in telling a story. It is instead an invitation to break free of a consecrated past and of the ways of living and valuing it validates, so as to make space for ways of being that don't constantly threaten to turn people into things.

WHY REVIVE THE LYRIC?

Claudia Rankine's *Citizen* and Craig Santos Perez's "Love in a Time of Climate Change"

YOU MAY HAVE HEARD EXPRESSIONS like the following: "This piece of writing is lyrical." "I'm going to see the play at the Lyrical Stage" (this is the name of an existing theater in Boston). "There's a lyrical quality to the visual images in this film." I am never sure what speakers mean when they use the word *lyrical* in such ways. It seems to refer to a kind of elevation of language beyond ordinary usage that is associated with the poetic. It suggests as well—especially in the case of film and print fiction—a marginalizing of character, action, and plot in favor of a forceful awareness of the present. Maybe *lyrical* means, then, that not much is going to happen. It might be pretty visually or make spectacular use of language, but whatever is being described is going to be slow. It might even be dull.

To say something is lyrical might also mean it's going to be like a poem. *Lyrical* and *poetic*: they are often synonymous. And together they suggest a kind of oomph to meaning, as if a piece of writing or a performance is heightening feelings and boosting awareness, albeit at the expense of a quick-moving story. Here is, for instance, how Seo-Young Chu defines the lyrical: "What makes a lyric poem 'lyrical' is a constellation of interrelated attributes that have characterized Anglophone poetry from the Renaissance (if not earlier) to the present. Lyric poetry is frequently soliloquy-like. Lyric voices speak from beyond ordinary time. Lyric poems are inhabited by situations and tableaux transcending ordinary temporality. Lyric descriptions are charged with depictive intensity. Lyric poetry is musically expressive. Lyric poems evoke heightened and eccentric states of consciousness."[1] What makes this characterization original—and quirky—is that it is being used to describe how science fiction (SF) narratives work: "SF is frequently soliloquy-like. SF voices speak from beyond ordinary time. Works of SF are inhabited by situations and tableaux transcending ordinary temporality. SF descriptions are charged with depictive intensity. SF is musically expressive. And works of SF evoke heightened and eccentric states of consciousness."[2]

There is no analogy in this argument. Science fiction is not like lyric poetry. Rather, Chu insists that it is another example of the lyric at work in creative expression. Even when not in verse form, it nevertheless remains lyrical in that even its prose begins to take on attributes of free verse. So while there may be relatively few (but a growing number of) examples of science-fictional poetry, its prose narratives—and movies and comics—require the lyric because it alone has enough power "to convert an elusive referent into an object available for representation."[3] By definition, science fiction is always interested in the "elusive referent" since it seeks to represent worlds that do not exist. The conflation of lyric and science fiction grants the latter more literary prestige while making the former seem more exciting. Stuff is going to happen. It's going to be wild. A lot of it is going to be improbable.

As much as I admire Chu's argument, I am wary of her use of the lyric. As Walt Hunter observes, the lyric "never had a stable set of generic traits or characteristics; the history of identifying them is checkered with moments of ambivalence and resistance to genre."[4] To make matters even more confusing, poetry itself has become so associated with the lyric, what Virginia Jackson calls the "lyricization" of poetry, that the meanings associated with the lyric keep proliferating.[5] Moreover, as Jackson and her coeditor, Yopie Prins, write in the introduction to *The Lyric Theory Reader: A Critical Anthology* about the essays in their collection, "For all of these critics, for all sorts of different reasons, the lyric is a fiction in which they find ways to believe."[6]

If *the lyric* lacks clear definition, as it has expanded in meaning to become more or less interchangeable with *poetry*, one reason may be all the uncertainty about what makes a poem a poem. There has been a century or more of intense use of free verse; avant-garde experiments in visual play, arbitrary restraints, and simple copying of existing texts; the growing popularity of prose poems; and so forth, which has exploded ideas of poetry, making it a fiction as well. Exemplifying this point by exaggerating it, the poet Kaveh Akbar made waves when he tweeted, "If someone hands me a bag of dirt and tells me it's a poem, it gets to be a poem. It might not be a poem that satisfies me intellectually or brings me any delight, I may not want to spend much time with it, but it's a poem because the person who built it called it a poem."[7]

The uncertainty about what poems are (you might say they are not bags of dirt, but what are your reasons for insisting on this exclusion?) suggests that contemporary poets aren't so much working with existing forms as creating new ones out of the remains of what came before. The lyric itself, then, is appealing because it has for so long been associated with ruin. Think of the poems of Sappho, who epitomizes the ancient lyric; they exist only as fragments. Likewise, in "Up Nursing," Hoa Nguyen writes in a fragmentary style:

> Pour hot water on dried nettles
> Filter more water for the kettle
>
> Why try
> to revive the lyric[8]

Andrew Epstein comments on this very short poem—the quotation is half of it—as a reflection on contemporary poetry. Its concluding question reveals its own answer: "*This* is why one must revive the lyric—to write and record and illuminate this constellation of detail and experience, to give life to the everyday experience of women and mothers in the contemporary world."[9] Another answer to the question "Why try / to revive the lyric[?]" in the explicit context of environmental concerns is offered by Margaret Ronda, who suggests the lyric is a way to train attention on a here and now so as to amplify "an uncanny sense of living on amidst accumulating planetary disruption."[10]

Similarly, Sonya Posmentier focuses on an environmentally sensitive African American literary tradition that refuses the kind of Anglo-American lineage for the lyric that scholars like Jackson and Prins seem to assume. She thinks of the lyric as giving expression to "vital modern concerns about the capacities of literary genre" and as taking part in a literary history "generated on the margins of American and European modernity."[11] For Asian American poets as well, the lyric swerves from the Anglo-American tradition by refusing to maintain its distance from the epic. In the case of *Dictee* (a foundational work of Asian American experimental poetry), for instance, Josephine Park argues that its author, Theresa Hak Kyung Cha, "revises both the lyric and epic" to show that their forms, and their differences from each other, "were never settled in the first place."[12] Why revive the lyric? Because it offers shifting understandings of literary history that can better accommodate the specificity of different racial groups.

For these latter critics, the lyric is intimately connected to a reimagining of the everyday as a refined attention to experiences—especially those experiences lived "on the margins of American and European modernity"—that might otherwise seem hardly worth commenting on, because they've already been devalued, and that can give way to something else, the exceptional and the extraordinary that is buried there. Under the pressure of the present, with its gross injustices and environmental pressures, contemporary poets like Claudia Rankine and Craig Santos Perez have found occasion to revive the lyric, or to make it lively in a way it wasn't before to the concerns that most press on their consciousnesses.

What follows starts with Rankine, to consider what it means for her to claim to be writing an "American lyric" in the titles of two major works, in particular her most widely read book, *Citizen*.[13] It then moves on to Perez, to think about how such a revival of the lyric might shape attention to climate change more explicitly. In focusing on these two poets, the chapter finds occasion to reflect on the quotidian force of racial microaggressions, the race-based critique of the human, the use of the simple present tense, and the ways in which reading the revived lyric can lead you to read other texts in a way that's attuned to the different modes of agency all around you. What follows should thus give you a solid sense of how I use the term *lyricism* and what makes it so powerful for making sense of the extraordinary transformations happening to the planet's ecosystems. This chapter is longer than most of the other chapters in this book because I want to explain what I find so appealing about the lyric and why I remain focused on it despite its many detractors.

THE LYRIC AND MICROAGGRESSION: CLAUDIA RANKINE

As Gillian White points out, discussion of the lyric has long been shrouded by the feeling of shame. Some of "the most ubiquitous, negative lyric stereotypes," which feed this feeling, include "solipsistic, rapacious ego, driven to mastery, narcissistic confessionalist, conservative both aesthetically and politically."[14] I am nevertheless drawn to the lyric, as many contemporary poets are drawn to it, because it directs attention not only to what is there. It sees what is there and something else besides—a "transcendence in the ordinary."[15] It speaks to the place of the human and makes a claim on behalf of the human to understand and act as part of a numinous world. This form is therefore also closely associated with ideas of the human, which are wrapped up in the interpersonal play between the I and you, the making of the individual, then, as something fundamentally relational and the uncertainty about where interiority begins and exteriority ends.

The lyric is part of a vast tradition of past creators and readers trying to make sense of the world all around them—blurring distinctions, foregrounding modes of expression, and demanding some kind of response—even as it is open to revival of its form. W. R. Johnson describes the ancient Greek lyric in similar terms:

> The listener can identify either with the *ego* ("I") or with the *tu* ("you") of the song, or he can identify with both almost simultaneously: he becomes, for the duration of the song, and perhaps beyond it, part of the lyrical moment, part of the lyrical discourse of praise and blame that reveals that moment; witnessing this compressed, dramatic instant, listening to words and the rhythms that illumine it, he is moved to ponder himself in relation to it. This process, in which the listener identifies himself with *all* that is sung, lyric shares, of course, with epic and drama. What distinguishes lyric from epic and drama in this regard are the extreme compressions of the things that are imagined.[16]

As this passage suggests, the lyric has often been thought capable of inducing an almost mystical state where conventional divisions falter. It is usually associated as well with compression, so that what matters is the moment and the image rather than larger expanses of time that require literary conventions like characters, story, and plot to fathom. But as the emphasis on "praise and blame" suggests, the lyric doesn't escape conflict. It seems instead to recognize conflict as itself constitutive of a moment, and it can cause those it captures with its hypnotic words and rhythm to consider these constitutive elements of the moment, which it suspends from an estranged vantage point.

Johnson promises a lot, and, inevitably, the lyric underdelivers. This is the argument that Ben Lerner makes in his short book *The Hatred of Poetry*—its notable brevity itself a possible example of lyrical compression even as its argument seems to replicate the very shame White focuses on. Poetry is so often openly hated, he reasons, because it disappoints in much the same way that ideas of individual human agency disappoint. An actual poem can never live up to the promise of an ideal poem. This is why so many contemporary readers are openly dismissive of poetry and of the lyric in particular (which Lerner seems to conflate with poetry, in yet another example of lyricization), a trait they share with many poets themselves.

Members of an avant-garde, for instance, are "intensive poetry haters" because they expect too much: "The poem is a weapon—a weapon against received ideas of what the artwork is, certainly, but also an instrument of war in a heroic, revolutionary struggle, whether of the far right (e.g., the Italian Futurists) or the far left (e.g., the Russian Futurists)."[17] And when it turns out, as it has repeatedly, that yesterday's avant-garde has become today's hallowed guardian of tradition, there is anger and disappointment at the ease with which it has been co-opted by the very establishment it sought to destroy. Its claims to political prowess appear feeble, and poetry is again shown to be making promises it can't keep. "This disappointment in the political feebleness of poetry in the present," Lerner observes, "unites the futurist and the nostalgist and is a staple of mainstream denunciations of poetry."[18]

How brave a poet must be, then, to continue to write poetry (it certainly isn't for the pay) and especially to return again to the lyric, which has promised so much but evidently failed to deliver. The poet Ilya Kaminsky addresses this problem in an interview about his work, in which he makes clear that he is writing a lyric that is also responsive to present-day pressures: "My native country, Ukraine, is currently at war. The country in which I am alive right now, USA, is currently harassing/bombing/taking advantage of more than half of this Earth's population. How do I address this, as a lyric poet? Do lyric poets address such things?"[19] I like how these quotations exemplify how thoughtfully poets like Kaminsky are approaching the lyric, as a kind of return accompanied by a big difference. Kamran Javadizadeh, in his study of Rankine and the turbulent relationship she has had with the post-Romantic lyric, which he describes as "a literary form of white innocence" for its attention to the self at the expense of larger social and historical forces, raises similar questions about what such a return with a difference might look like. "Once the idea of a transcendent lyric subject—the end result of a century and a half of lyricization—has been exposed as a form of white innocence," Javadizadeh asks, "how can a poet retain the intimacy allowed by the lyric tradition without replicating its pernicious political effects? Why even try?"[20]

I like the idea that it's possible to read *Don't Let Me Be Lonely* and *Citizen* as Rankine's response to these questions. Both volumes are subtitled *An American Lyric*, which confounds Lerner because for him neither contains anything that is "traditionally associated" with this form, namely, "brevity, intensely felt emotion, and highly musical verse."[21] He gives the following example: on the last page of part I of *Citizen* (the volume is divided into seven distinct parts), the speaker relates how she went to visit a new therapist, who was white, and the therapist did not recognize her as a patient. "At the front door," Rankine writes, "the bell is a small round disc that you press firmly. When the door opens, the woman standing there yells, at the top of her lungs, Get away from my house! What are you doing in my yard?" The page ends with the sentence, after the therapist realizes the speaker is her new patient, "I am so sorry, so, so sorry." [22]

The sentence is left there on the page. As can be seen in figure 2.1, a large space of white glossy paper surrounds it, and it's not clear who is speaking or even whether these words are being spoken. The passage was written entirely in the second person, so that use of the "I" seems to repeat the therapist, who says in the previous sentence (and it's clear that she is the one speaking), "I am sorry." But is it still the therapist who is speaking at the end, or is the poet repeating it back to the therapist? Or maybe it is the poet much later in time, looking back at this incident, thinking to herself how she feels? Who is the sorry one, and to whom is the apology given?

Lerner concludes, "What I encounter in Rankine is the felt unavailability of traditional lyric categories; the instruction to read her writing as poetry—and especially as lyric poetry—catalyzes this experience of their loss, like a sensation in a phantom limb." [23] I cannot emphasize this enough: I strongly disagree. I don't feel a sense of loss at the level of form when I read Rankine's poems because they evince a lively and creative reinvention. The repetition of "I am so sorry, so, so sorry" is a dramatic example of compression that resonates in the mind of the reader. Maybe it's not exactly musical, but it has an incantatory power that few readers are likely to forget. The doubling of *sorry* and tripling of *so* and the quintupling of the alliterative *s* sound in both words contribute to the sense that a thought is being evoked, and repeated, a sibilant echoing that lingers long after the pages of the book have been closed. I often think about this line when I'm watching yet another viral video of a racial encounter gone horrifically awry. It also rings in my head when I think about how weather patterns are changing around me. This echo is mostly directed at all the young people around me and the animals and plants and trees as well, all of whom (or is it which?) will have to struggle with what's already here and what's to come. "I am so sorry, so, so sorry."

I also don't feel a sense of loss at the level of content. The scenes of racial conflict and accumulated injury these poems evoke are not scenes of loss, for they are powerful precisely because they describe an endemic and ubiquitous racism. As Rankine makes clear, there was no time before in the past several centuries when these kinds of conflicts and injuries did not occur. There's no place you can go where you won't run into these kinds of painful social interactions. Or, as I put it in the introduction, loss and absence are constitutive of the speaker, not an aberration that needs to be overcome. You can't lose what you've never had.

Even in the example Lerner gives, then, there's a notable emphasis on "brevity" and "intensely felt emotion." The whole anecdote occupies three-quarters of the page, in three short paragraphs and a final line. The words are thus organized to resemble stanzas as much as paragraphs. The words appear in large font, and there are prominent space breaks between the paragraphs. This presentation suggests that something about the whiteness of the page is as important as the appearance of the text itself, a point reinforced by the careful use of contemporary visual art and images from television broadcasts, which frequently punctuate the volume's pages. Indeed, when the book is open to this poem, the text appears on the verso page while the recto displays a photograph of Kate Clarke's statue *Little Girl*, which combines the body of a caribou with the face of a person (see figure 2.2). The figure itself seems to be stuffed, as if offering some kind of commentary on taxidermy. The page also radically decenters the image of the statue to the lower right corner, so what dominates on the recto is white space.

Everything about this spread calls on the reader to pay attention not just to the words but to their presentation in the book, so that meaning appears in densely compacted form, layered not only in the words themselves, their syntax, their patterns of stressed and unstressed syllables, and their layout, but in the negative space around the text and the visual art that's been carefully selected to offer commentary on what has been written. The poem is itself, then, as much an example of visual art as of poetic expression, and more and more, as I contemplate it, has less and less relation to prose.

This kind of intense experiment with form can easily be overlooked because Rankine's words are deliberately accessible, especially in the first two parts. Part I comprises about a dozen short anecdotes, each centering on a moment of misrecognition and prejudgment based on the speaker's race, crystallizing singular moments of excruciating but minor insults. They are all composed in the second person, so that readers are asked to place themselves in the position of the one to whom these events are happening. There is no attempt to make sense of what is happening in these opening anecdotes. These are not expositions. They are descriptions. The emphasis is on a factual account of what happened.

These anecdotes reveal Rankine to be a master chronicler of racial micro-aggressions who elevates what can be easily overlooked or dismissed into something to consider at length and to understand as profound. Racial

The new therapist specializes in trauma counseling. You have only ever spoken on the phone. Her house has a side gate that leads to a back entrance she uses for patients. You walk down a path bordered on both sides with deer grass and rosemary to the gate, which turns out to be locked.

At the front door the bell is a small round disc that you press firmly. When the door finally opens, the woman standing there yells, at the top of her lungs, Get away from my house! What are you doing in my yard?

It's as if a wounded Doberman pinscher or a German shepherd has gained the power of speech. And though you back up a few steps, you manage to tell her you have an appointment. You have an appointment? she spits back. Then she pauses. Everything pauses. Oh, she says, followed by, oh, yes, that's right. I am sorry.

I am so sorry, so, so sorry.

FIGURE 2.1 AND FIGURE 2.2 A two-page spread from Claudia Rankine's *Citizen* features a lyrically compressed text on one side and on the other a photograph of Kate Clarke's statue *Little Girl*. In Rankine, *Citizen*, 18–19.

microaggressions are, according to psychologists whose research focuses on race and ethnicity, minor incidents that may or may not be about race but that, to those who encounter them, can feel demeaning, exclusionary, and, in the accumulation of such incidents, psychologically damaging.[24] Let me give you a few examples derived from everyday experiences, which Rankine's thoughts on microaggression put into a new light:

> You go to buy a tie at a department store, and the salesperson fails to register that you are a customer because you don't look like the mostly white and affluent clients that shop there.
>
> Your colleague, with whom you've attended several meetings and have worked together on at least a couple of projects, mistakes you for another Asian American faculty member.
>
> You are at a conference, and it's late in the evening (and you tell yourself later you were tired). You run into someone you know in passing and mistake him for another prominent Filipino American scholar in your field, doing to someone else exactly what you've complained others have done to you.
>
> You and your family are standing on the sidewalk, perhaps a little too close to the street, talking about where to go next, when a car full of young white men drives by and one of the men yells at you from an open window, "Get back, n*gg*r."

These are minor incidents (as the prefix *micro-* insists) in the sense that they happen quickly and can leave you feeling powerless—and not in the sense that they are insignificant. As you may have guessed, all of these incidents happened to me, and, in that one embarrassing example, I was the one who committed the act. It's maddening that it's a challenge to say whether they were racial in content—well, except for the last example—and, if they were, how deliberate they were.

More important still, how are you supposed to respond if you are on the receiving end? If you make a ruckus, others respond in outrage and defensiveness. The very mention of racial microaggression as a concern is often greeted with derision and dismissed as obviously frivolous—and as such it belongs in the aesthetic category of the cute, of which the lyric poem is a salient example, for what defines racial microaggression is its smallness, its diminutive status, and the will to make it even smaller and more diminutive.[25] Racial microaggressions and the lyric poem are thus connected to each other by the cute. They are both compact, the emotions are highly felt, and the words that are often spoken in such encounters ring in the ear loudly and stay there, ready to be recalled with the slightest prompting. If what was spoken was a song, it would be called an earworm.

It's also possible, of course, that you are misreading the intent. Maybe there is no aggression in the social interaction. If you stay silent, though, all you are left with is your suspicion and frustration, and you can find yourself exploding later on. Little events have big psychological effects. That these effects are so often ignored and considered not worthy of serious attention suggests how much the everyday itself is understood as unimportant, a mere container that can't accommodate conflict or discomfort.

Given the fraught dynamics involved in trying to call attention to the everyday in this way, the opening of Rankine's *Citizen* is remarkable for how persuasively she can dissolve such doubts—what might be called *microdenials*. The considerable skill required to produce this effect can thus be easily overlooked. And, certainly, part II actively encourages readers not to focus on the artistry at work in these poems by the way it reads like a tightly constructed short essay. But as the book progresses, as can be seen in the accompanying table, each part gives way to more and more complex presentations. There is a careful building up of lyric structure that intertwines with the theme of racial microaggression, making you aware as the book progresses that what is important is not the isolated events but the way they are part of something larger and more systemic. To pay attention to them, and to insist on the right to pay attention, is to impugn a whole structure of meaning. As table 2.1 helps illuminate, racial microaggressions matter because they are part of something larger and systemic, and what makes *Citizen* such an outstanding work of creative expression is how Rankine makes use of the lyric to build awareness of this structure.

Every part of *Citizen* thus tries to process what it means to sit with the uncomfortable feelings conjured by recognizing the intrusion of race into the everyday, racism itself being a system through which others exercise their power in specific forms—such as the bad calls umpires deliver to Serena Williams and the deaths police officers deal to so many Black people. There are moments of happiness and pleasure as well as pain and recognition of injury, and the contrasting sensations are brought together as a kind of ecstasy in living: "Every day your mouth opens and receives the kiss the world offers, which seals you shut though you are feeling sick to your stomach about the beginning of the feeling that was born from understanding and now stumbles around in you—the go-along-to-get-along tongue pushing your tongue aside."[26] As a depiction of an ecstasy in living, this passage evokes intense frustration and unpronounced longing as well. There is the urgent need

TABLE 2.1 Description of Parts in Claudia Rankine's *Citizen*

PART I	The text contains about a dozen short anecdotes, each centering on a moment of misrecognition and prejudgment based on the speaker's race, crystallizing singular moments of excruciating but minor insults.
PART II	The text is presented as a tightly constructed short essay.
PART III	The text returns to the short-anecdote format of the first part but after a first long piece remains consistently shorter and more intense in its focus.
PART IV	The text is organized into isolated paragraphs and monitors the speaker's bodily responses—sighs, the breath, headaches, numbness, the feel of the mouth—to watching a tennis match on television.
PART V	The text largely gives up on paragraphs and instead consists mostly of a single sentence or double sentences.
PART VI	The text chronicles the many recent events in which Black people have been neglected, abused, and murdered, from the bodies found in New Orleans in the wake of Hurricane Katrina to the death of Trayvon Martin and James Craig Anderson, the harsh indictments of six black teenagers accused of physically assaulting a white teenager in Jena, Mississippi, the use of stop-and-frisk policies by the police, and the demand that President Barack Obama publicly share his long-form birth certificate.
PART VII	The text tries to process all that came before, especially in the previous part, by turning to notably short lines, sometimes a mere word, which overall seems to resemble more familiar forms of the lyric.

to speak and the powerful social demand to go along to get along. There is, then, in this passage a wrestling with an everyday that makes speaking seem an insurmountable challenge. It's as if a stranger's tongue has physically pushed aside your own.

AN ANTHROPOLOGICAL RECKONING

The way Rankine focuses on the here and now in all of the different parts of *Citizen* concentrates attention on incidents of racial microaggression, so that a coherent claim emerges that what happens at the level of the everyday has major repercussions that go beyond any single moment. The drama of the everyday doesn't just remain at the level of the everyday; the everyday itself is shown to be so much more than readers might at first assume. The everyday is composed, as Christina Sharpe has argued, by the "weather" of anti-Blackness. As she puts it, "In my text, the weather is the totality of our environment; the weather is the total climate; and that climate is antiblack."[27] But it would be a stretch, despite Sharpe's analogous use of weather, to claim that Rankine's poetic reflections on the everyday have anything specific to say about climate change. I am unable to read *Citizen* as a direct comment on the latter. There are limits to what reading for climate change can reveal.

Citizen might thus be thought of as participating in a form of denial, especially when part VI begins with an explicit invocation of Hurricane Katrina without reference to this larger phenomenon. It takes work to talk about this event in particular without talking about climate change, for it was one of the very first disasters to break the smooth silencing of discussions of this phenomenon in U.S. mainstream media accounts of extreme weather events. For this reason I struggled with the decision to include such a lengthy discussion of *Citizen* in this chapter.

I don't want to press this point too much. Not every literary work has to make explicit reference to climate change or environmental problems more generally to offer something useful for readers who care about such topics and want to amplify awareness of their challenge. As Kate Marshall argues, critics interested in climate change often fall prey to "a demand for content." She describes this demand as the belief that critics should act as collectors, creating lists of literary works in which the topic of climate change is easy to identify, central to the stories they tell, and explicit in the connections they make. A necessary complement, she insists, is the development of reading practices that are sensitive to subtle traces and hybrid forms. What is needed are "good readers" and "good aesthetic responses to the world as it is." What is needed is a focus on both reading *and* making.[28]

My focus, then, is on how Rankine models through her revival of the lyric a way of apprehending the everyday that doesn't hesitate to pay attention to the disturbing conflicts and resulting injuries that are too often buried in silence. There are many heavy psychic costs to so much attentiveness, which *Citizen* explicitly acknowledges and explores in depth, and one such cost is a recognition of how race impinges on what it means to be human for the speaker. The human is always presented in the book as an open question. What does it mean to be human? And closely aligned with this question is another: What kind of agency can you have when your humanity is in so much doubt?

In thinking about these questions, I find it instructive to linger for a moment with Jane Bennett's most recent book, *Influx and Efflux: Writing Up with Walt Whitman*. It directly addresses the problem of human agency from a new-materialist perspective by describing the shape of this agency operating in a world of vibrant matter. It focuses primarily on Walt Whitman's poems, finding in them a quirky being in the world that draws affect from physical posture, pulsates with sympathetic flows of energy, and withholds snappy judgment in favor of nonchalance. It further elaborates such thoughts with discussion of the philosopher Alfred North Whitehead, the French surrealist Roger Caillois, the critic Harold Bloom, and Henry David Thoreau, which invites readers to think of the human "I" as constantly drawing in influence from elsewhere and exhaling it out in subtly changed forms. This is the "influx" and "efflux" of the book's title. The "mode of subjectivity and action" it thus conjures, based on readings of these authors, acknowledges how "the forces of nonhuman agencies and the ubiquity of stupendous, ethereal influences . . . become more felt, and, given more their due, become slightly more susceptible to being inflected, for example, toward an egalitarian politics."[29]

I greatly admire the originality of Bennett's ideas and find her efforts to break the mold of often-stultifying scholarly writing courageous. At the same time, I am frustrated by the ways in which its suspicion of a strong human agency and lack of careful thinking about human differences lend support to a quiescent form of politics, as in the emphasis on nonchalance and the slightness of the effects it attends to. I am even more frustrated by Bennett's archive, which remains predominantly white, male, and Euro-American. Her stated concern for egalitarianism, and support for antiracist and antifascist politics, would be better served if her archive were more diverse and if she were in more direct conversation with the many critics, *especially* nonwhite critics, thinking deeply about such politics. Indeed, it is deeply unfortunate that of her rare references to African American thinkers, her most explicit—"Henry H. Lewis, Simon Foreman Laundrey, Lucretian [*sic*] Mott, and Frederick Douglass"—is made as part of a recuperation of nineteenth-century phrenology from associations with scientific racism. What these figures have to offer on their own to a discussion about human agency is not the point; rather, Bennett mentions them to help keep the focus on Whitman and his use of "phrenological terms and practices."[30]

In many ways, *Influx and Efflux* feels to me like a missed opportunity because it does not more directly engage the many brilliant provocations offered by scholars of race around the very topic of the human. They have produced accounts of the human that Bennett should have considered, and responded to, in her own work. Climate change's rupturing of the world, in particular, has called for a reckoning with the models used to make sense of the world as it exists, and in their place what is emerging is a suspicion of the human as a concept invented in Europe during a period of global exploration and conquest. As the historian Dipesh Chakrabarty observes in an often-cited article, "The fact that the crisis of climate change will be routed through all our 'anthropological differences' can only mean that, however anthropogenic the current global warming may be in its origins, there is no corresponding 'humanity' that in its oneness can act as a political agent."[31]

Chakrabarty's article is cited so widely because it homes in on a central problem that Bennett sidesteps. Current concepts of the human, with their emphases on freedom and individuality, did not emerge in Europe alone but as part of a convergence of events happening in the Caribbean. As Lisa Lowe argues in an especially riveting account of this originating moment:

> Liberal forms of political economy, culture, government, and history propose a narrative of freedom overcoming enslavement that at once denies colonial slavery, erases the seizure of lands from native peoples, displaces migrations and connections across continents, and internalizes these processes in a national struggle of history and consciousness. The social inequalities of our time are a legacy of these processes through which "the human" is "freed" by liberal forms, while other subjectivities, practices, and geographies are placed at a distance from "the human."[32]

The idea of the human cannot be shorn from the history Lowe references in this passage, which implicates its grandest claims in the violent expropriation of land, the equally violent movement of people as labor, and the rise of the plantation.

The geographer Kathryn Yusoff seconds this point when she observes that geology "is a category and praxis of dispossession. It has determined the geographies and genealogies of colonial extraction in a double sense: first, in terms of settler colonialism and the *thirst* for land and minerals, and second, as a category of the inhuman that transformed people into things."[33] It's partially this way of thinking about land as geology that has left contemporary environmentalism susceptible to what Sarah Jaquette Ray describes as "discourses that make the exclusion and exploitation of those deemed other the cost of protecting the environment."[34] Predating these statements and in many ways providing the intellectual foundation for them, Sylvia Wynter comments on the process by which some humans are "overrepresented" as human, dehumanizing others, so that "non-West, nonwhite peoples can only, at best, be assimilated as honorary humans (as in the case of the 'developed' Japanese and other lighter-skinned Asians) and, at worst, must . . . forcibly be proscribed from human status by means of the rapidly expanding U.S. prison-industrial complex."[35]

No wonder, then, that the very idea of the human is being questioned by scholars of race, especially in African American studies. Alexander Weheliye, for instance, explicitly sets out to find alternative "genres of the human" (Wynter's phrase) that actively maintain the possibility for "lines of flight, freedom dreams, practices of liberation, and possibilities of other worlds."[36] Likewise, Zakiyyah Iman Jackson considers how "the severe limitations of liberal humanism" have led to "a radical questioning of 'the human.'" She continues, "This questioning is suggestive of a desire for, perhaps, a different 'genre of the human' or may even signal, as I propose, an urgent demand for the dissolution of 'human' but, in either case, is not simply a desire for fuller recognition within liberal humanism's terms."[37] It might be said that Bennett is *also* interested in a similar project, in which the human is freed from the confines of a constricting liberalism. And yet the difference remains that Bennett assumes that the human names something quintessential, a "oneness," to use Chakrabarty's word, that her careful reading of canonical Euro-American texts can tease out. The problem with the human, then, is its separation from its surroundings and antipathy to influence and not also its separation from itself. Weheliye and Jackson, in contrast, clearly reject such a starting place and understand the very category of the human itself to be fundamentally exclusionary. It is founded on racial differences, especially on anti-Black racism.

Any practice of sustaining attention to climate change must thus not only reckon with the ways in which the dominant models for making sense of the world are "genre flailing," as Lauren Berlant puts it, but also be mindful of how the human itself, as sovereign and separate from the environment, has been produced by a history of violent expansion and expropriation of peoples and resources.[38] As Patricia Stuelke observes, building on Berlant's argument:

> Amid the floods, famine, and fire of accelerating climate disaster, worsening refugee crises, unbounded global war, mass incarceration, femicides, the resurgence of white supremacist movements, and the crushing burden of work and debt, the aesthetic and social forms people share are no longer sufficient to sustain them in the face of the "violence of the world," and so we fumble around for new imaginaries that might hold us together and propel us toward the possibility of just and livable life.[39]

To sustain attention to the forms of organized injustice that contribute to the present's environmental emergency is to realize how many other forms of organized injustice exist alongside, and are interwoven with, them.

In the flailing search for "new imaginaries" that make denials of climate change harder to engage and attention more common, and in the process allow those who may not possess a lot of agency to acquire more of it, Rankine offers a lot. She offers an understanding of the human as fraught and fragile, with the everyday itself a series of potentially traumatic encounters that can viscerally remind those who are Black like her that they don't belong. The everyday thus needs to be navigated carefully:

> Though a share of all remembering, a measure of all
> memory, is breath and to breathe you have to create
> a truce—
>
> a truce with the patience of a stethoscope.[40]

Reading *Citizen* for climate change might offer, then, a strong critique of the kind of claims about the human and human agency that Bennett makes, one that seeks to found a stance that everyone can share as if the human itself wasn't already a kind of ruin, a concept passed down to the present as fragments even if some have the luxury to imagine something more whole. It reminds me again of the significance of Chakrabarty's observation that there is no one humanity capable of acting in a way that decisively addresses the challenges of climate change. When I use the word *human*, I think of it as implicitly asking a question. What alternative genres can it name? For me, the lyric asks the same question because it, too, like the idea of the human, is founded in ruin.

As much as I find Rankine's poetry instructive, I worry that, in focusing on *Citizen* so much in this chapter, I have promised to think about the lyric and climate change together in an explicit way and then offered instead only a discussion of the lyric that is primarily focused on the everyday, racial microaggressions, and critiques of the human. This concern leads me to focus on the work of Craig Santos Perez, which is much more explicit about its interest in climate change and is as worthy of attention as Rankine's poetry. The following two poems, for instance, appeared together in the *New Republic* under the title "Love Poems in the Time of Climate Change" and so directly reference the phenomenon I promised to discuss.

The first, subtitled "Sonnet XVII," has a strong first-person speaker, an often-repeated "I," and is addressed to a second person, the often-repeated "you." It's not clear, however, as the poem progresses who the I and the you are. The you becomes by the final stanza of this three-stanza poem less a person and more a personification—but of what I'm not sure:

> I love you without knowing how, or when, the world will end—
> I love you naturally without pesticides or pills—
> I love you like this because we won't survive any other way,
> except in this form in which humans and nature are kin,
> so close that your emissions of carbon are mine,
> so close that your sea rises with my heat.

The second poem, "Sonnet XII," begins by naming what it addresses without ambiguity:

> Global woman, waxy apple, record heat,
> thick smell of algae, burnt peat and sunset,
> what rich nitrogen opens between your native trees?
> What fossil fuels does a man tap with his drill?[41]

It's important that these are love poems, for the object being addressed is emphasized much more than the speaker. They are not explorations of the speaker's subjectivity but apostrophes that attempt to think with and about a world beyond the speaker that calls forth a structured literary response. Even the verb tense is a response to this object focus.

In trying to make sense of what's happening in these twin poems, I find it useful to think about Jonathan Culler's argument—in his book-length study of the lyric—that creative writers are self-conscious in the way they read and respond to past writers. Just as important, literary forms, once developed, can be used by anyone in any subsequent period and are not therefore like a "sociopolitical configuration." "Who could have expected," he muses, "the villanelle and the sestina to resurface as they did in the twentieth century? Lyric forms are not confined to one historical period but remain available as possibilities in different eras."[42] This observation applies as well to Agha Shahid Ali, who often wrote in the ancient form of the *ghazal* and helped to promote it in English.[43]

Culler is not saying that the lyric, or any genre, is static. Rather, genres move through time in a different way from other concepts or objects. By attending to genre in particular, Culler believes scholars can arrive at a literary history that is respectful of this different sense of temporality, one that allows them to think of literature as being marked by "the modifications of genres, the rise of new genres, and the eclipse of the old" rather than "as the succession of individual works."[44] Thinking of the lyric as a genre with its own way of moving through history allows Culler to claim "that there is a Western tradition of short, nonnarrative, highly rhythmical productions, often stanzaic, whose aural dimension is crucial."[45] What is missing from this definition is the focus on a subject. In his or her or their place is an emphasis on the "aural dimension" of the lyric, one that depends for its effect on rhythm.

A focus on rhythm is crucial to Culler's claim that the lyric does not seek to mirror action, as the epic and drama were said to by Aristotle, but rather seeks to be its own event. It thus prefers enunciation in the simple present tense and evokes in this way a presence that does not require the narrative apparatus that a focus on a subject entails. Indeed, for Culler, the subject who speaks in a lyric poem may be more important than who, or what, is addressed. Referencing new-materialist speculation about the agency of things and the independent existence of objects, Culler observes, "The poets, though, were here first. They have risked embarrassment in addressing things that could not hear in an attempt to give us a world that is perhaps not more intelligible but more in tune with the passionate feelings, benign, hostile, and ecstatic, that life has inspired."[46]

Not only a beloved other or the reader but a wide variety of animals and objects are often the object of the lyric's address. And sometimes, as in Elizabeth Bishop's "Roosters," what is addressed responds:

Each screaming
"Get up! Stop dreaming!"
Roosters, what are you projecting?[47]

And at other times, as in Frank O'Hara's "A True Account of Talking to the Sun at Fire Island," the object is first to speak:

> The Sun woke me this morning loud
> and clear, saying "Hey! I've been
> trying to wake you up for fifteen
> minutes. Don't be so rude, you are
> only the second poet I've ever chosen
> to speak to personally.[48]

To take a more recent example, it's the LP's turn to speak in Morgan Parker's "My Vinyl Weighs a Ton":

> Shut down shut up slip me out of my sleeve
> I have come from the grasses of California.[49]

I am drawn to Culler's understanding of the lyric for the ways in which this lyric can speak from an inhuman or nonhuman position that asks its readers to experience a very different world in the here and now than the ones they may be accustomed to inhabiting. Rather than being a humanistic literary genre, one focused on the expressivity of an individual subject, the lyric might spell trouble for the human. I mean *trouble* in the way Donna Haraway means it, "to stir up," "to make cloudy," "to disturb." As she explains, "Staying with the trouble requires learning to be truly present, not as vanishing pivot between awful or edenic pasts and apocalyptic or salvific futures, but as mortal critters entwined in myriad unfinished configurations of places, times, matters, and meanings."[50] By adding "the" before "trouble" in her book's title, Haraway makes it clear that she cares about a specific disturbance, environmental catastrophe.

Following Culler's lead, I want to focus on how Perez's poems are written in the simple present tense. In everyday speech in English, when speakers speak of the present, they more often than not use the present progressive. So already the lyric penchant for the simple present tense is a departure from the everyday. When Culler tries to explain this convention, he observes, "In English, to note *occurrences* in the present, we use the present progressive tense: 'I am walking.' When we encounter the unmarked nonprogressive present tense with occurrences, we can guess that we are dealing with a foreigner or a poem."[51] *I am walking* versus *I walk*: the latter signifies that you are in the presence of "a foreigner or a poem," which also implies that "I" am not a foreigner and not a poet. To be a poet, then, is to be like—or is it just to be?—a foreigner, who in turn betrays his or her foreignness by a lack of familiarity with the well-worn conventions of English language usage.

I am no fan of Culler's sloppy equation of the foreigner (in the United States?) with nonstandardized use of English (must the foreigner always come from a non-English-speaking country?). Nevertheless, I am tantalized by the suggestion that a poet is akin to a foreigner in the United States, in that both are out of place in English, and as a result the poet charts a disturbing relationship to his or her conventions. I imagine that Perez, a native Chamoru of Guam who has written many poems about the legacy of colonialism in the Pacific and the struggles of Pacific Islanders, would be delighted by this suggestion, for it would mean his choice to write lyric poetry was a good one. Although the United States came to Guam, its conquest of this island has made the Indigenous population there a kind of foreigner in their own land. In this spirit I would like to call the lyric use of the simple present tense the *foreign present*.

If the foreign present is a staple of the lyric, as Culler argues, it's worth noting the ways in which Perez diverges from the conventions of the lyric as well. For instance, neither "Sonnet XVII" nor "Sonnet XII" is a conventional sonnet. While they are each fourteen lines long, none of these lines follows any rhyme scheme, much less the strict schemes most associated with the sonnet in English or Italian. The meter is also not regular. In addition, the numbering suggests these poems are part of a larger set, but it's not clear where this larger set can be found. As a result, the poems feel like fragments. They are the ruins of the fullness they can only allude to. Moreover, these poems are numbered but not presented in a sequential manner. That is, the higher-numbered sonnet *precedes* the lower-numbered one, and not the reverse, as a reader might expect. This upsetting of what might be called *poetic order*—if it's possible to speak of such a concept anymore, if one ever could—thus requires readers to listen to these poems in their own self-imposed terms.

And if readers try to do this, they are likely to find the lines of these poems pleasant to listen to because of their unmistakable rhythmic, but not regular, qualities. "Sonnet XII" in particular opens with a line that contains three short phrases, each of which contains two pairs of stressed and unstressed syllables in succession, with the third phrase leaving out the final unstressed syllable for emphasis. The regularity of these trochees calls attention to the syllable that isn't there at the end of the line, which suggests less a hard caesura for dramatic effect, the purpose for which a catalectic is often employed, and more the conjuring of something missing, the loss of a pattern that has failed to form. Just say the words again aloud and notice how difficult it is not to chant them in a rhythmic way or to feel that last missing syllable: "Global woman, waxy apple, record heat."

Right away, this rhythm provides a kind of incantatory or ritualistic power to the whole poem. In addition, while both poems reference an explicit speaker, the speaker is an abstraction, and in the second poem there's an interchanging of "I" and "we" that suggests a disinvestment in a lone subject in quiet contemplation in favor of a focus on a collective struggle with the issues the poem raises. What is more, these issues in both poems are the occasion for their existence. They are addressed to the problem of climate change, and what they speak about is not the inner struggles of the subject but the public challenges that you, as the reader, share with every other reader.

THE AGENCY OF THINGS

Only "Sonnet XVII" makes it into Perez's volume of poetry *Habitat Threshold*, this time under the title "Love in a Time of Climate Change."[52] In being thus included, the poem changes meaning. While before I read it as a love poem addressed to another adult, its placement in a collection of poems occasioned by the birth of the speaker's daughter suggests this poem is actually addressed to her. Resituating the poem in this way may make it seem more conventional than what I have been describing it as. Rather than refashioning the lyric in a dramatic fashion, it may merely return the reader to a familiar set of concerns about the human, the subjective, and the individual, with the infant acting as a symbol of what Lee Edelman calls "reproductive futurism."[53]

The very first poem announces this very kind of psychic investment, as it focuses on the speaker's daughter as a fetus. "The Age of Plastic" begins:

> The doctor presses the **plastic** probe
> against my pregnant wife's belly.
> *Plastic leaches estrogenic and toxic chemicals.*
> Ultrasound waves pulse between **plastic**,
> tissue, fluid, and bone until the embryo
> echoes. *Plastic makes this possible.*[54]

Environmental concerns are literally highlighted in this passage by putting uses of *plastic* in bold, when the other words are faded. And while plastic itself doesn't cause climate change, it is made of oil, and its production is energy-intensive. Such connections are encouraged by the paratext in the volume: the page facing this poem contains a graph (figure 2.3) representing

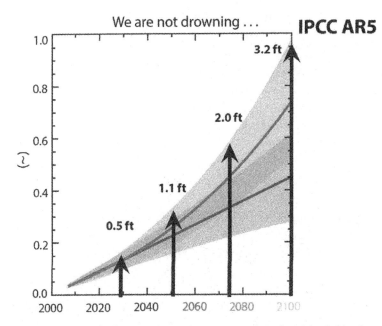

FIGURE 2.3 Facing the first poem in Craig Santos Perez's *Habitat Threshold* is this graph projecting future sea-level rise based on data from the fifth assessment report of the Intergovernmental Panel on Climate Change (2014). In Perez, *Habitat Threshold*, 10.

the projected sea-level rise, and on the right margin of the poem there's a quotation from Roland Barthes inviting critique of the cultural meaning of plastic.

In this way, the first page of the volume encourages readers to think about climate change as a phenomenon that is intimately connected to the human body and its capacity for reproduction. It also encourages thinking about the ways in which the body and the environment are inextricably connected, so that the chemicals in the plastic can "leach" through the skin at contact, potentially triggering what Heather Houser calls "ecosickness": "It is a pervasive dysfunction; it cannot be confined to a single system and links up the biomedical, environmental, social, and ethicopolitical; and it shows the imbrication of human and environment."[55] All of this hinges on the investment in the child as a figure of the future, the anxiety this poem expresses being connected to the potential damage that might be inflicted on both mother and fetus, so that heterosexual reproductivity links data visualization to verse and analysis. The very emphasis in the second line, "my pregnant wife's belly," makes explicit what is at stake. At the same time, there's something about the plastic itself that the poem is not subtle about calling attention to. The bold makes the word stick out on the page and moreover insists that it is a noun that can carry an agentive verb. The plastic "leaches," and it "makes." The plastic, then, is capable of agency. It might not be as deliberate as the kind humans practice, but it nevertheless has effects on the world that need to be attended to, which suggests a messier frame than the one proffered by reproductive futurism. Here, then, is an example of climate lyricism where anthropocentric habits of expression turn back onto themselves.

This kind of thinking about the agency of things seems especially vivid in this passage because of its use of the lyric and the way it invites thought about the divide between the human and the nonhuman. The passage recalls for me other moments when a piece of writing or filmmaking caught my attention in a similar way, which extends my interest in the lyric beyond a concern with genre to encompass habits of attending. The first example is a journalistic description of Staten Island just after Hurricane Sandy passed over it in 2012: "Shrubs and saplings had been cut off at the roots—not cleanly, but as if scratched away by fingernails. Deep gouges in the banks undercut fences and asphalt biking trails, and the scrubby trees far above the usual high-tide line hunkered down as if some massive creature had slept on them. Shreds of plastic bags hung among the branches everywhere, while the ocean, distant and calm at low tide, offered its quiet wavelets and asked, 'Who, me?'"[56] The words that leap out of this passage are words ordinarily reserved for human, or at least some kind of animal, agency: "scratched," "hunkered down," and "asked." The point might be made a little too emphatically, especially in the way the action is connected through simile to an organic being ("fingernails" and "creature"), as if the journalist doesn't trust the reader to get his meaning. The words "gouges" and "shreds" are used as nouns but also connote human or animal action. As a result of such word choices, the landscape becomes a scene of forces mimicking what is ordinarily thought of as human agency, and until the end of this passage, the word choices allow a slipperiness between the human and nonhuman, an in-between that has more often than not been occupied by nonwhite people. But the slipperiness gives way at the end, as the source of this agency, the ocean, is imagined not only to have the ability to enact great violence but to dissemble with a threatening coyness. The ocean does not merely speak in this passage. It lies.

The rhetorical flourishes found in this quotation and its heavy dependence on personification are some of the things I remember most vividly about the readings I did in writing this book. In such descriptions, things seem capable of action despite their inhumanity, and often, as in the case of Hurricane Sandy, they act with more force than humans can comprehend, even as I work hard to remind myself that the human as a category is racially exclusionary.

The quotation that describes Kath in front of a field laden with meaning, found near the end of Kazuo Ishiguro's *Never Let Me Go*, evokes a similar kind of moment for me, albeit more subtly:

> I was thinking about the rubbish, the flapping plastic in the branches, the shore-line caught along the fencing, and I half-closed my eyes and imagined this was the spot where everything I'd ever lost since my child-hood had washed up, and I was now standing here in front of it, and if I waited long enough, a tiny figure would appear on the horizon across the field, and gradually get larger until I'd see it was Tommy, and he'd wave, maybe even call.[57]

It would be incorrect to say an explicit personification is employed in this long sentence, but there's nevertheless the sense of a kinetic being. "Flapping" suggests action, even if not driven by a sentient will, while "shore-line" invites comparison to the motion of the waves as they repeatedly remake sand and rock. The waves push out and draw back, a movement imitated by the syntax of this passage, which hints at a perception of time on Kath's part that the past can come back to her instead of always receding in a single linear direction. The flapping and the shoreline are manifestations of the field itself, which Kath is standing in front of and contemplating, as if the field was the source of some mysterious agency. In the distance is Tommy, a clone like Kath who occupies an in-between between the human and nonhuman, whose agency (especially as he has died long ago) is as whimsical as the agency of the field.

As another illustration of the way personification grants agency to things, troubling the boundary between the human and nonhuman, I turn next to what may be the most memorable moment in Michael Pollan's deservedly well-known book *The Omnivore's Dilemma*, his description of the corn at the base of the United States' industrial food system (itself a significant contributor to global warming). I've taught this book to students for years, and this passage in particular stands out in my mind: "Basically, modern hybrids can tolerate the corn equivalent of city life, growing amid multitudes without succumbing to urban stress. You would think that competition among individuals would threaten the tranquility of such a crowded metropolis, yet the modern field of corn forms a most orderly mob. This is because every plant in it, being an F-1 hybrid, is genetically identical to every other. . . . There are no alpha corn plants to hog the light or fertilizer." Later in the same chapter, Pollan returns to his conceit of the anthropomorphized corn: "And then of course there's the corn itself, which if corn could form an opinion would surely marvel at the absurdity of it all—and at its great good fortune."[58]

I want to give one final example, because I want to sample a large variety of expressive modes. This one focuses on images and sounds. It comes from the critically acclaimed independent film *Beasts of the Southern Wild*. Intercutting the narrative of a Black man and his daughter living in an impoverished tidal community threatened by floods (modeled on the Isle de Jean Charles on the jagged southern coast of Louisiana) and by dams meant to protect a more affluent—and less racially heterogeneous—nearby community are scenes of icebergs breaking apart and falling into the ocean on the other side of the planet. As these icebergs break apart, they awaken giant boar-like creatures that march across an abstract landscape, until at the very end of the film they face the Black girl—I don't write "African American" because it's not clear to me what timeline the movie is set in or if in this timeline the United States exists—who snarls angrily back at them, while in the background rousing music blares signifying something momentous is occurring that requires the viewer's utmost attention.

Rather than confrontation, however, the film suggests that something more communicative occurs, a moment of mutual acknowledgment. What at first seems threatening turns out narratively to be more profoundly contiguous, a metonymic line drawn between melting ice and charging animals and snarling human. The Black girl seems somehow to have come face to face with the melting ice as embodied by the animals and in doing so gives recognition to the animals as the manifestation of the ice's changing form and the water's growing force. There's continuity in this encounter rather than conflict or demarcation.

Attempts like these to describe a being that clearly lies outside ordinary habits of perception—a leaching plastic, a lying ocean, a time-traveling field, a city of corn, ice–animal–Black girl—seem to strive to capture what Seo-Young Chu calls an "elusive referent." If so, they don't so much decenter the human as they recognize how humans, a concept increasingly turbulent with dispute, fit into a world they have always been a part of. They are a warning against claims to mastery *and* a creative description of how humans can make sense of and exert their agency in an environment full of animistic wonder. Because such moments of recognition are difficult to arrive at, elusive as they are, their occasion needs to be multiplied. Recognition has to happen again and again, a practice of being aware of how the everyday offers opportunities for such witnessing that is active and purposeful. The revival of the lyric as exemplified by Rankine and Perez offers such occasions in highly condensed forms, so that they contribute to the making of habits of attending.

WHY STAY WITH BAD FEELINGS?

Ilya Kaminsky's *Deaf Republic* and Tommy Pico's *IRL*

A CONFESSION, IN KEEPING WITH THE TRADITION of the lyric after the nineteenth century: whether warranted or not, I felt comfortable in the early years of my career moving across discussions of novels, autobiography and memoir, journalism, films, and television shows, but I drew a bright line beyond which the study of poetry lay. The latter seemed daunting, the province of specialists who had dedicated themselves to a deep knowledge of prosody, literary experimentation, extensive memorization, and a genealogy of mostly white poets with its own, often-obscure systems of valuation. The more contemporary poetry, in particular, felt the most difficult to read, much less write about, for it hadn't been discussed in the courses I had taken in the past, often didn't look like the kind of poetry I had been exposed to, and was full of controversies and divisions I was only somewhat aware of. Trying to read it, much less write about it, felt as if I was trespassing on someone else's property—the someone else being specialists and gatekeepers who were not inclined to be welcoming, especially for nonwhites.[1] I suspect that for many critics and avid readers alike, these feelings are familiar.

As I sought to think more deliberately about climate change as a topic for literary study, I read more poetry than I ever had before—most of it contemporary and written by very racially diverse authors. This poetry has altered my sense of the world and of my place in it. I became more alive to the cadences around me, to the rhythms of the days and seasons and my body's movement through the city in which I live. Everywhere, I felt music greeted me, and I became more conscious of the beats Jonathan Culler calls attention to in his book on the lyric, many discordant and harsh, which made me stop and contemplate what exactly I was experiencing. Meditating on Wallace Stevens's claim that "the poem must resist the intelligence / Almost successfully," Culler writes, "Usually this is taken as a warrant for obscure poetry, but poetry can resist the intelligence without being obscure: by offering linguistic echoing without obvious thematic purport, and by so doing get under the guard of intelligence, as it were, into memory, where it can provide form for the mind to espouse."[2] A "linguistic echoing" is what I experienced, my very motion through space humming to a beat that existed in memory and was not always processible by my mind. The poetry helped me to form new habits of attending.

I also lost a lot of sleep and felt agitated and anxious. What others viewed as ordinary I began to think of as menacing. My attention, forcibly arrested on the topic of climate change with the drumbeat of contemporary verse as an aid (and because of the discipline required to write this book), made me aware of the severity of the environmental concerns pressing down on the present and the urgency of finding ways to address these concerns, often against entrenched structures of power designed to protect a ruinous business as usual. The seasons in the Boston area seemed to have lost their shape; the rain came as downpours, and then no rain came for days and even weeks; the temperature swung wildly, and if it snowed, it would be a blizzard that made everything white for what seemed only a day or two before melting away. December and January were often mild, while February became the fiercest of winter months, and cool weather dominated through March and April and into May.

In the spring I became aware of the disorder of the local flora. Miniature Japanese maples, cherry trees in blossom, gingkoes, and even bamboo spoke to the ways in which homeowners were planting for aesthetic pleasure from a global selection of trees. And, indeed, if I thought about it further, I became aware of how the very idea of an invasive species ignores how much of the flora and fauna around me originated from elsewhere, a transformation that dates as far back as the arrival of Christopher Columbus and the subsequent mass death of native populations in the Americas. Even the earthworms in the courtyard of my building are European settlers.[3]

In parallel with such thoughts, I especially came to value the poetry that doesn't indulge in overly pretty language. This poetry labors to ground its readers in the mundane and refuses the epiphanic moment or a sudden turn at the end that promises insight. More often than not, the insight that's offered in such a turn is fleeting—a feel-good moment that's incompatible with a present that requires dwelling in feeling bad. Climate change needs a slower burn of attentiveness, a willingness to sit with discomfort that doesn't fit too neatly into narrative plots, a returning again and again to contemplation. These are the demands of an everyday attention that is continually locked in a wrestling match with everyday denial.

In this chapter I want to focus on feeling bad as a daily experience and the way poetry encourages it. I look first to Ilya Kaminsky's extraordinary book of poetry *Deaf Republic*. In this section I expand further on the point I made earlier, that readers should not just look for literature that speaks explicitly about climate change (which is the rationale for my discussion of Claudia Rankine's *Citizen* and Kazuo Ishiguro's *Never Let Me Go*). Instead, readers should seek to make their interest in climate change explicit, asking about everything they read what it has to offer to an understanding of this topic. Next, I turn to the example of Tommy Pico, whose poetry I find myself rereading often for its accessibility, candor, and humor. There's something deeply appealing about these traits, which draw readers into an experience of the everyday that is at once unique to the speaker of his poems and generalizable, so that many different kinds of people might feel invited to share in these experiences and to recognize some of their own struggles in them. There's one moment in particular, in his first book of poetry, entitled *IRL*, that crystallizes for me the need to share bad feelings rather than keep them all to myself. The goal of focusing on the everyday is not to make thinking about climate change tolerable, which would be its own kind of everyday denial, but to sustain an awareness of how terrible it is.

TOWN WATCHES EARTH STORY

The poems in *Deaf Republic* conjure an imaginary town named Vasenka, which is part of a country at war and occupied by foreign soldiers. Few of the soldiers know the local language. They are brutal and violent. They lack names or other markers that might set them off from each other and make them unique in some way. The first half of the book focuses on Alfonso and his pregnant wife, Sonya, beloved puppeteers who perform their shows in the town square. During one of these shows, the soldiers arrive and, in an altercation with a deaf boy, shoot him dead. The town's residents, in defiance, suddenly become deaf and develop their own sign language to communicate with one another.

Their deafness—whether an actual physical change that happens to them or a deliberate pretense taken up as a form of protest—suggests the precarity of their lives. Ordinary economic concerns are superseded by a constant threat of violence and death, and it's never clear who will be subject to such cruelty. Just after Sonya gives birth, she is rounded up by the soldiers, sexually humiliated, and murdered. Deranged by grief and anger, Alfonso agrees to murder a soldier captured by the townspeople and is subsequently hung. The second half of the book focuses on Gayla, a sexually attractive middle-aged puppet-theater owner, whose female puppeteers attract soldiers into their rooms only to murder them. When the deaths are discovered, the soldiers kill many of the town's women in retaliation, and the townspeople eventually turn on Gayla for bringing this misfortune on them. Sometime after her death, their country surrenders, and the war ends.

I focus on the story this book tells because it is a harrowing tale of failure, with the town members behaving in ways they regret, as the book makes explicit. Regret leads to denial and to an everyday full of a refusal to dwell on bad feelings. "Years later," one of the last poems observes, "some will say none of this happened; the shops were open, we were happy, and went to see puppet shows in the park." History has been rewritten, at least by some, the unpleasant parts the book narrates written out, and in its place a rosier picture of daily life has been imagined. The poem continues:

> And yet, on some nights, townspeople dim the lights and teach their children to sign. Our country is the stage: when patrols march, we sit on our hands. Don't be afraid, a child signs to a tree, a door.[4]

The arc of this story does not follow a familiar plot. There's no movement toward a goal; rather, humiliation pervades it as the country loses the war it has been fighting and the townspeople must accept the occupation of their homes by a foreign power. Clearly, the presence of the soldiers continues to be intrusive, as their "patrols" intimidate the townspeople and make them retreat into silence and denial. What remains of their resistance is muted, physically, and even their mute forms of communication are further restricted when they feel threatened. Literal denial, then, can be understood as a protective strategy, a way to survive in a situation the townspeople no longer feel they have the ability to alter.

What, then, does the child signing "to a tree, a door" signify? Since these are lines from a poem that tells this story in a highly compressed form (sometimes what happens is signified by the title and not the text that follows), the reader is asked to linger over the meaning of a tree and a door. Grammatically, the quotation presents these two objects not as alternative possibilities. The child is not oriented toward either a tree or a door but rather toward a tree that could also be a door. The two objects are interchangeable and perhaps even the same thing, at least from the perspective of the child. This suggests that both objects stand in for the same meaning, or whatever quality they have in common.

Perhaps, then, what the child signs toward is the possibility of something different, a way out either in the slowness of time that a tree can refer to or in the movement across a threshold that the door (which might very well be made of wood) suggests. These possibilities are outside the frame of the book itself, and of the story it tells, because the book restricts itself to a narrow band of time, years during which what has been narrated retreats into the past, and the present becomes life in the consequences of these events. It remains unclear what lies beyond this band of time, the years ahead when the child will continue to grow and perhaps, through the knowledge of signs, retain some memory of what happened. There is, in this image, the suggestion that time continues, and what may seem like the end of the story is merely its perpetual middle. What might seem like defeat and victory in the now of this moment is transitory in the greater expanse of time gestured to by this sentence.

But the reader needs to take care and not read in such a moment the promise that the townspeople can regain what has been lost. There's no going back to a prior, more pristine state of being, not after all they have been through, and given the way the town has acted, the suggestion remains that there was no ideal past or moment of purity to go back to. Even the moment when Alfonso kills the soldier is deliberately marked not as triumph, the fineness of the rebellion engaged in a righteous form of violence against the invaders, but, rather, as something the townspeople will later feel shamed by, something some will eventually deny happened.

While they "are cheering, elated," the speaker of the poems ends at some future date, when their lives will have ended and they will—in a dramatic reversal of common eschatological thinking—get a chance to put God on trial. These are perhaps some of the most memorable lines of the book:

> At the trial of God, we will ask: why did you allow all of this?
> And the answer will be an echo: why did you allow all of this?[5]

The first time the question is asked, it seems the townspeople want to know why they had to endure the horrors they have endured. There is in this iteration of the question the sense that agency lies elsewhere, as well as the fault. There is also, in the ambiguity of the "this" that ends each line, the possibility that the antecedent is not the occupation but rather Alfonso's murder of the soldier. They will remember that act as being as horrible as everything else that happened. God's response, the second iteration of the question, suggests that agency has not been limited to an elsewhere but that the townspeople themselves have acted. They made choices that led to the horror they endured, including the decision to murder the first soldier and to turn to Alfonso to carry out their will. When Alfonso is hung for this deed, the wind also has agency:

> In the Central Square, Alfonso hangs from a rope. Urine darkens his
>   trousers.
>
> The puppet of his hand dances.

The spare quality of the description invites the reader to imagine the details—the way the body twists on a rope, circling with the residual force left by the violence of taking the support from under the body and the body itself spasming and twitching as it dies, and then the ways in which the wind might gently caress the body, prompting the hand, so centrally a marker of human agency, in particular to dance. The same imagery of the wind exerting its force on what is now an inanimate object is repeated throughout the book, which reinforces the sense that the wind is making the hand move in this moment. When Sonya is put on display for the soldiers, "snow swirls in her nostrils."[6] When Alfonso is taken by the soldiers, "a t-shirt falls off a clothesline and an old man stops, picks it up, presses it to his face."[7] The townspeople, reflecting on Alfonso's death, proclaim, "Let us wash our faces in the wind."[8] Later, as the rebellion starts to grow more violent,

> Wind swept bread from market stalls, shopkeepers spill insults
> and the wind already has a bike between its legs.

While, before, the wind has been a subtle presence, exerting pressure on light objects—snow, a T-shirt, Alfonso's hand—in such a way that its force could be debated (What causes the snow to swirl? What caused the T-shirt to fall and the hand to dance?), it is now fully personified. But still, even this explicit manifestation of its force is not strong:

> The wind is helpless
> with desire to touch these bonnets and socks.[9]

All of these moments seem to revolve around the image of Alfonso's hand dancing. If the wind is indeed what moves the hand, is it the wind or the hand that has the most agency? Are they the same force? There is, in other words, a sly suggestion in the book that human agency is not the only force at play in this narrative, even as human agency is also not negligible; this undermines claims of individual mastery over the self while simultaneously not discounting the possibility of individual will completely. And, indeed, Alfonso's hand is described as a puppet, which reminds the reader that both Alfonso and Sonya were puppeteers and that Gayla is a puppet-theater owner. It's not difficult to decipher how the figure of an object that is primarily associated with the illusion of animation by hidden hands quizzes ordinary ideas of agency—what animates and what is animated are often different, and the former is often disguised or invisible.

As Mel Chen points out, the very word *animate* is associated with animacy, which linguistically is a "prevalent conceptual structure and ordering that might possibly come out of understandings of lifelines, sentience, agency, ability, and mobility in a richly textured world."[10] What is most animated is considered most alive and most capable of directing action. And the hierarchies such a privileging of animacy creates cannot be divorced from "the spread of Christian cosmologies, capitalism, and the colonial orders of things," which not only differentiate between the human and nonhuman but regulate who can be considered human among *Homo sapiens*.[11] The slowly building force of the wind in Kaminsky's poems suggests, subtly, a questioning of these kinds of hierarchies. The sources of animacy and agency are not easily divinable, the wind seems to sign.

It is a little more difficult to puzzle out how the figure of the puppet calls further attention to the hand, which is graphically depicted throughout the book in illustrations of the different signs the townspeople invent and learn to make. In each illustration the meaning of the sign the hands make is described with a helpful caption. Only at the end, when the main story is over, does the book present four illustrations of hands making signs without captions. The reader is required at this moment to remember, or to flip back to previous illustrations, to make sense of what the hands are communicating. As the accompanying reproduction (figure 3.1) shows, the top illustration is the sign for "town"; the second, "the town watches"; the third, "earth"; and the bottommost, "story." The notes at the end of the book tell the reader that these are not taken from any single existing sign language but are rather derived from several ("Russian, Ukrainian, Belarussian, American Sign Language, etc.") and that some signs were merely "made up" to evade the occupiers' prying.[12]

The sign for "story," for instance, is different from that in American Sign Language and, as far as I can tell, those in the other sign languages the book mentions. This suggests it's one of the signs the townspeople invented, in which case it's noteworthy that the sign for "story" used on this page is two hands that are at first open and then closed, as if a book has been shut—a reversal of how "story" was presented earlier, as two hands first closed and then open. "Story" thus does not refer at this moment to an opening up of meaning but to its closure. In the final gesture of the page, there is a recognition that something about the very idea of a story itself makes telling impossible. Something inevitably goes untold. There is also, in the way "story" can be two hands opening *or* two hands closing, the suggestion that storytelling itself is part of an ongoing series of openings and closures. It doesn't simply come to an end but is part of something larger, a seemingly endless movement through time.

Perhaps what goes untold at this book's moment of temporary closure is conjured directly at the start of *Deaf Republic*, in a framing poem that discusses the war from the perspective of the United States. There, people

protested
but not enough.

The United States, too, seems in this poem to be in turmoil, "falling" "invisible house by invisible house" so that

in the sixth month
of a disastrous reign in the house of money,

in the street of money in the city of money in the country of money,
our great country of money, we (forgive us)

lived happily during the war.[13]

The "happily" in this final line suggests something that explicitly has to be forgiven, for a state of everyday denial has actively turned attention away from the war the rest of the book narrates, to be instead occupied by the mindless pursuit of wealth. This mindless pursuit of wealth, accompanied by a happiness maintained by the arduous work of turning away from what is unpleasant or disturbing, has also led to "a disastrous reign," which conjures the sense that the United States is itself in the midst of political instability. How far away, then, is the occupation, the rebellion, and the violence on all sides narrated in the main poems of this book from a country already distracted and focused only on individual gain?

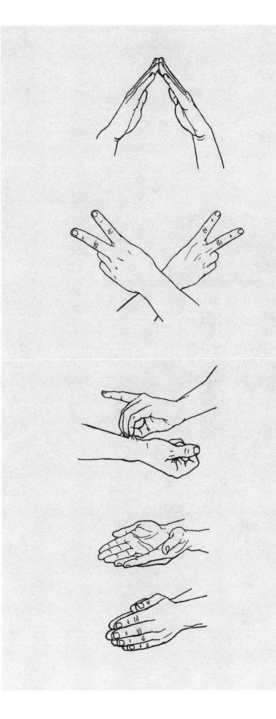

FIGURE 3.1
The topmost
drawing on this
page from Ilya
Kaminsky's *Deaf
Republic* is the
sign for "town";
the second, "the
town watches";
the third, "earth";
and the bottom-
most, "story." In
Kaminsky, *Deaf
Republic*, 73.

Deaf Republic ends with another framing poem, returning the reader to the United States, this time to consider the highly publicized incidents of police murdering African Americans:

Ours is a country in which a boy shot by the police lies on the pavement for hours.

We see in his open mouth
the nakedness
of the whole nation.[14]

Nevertheless, despite what such spectacles communicate about the turmoil the country has been plunged into, the everyday and its distracting rhythms reassert themselves:

All of us
still have to do the hard work of dental appointments,
of remembering to make
a summer salad.[15]

In both the first and last poems, then, Kaminsky foregrounds the sense of distance from tragedies happening both outside the country, in a faraway country, and inside the country, in a nearby community, and the ways in which most Americans cannot keep their attention on either. They are acknowledged and even discussed candidly, but what is missing is any sense that they entail more from the citizenry, maybe even a disruption of the everyday. As story, they are best represented by the image of open hands closing. And so while Kaminsky's poems might not have anything explicit to say about climate change, they gesture profoundly to what lies outside the way people frame their sense of the everyday, and they invite speculation about what is being foreclosed. This is an important gesture, if only because it makes the reader more aware of how the avoidance of bad feelings prevents a necessary openness to the many sources of collective heartache.

SHARING BAD FEELINGS

I might have overlooked the story had I not spent a semester teaching in Venice in the spring of 2016. On October 29, 2018, the famed Piazza San Marco was under three feet of water. For weeks, rain fell all over Italy. Across the country, winds exceeded a hundred miles per hour. By the time the storms ceased, about 250,000 acres of pine trees had been flattened, and about thirty people had died. In Venice itself, the mayor said the damage would amount to over a billion dollars.[16] The prefect decreed the closing of public buildings, including schools and universities—an unprecedented move, a resident told me. A year and a month later, the flooding returned, this time much worse. About 85 percent of the city was under water. I can easily imagine in both cases the alarm the rushing waters raised for the people who live in the city, but then again, for people elsewhere, heavy rain, flooding, damage to buildings, and disruption of civic institutions are becoming mundane events routinely reported in the news, and this level of destruction hardly seems worth singling out unless it dramatically exceeds what has come before.

Even in Venice, these events might not have felt all that momentous. The city floods regularly, especially from October to January and during full moons, when the tides are at their highest. Tall, narrow walkways on metal legs can be found stacked up along its busy pathways, ready to be laid out end to end for the *alta acqua*, literally "the high water." Long-term visitors are encouraged to get tall waterproof boots. A viral video after the 2018 flood shows people in a restaurant going about their business in what looks like a foot of standing water.[17] Diners wait for their orders. Waiters in black ties pick up pizzas at the counter. Friends greet each other with big smiles. The flooding was unusual for how high it was, but it could hardly be said to be unexpected or unusual. People live with the high water as best they can and keep going on with their lives.[18]

I recognize why anyone would want to avoid talking about climate change all the time and how thinking about it too much can overwhelm. The demand to pay attention can feed the worst traits of "environmental art, activism, and discourse," which, as Nicole Seymour argues, so often can be characterized with descriptors like "sanctimony," "self-righteousness," "being out of touch," and "unrelatable."[19] I often feel this way myself, an exhaustion with the feeling that I am not maintaining the right kind of feeling; in writing this book, I have had to step away from it frequently and find something to distract myself with. Sometimes, it was a relief to write about works like *Deaf Republic* or *Citizen,* neither of which mentions climate change explicitly, but then I had to shake my head loose and remind myself to focus. Denial, at least the kind that means not thinking about a problem (even if I am thinking about other problems), may be necessary, if only to give the mind a rest—so the point in discussing denial is not somehow to dispel it permanently. But it is also important to feel overwhelmed and to dwell on such a feeling so as to appreciate the enormity of what is happening, because only in this way can everyday denial give way to everyday attention. Without a sense of urgency, there can be no commensurate awareness of the enormity of the challenges climate change poses to everyone, and every living thing, on Earth.

In Tommy Pico's *IRL*, the speaker Teebs—a nickname the author also often goes by—confronts how denial goes beyond respite and becomes regulated by social conventions, so that, as for the Venetians in the storm, everyday life exerts a normalizing force. He finds himself at a ritzy party in the Hamptons where he feels out of place and keeps reminding himself, "*Keep it light keep it light.*" He says this to himself when another guest tells him he plans to move to Thailand to be with his "half / Thai girlfriend." In response, Teebs goes on and on about the coup and the protests there.[20] This encounter leads him to

think about death and climate change:

> Confront the swirl-
> ing panic of Do I Live, or
> leave—For ppl like us, isn't
> this always the question
> at the bottom of every
> question.
> Make a decision to cut
> emissions b4 greenhouse
> gasses turn into
> Venus. Let's be realistic.[21]

The use of short lines makes the pace fast. There's also the recognition in the first few lines that the speaker (Pico is Indigenous and queer) feels different from the other guests and that the reader is like the speaker in this feeling of difference (regardless of whether they are exactly like him). And in thinking about the weighty topic that is about to follow, there's the recognition that what's at stake is, for some more than others, an existential challenge—"Do I Live." Climate change kills, but not uniformly. It discriminates in its murderous violence between the poor and the rich, and between the people of color who are more likely to be poor and less protected by the state ("ppl like us") and the wealthy white partygoers.

Pico's use of colloquial abbreviations often found in social media, such as "ppl" and "b4," adds to the sense, however, that such weightiness cannot be held in mind too long. After the question, "Do I Live," there's the option to "leave." The short lines and the abbreviations further connect this passage to the flow of contemporary everyday life, with its many electronic distractions and twists of thought. This is not a physical leave-taking but a mental leaving. The mention of climate change is part of this flow. It doesn't nec-

essarily stand out and is as much an intrusion into the smooth running of
social occasions as Pico's references to political oppression and mass protest
are at a swanky party. What follows "realistic" at the end of the above quotation doesn't only lead to greater self-awareness. Being realistic can lead to
a vision of cataclysm:

> New York is drained
> of moisture and combusts.

But just as easily, and probably more likely, it can lead to something quotidian:

> I turn left
> and go to the gym.[22]

In these verses, the apocalyptic and the everyday exist in a cozy relationship to one another. The former erupts in thought in uncomfortable ways but
is forgotten and left behind with ease. It even gives a slight thrill that helps to
break up the dullness of a day. To be "realistic" means to recognize how such
concerns get normalized and become something not to dwell on for long.
Such concerns belong to what Henri Lefebvre calls, at the start of his foundational three-volume study of the everyday, "the weird and the bizarre," which
are "at one and the same time familiar yet surprising."[23] The careful patrolling
of boundaries, where crossings are modulated to preserve a sense of what is
familiar more than to carry beyond to something completely disorienting,
is what Jacques Rancière calls, in another frequently referenced study of the
everyday, "the distribution of the sensible," which "simultaneously discloses
the existence of something in common and the delimitations that define the
respective parts and positions within it."[24]

Kathleen Stewart calls the same phenomenon a "refrain," or a "scoring over
a world's repetitions. A scratching on the surface of rhythms, sensory habits,
gathering materialities, and durations." Against such a habit of making worlds,
Stewart proposes the existence of "bloom spaces," a way of occupying such
worlds that acknowledges the demand for "collective attunement and a more
adequate description of how things make sense, fall apart, become something else, and leave their marks, scoring refrains on bodies of all kinds—
atmospheres, landscapes, expectations, institutions, states of acclimation or
endurance or pleasure or being stuck or moving on."[25] If so, the existence
of bloom spaces and the constraints (rather than the possibilities) that accompany them are more apparent for those who are not thought of as fully
belonging to this kind of everyday. For instance, as Ju Yon Kim informs her
readers, late nineteenth-century Chinese immigrants to the United States,

who claimed the right to reentry based on their already existing citizenship, "had to establish their identity through the mundane, namely through their familiarity with the prosaic details of the lives they claimed on paper. American citizens had to demonstrate their status partly through clothing and mannerisms that evinced their time in the United States."[26] The everyday is not something you and I simply experience; it is a hailing, a discipline, a force of alienation.

As Pico's poetry dramatizes, the balance between inattention and attention in such an everyday tilts wildly toward the former. Avoiding the subject as much as possible in social occasions as well as in public forums is the expected norm, and such studied avoidance gives more power to those who insist there is no problem at all. In a room full of strangers or even casual acquaintances in the United States (or elsewhere), there is little possibility of sharing a wry acknowledgment, a witty or ironic statement, or even a knowing look. Such small exchanges are important, if only so no one feels crazy for noticing how out of joint everyday experiences have become.

But the conditions for even such tacit acknowledgment seem to be missing from the party Pico attends. To talk about climate change takes a tremendous amount of energy and involves a heavy social cost in such surroundings, so much so that it rarely comes up in conversation. And even if such conditions did exist, what would be acknowledged would very much be like Pico's "cut / emissions b4 greenhouse gasses turn into Venus," a moment of alarm carefully calibrated to provide a sharp sensation without being debilitating or disruptive. Its exaggeration provides alarm and enables easy dismissal.

According to the rules of civility, it's appropriate to discuss climate change in specialized circumstances but not in more mundane situations or in popular venues or in performances of the everyday. To do so is to break a social taboo, in the same way Teebs talking about coups and protests in Thailand while he attends a party on Long Island is an obvious faux pas. There should be a name for this kind of everyday encounter, when you flaunt convention and risk censure to talk about something that's usually considered out of place in an ordinary conversation. Sara Ahmed offers one possible name when she writes about how feminism often involves becoming conscious of unhappiness and in the process refusing a happiness that covers up the structural reasons for this unhappiness. Such feminism is often characterized as killing joy, and in the teeth of such a characterization, Ahmed wonders if it's possible to resignify the meaning of being a killjoy: "We can talk about being angry black women or feminist killjoys; we can claim those figures back; we can talk about those conversations we have had at dinner tables or in seminars or meetings; we can laugh in recognition of the familiarity of inhabiting that place." To this figure of the feminist killjoy, which Ahmed has worked so hard to teach her readers to celebrate, I want to add the figure of the climate killjoy: the one who, in insisting on talking about climate change and all that it entails, finds "solidarity in recognizing our alienation from happiness, even if we do not inhabit the same place (as we do not)."[27]

This is hardly a new application of this term, for environmentalists have long been characterized as killjoys. Seymour, again, speaks explicitly about this when she argues for a "bad environmentalism" founded on irony and irreverence and explicitly opposed to sincerity and purity. The examples she champions thus "actively anticipate, and attempt to change, the 'killjoy' reputation of environmentalists, at a time when public sentiment toward activists runs vitriolic."[28] Pico's IRL shows, at least to me, how one might not tiptoe around public sentiment but rush right against it. This doesn't mean giving up on irony or irreverence, qualities the speaker in this book has in abundance, but rather making use of both in insisting on talking about what others don't want to talk about.

If Pico is one example of a climate killjoy in writing about climate change in his long poem, here is another: the journalist Elizabeth Rush recalls walking along the shore in Rhode Island and contemplating the trees that can no longer survive as salt water reaches their roots. She asks a stranger if he knows what's happening to the trees. She then tells him everything she's recently learned about the tupelos and about the way the rising salt water over the past fifty years has slowly killed these trees that used to flourish all along the East Coast. Now they're just what coastal landscape architects call *rampike*, dead tree trunks that have had all their bark stripped from them, "looking as if pecked by ravens."[29]

She can't help herself. She is like the figure of a hand caressed by the wind in *Deaf Republic*, both moved by it and, luckily for her, capable of moving in response. She shares what she knows, and as she talks, the stranger "shifts from foot to foot, anxious to break away."[30] It's not fair to say that Rush takes joy in making the stranger uncomfortable, but she does it anyway. She feels the need to talk and in meeting this need—a significant act of the will—forces a conversation that no one seems to want because it threatens the pleasantness of the day and the enjoyment of a scenery that is pretty to look at so long as you don't look too closely.

HOW SHOULD I LIVE?

Inattention and Everyday-Life Projects

THE CLAIM I HAVE BEEN MAKING, that climate change requires a practice of sustaining attention occasioned by the revival of the lyric and focused on feeling bad, is counterintuitive. After all, there is a wealth of reliable, readily available information about this phenomenon. There are books and articles, documentaries and official reports, even podcasts and YouTube videos that will explain every facet of it to you in as much detail as you can stomach and at whatever level of difficulty you feel comfortable with. Much of this information is available with a few clicks of a keyboard, and it would take several lifetimes to consume all of it. The lyric is hardly the dominant genre or mode for these sources, and yet they excel in informing audiences about their subject and can often do so in entertaining ways that don't just leave you feeling awful.

If this material is still not enough to convince you that this phenomenon is something to be concerned about or if you feel for whatever reason that you'd rather not read or watch any of it (there are a lot of days when I'd rather not as well), you can just go outside and experience its effects for yourself. Extreme weather events are becoming more common. The seasons are losing their definition. The temperature dips and rises in unpredictable ways. Sunny days bring flooding in many coastal areas, especially on the East Coast of the

United States. The rain is heavier, downpours more common, and droughts more severe. Everywhere, there is the problem of too much water and not enough water. And the heat, which I personally dread the most, often lingers on and on, making even the simplest forms of physical exertion more annoying than I could have imagined. Just breathing can be laborious and strained. The very tempo of the natural world no longer swings the way it used to when I was young—and if you are young, my heart goes out to you, because you will never know its former tempo.

Nevertheless, I have met many who insist climate change is no big deal. They might not assert that the science is wrong, but they aren't alarmed by the changes happening around them and don't worry too much about what's to come. Many years ago, the father of my son's friend came to pick her up from a playdate. The weather had been acting strange in a predictably off-kilter way, and I said something about how warm it was for winter. "We live in New England," he said. "I'm all for more global warming." I laughed uneasily and decided it was best to let it go. It was obviously a joke, but as a joke it revealed a refusal to take climate change seriously. The memory has lingered, and I keep wondering if I should have said something more, but I'm not sure what more I could have said. Lately I've been asking myself, Maybe this kind of joke isn't always a destructive denial but an emotionally manageable way to admit what is happening?

Underlying this question are several more related but unspoken ones. How should I respond to the phenomenon of climate change? Is it okay to joke, and if so, on what occasions is it permitted, or am I required to maintain a constant serious affect? Should I always be trying to find ways to minimize my impact on the world around me and on the fragile climate? What if I fail? Does anything I do make a difference? These are some of the questions I investigate in the first half of this chapter, exploring the ways in which inattention to climate change flows from a lot of different reasons. It's not just because people don't believe it's happening or don't want to believe it's happening. It's also because they don't know what to do about it. This means that for even the most committed, attention to climate change can be easily attenuated, the bad feelings too much to bear, and the world full of a lyricism that makes them want to turn away from what it signifies.

In the second half of the chapter, I discuss what people can do. Even though what I'm proposing will not have a measurable impact on efforts to mitigate and adapt to the effects of climate change, engaging in what Andrew Epstein calls "everyday-life projects" can connect thinking with doing so that they sustain each other, acting as a kind of feedback loop for attention. Consider these projects as informal experiments in living and, as such, building material for imagining in as concrete a way as possible how to live differently. This imagining, in turn, can contribute significantly to the democratization of human agency. Because individual actions do not affect climate, you have the freedom to be easy on yourself. Don't be upset if you fail to do the things you set out to do or if you find you have to revise your goals downward. It is not virtue you are after. It is a practical working out of alternative ways to live your life in the belief that alternatives become more compelling the more you've figured out what they entail. It may sound simplistic or tautological when I put it like this, but it gets right to the point I'm making in this chapter. You act by acting.

THE DYNAMICS OF INATTENTION

To begin with the basics: if you do not feel concern about climate change, let me assure you that you are not alone. Your perspective is understandable, maybe even reasonable. Indeed, there are many reasons you might feel this way. The most obvious is that corporate-run news in the United States rarely mentions this phenomenon in its reporting on events, opinion pieces, or talk shows (I can't speak about what the news is like in other countries). Every once in a while, and with increasing frequency, an article or a show breaks through the silences that surround the subject, usually connected to some sensational event, but the norms of civility—the kind that govern the lives of Kath and her friends in Kazuo Ishiguro's *Never Let Me Go* or torture Teebs so much at the Long Island party in Tommy Pico's *IRL*—reassert themselves promptly.[1] These norms insist that discussion of climate change is beyond the pale of polite conversation and outside the boundaries of everyday concerns. If you've been paying any attention to the way the news frames race and racism, you already have a strong understanding of how these norms work. It's not that climate change is never mentioned, but a lot of care is put into context, language use, and prominence. You have to pay special attention to the application of active and passive verb constructions, especially in phrases like "officer-involved shooting."

A slightly less obvious reason that you might find any discourse about climate change difficult to take seriously is the way in which popular television series and movies, with all of their rousing apocalypticism, infrequently mention or make direct reference to it. When they do, climate change is almost always associated with fantastical situations involving titanic monsters, alien invasions, or a world inhabited by super-powered beings. The second-to-latest Godzilla movie might make a big deal about the environmental problems besetting the world (while offering a fantasy of solving these problems), but the weather in the most recent remake of *A Star Is Born* is unremarkable and serene.[2] Climate change figures, if at all, in stories of the extraordinary and fantastic, while its absence is associated with the realistic.

And, really, how can you feel a sense of urgency about the severity of this phenomenon, much less the urge to chat about it with someone you barely know, if no one around you treats the subject as if it matters, at least on a day-to-day basis? Take what I've learned from my students as an example. Many have grown up in social circumstances where talk about climate change has been considered out of bounds, maybe even rude. As a result, my students lack, generally speaking, an appreciation for the scope and urgency of the crisis they have grown up with—although this, too, might be changing fast, as the effects of climate change are becoming more pronounced. This is a kind of active not-knowing encouraged by social rules they readily acknowledge when I make note of them: for example, avoid conversation about controversial topics; try to be respectful of differences of opinion, especially when they are deeply held; don't be a downer at social occasions by bringing up heavy subjects. These are mostly admirable traits, founded as they are on the desire to be considerate of others' feelings (as well as some defensiveness, in the sense that saying the wrong thing to the wrong person can hurt a person's economic opportunities). Their wide adoption shows how thoughtfully my students have been raised. These same traits are also a trap when it comes to a topic like climate change—or racism, sexism, homophobia, wealth inequality, ableism, or transphobia. Civility leads to quiescence.

The alarm that surrounds specialized discussion of climate change thus doesn't match the way the people around you are reacting to it. You may, for instance, have heard that panic helps no one. While it's true that panic can be counterproductive to addressing any issue, it at least shows a concern commensurate with the enormity of present-day environmental crises. Panic, alongside other strong emotions like terror, fear, anxiety, and anger, is preferable to cool disregard, but the latter reigns over the everyday. And because cool disregard reigns, you may easily feel there are more immediate concerns to worry about, like growing economic precarity; the rising tide of authoritarian governments and ethnonationalisms; the erosion of women's reproductive rights; police violence against Black, Indigenous, and Latinx peoples; mass incarceration; the rolling back of immigrant and refugee rights; hate crimes against Asians and Asian Americans; the epidemic of opioid addiction; other kinds of epidemics; the wave of migrants at the borders of so many nations; the suffocating ubiquity of plastic waste; and so on and so forth—as if these concerns can be understood separately from one another.

There's no shortage of topics to be concerned by, and most of these topics have a relevance that is much harder to deny than that of something occurring at temporal and spatial scales that are difficult to comprehend. You know people who can't find a steady job. Maybe you can't find one yourself. You tense up and feel nervous when a police cruiser pulls up behind you. You've read the graphic accounts of how migrant children are separated from their parents at the U.S. border and put into what I can only think of as concentration camps, and you are haunted by the inhumanity they detail. You saw the video of a straw being extracted from the nose of a sea turtle, blood streaking down its face, and have read stories of whale and albatross carcasses with stomachs full of plastic. You have most definitely experienced the difficulty of living—and in too many cases the sadness of witnessing those who did not live—through the global spread of the coronavirus disease that began in 2019 (COVID-19 for short). In contrast, worry about a crisis that is more often than not described as probable in some ill-defined future struggles to elicit the same kind of visceral response.

Less obvious still, devoting a lot of attention to climate change, while emotionally difficult, opens up the likelihood that you will have to change the way you live your life. You may not want to consider where this implication leads. The use of fossil fuels makes contemporary life, especially for the most well-off, possible in the way it's currently configured, from heating or cooling your home to enabling fast travel across vast distances and powering the electronic devices that are your constant companions. Fossil fuel use is so pervasive, and so many daily activities are dependent on it, that you find it difficult to imagine living without. Even plastic is made from oil. Indeed, living without fossil fuels might not feel like living at all. "We experience ourselves, as moderns and most especially as modern Americans," Stephanie LeMenager observes, "every day in oil, living within oil, breathing it and registering it with our senses."[3] Proponents of business as usual have it easy, for no one wants to give up what they have already taken for granted.

You may tell yourself, pausing to consider what you don't want to give up, that individuals choosing to have one less child or no children at all, to go without flying, to avoid driving, and to eat no meat or less meat—which are the (non)activities one study claims have the greatest individual impact on emissions—is ultimately negligible, given how enormous the problem is.[4] You wouldn't be wrong. A meaningful impact on global warming requires, first and foremost, a massive reduction in fossil fuel use. The focus on what you can do as an individual inevitably falls into consumer fallacies, so that making lifestyle choices become both a marker of your concern for the environment and a statement about your social class. You have the means and the education to live in self-conscious ways that might inconvenience you but aren't an insuperable burden. In any case, no matter how fastidiously you live your principles, it amounts to nothing compared to the scale of the crisis. So why not just live with the luxuries that oil affords, enjoy what you have, and in the meantime fight for more comprehensive policies?

Here is what I think of as the heart of the problem of denial. You may know a lot about climate change already and worry actively about its consequences. You may even be losing sleep over it. You might talk about it with like-minded friends and yearn earnestly for more robust public discourse. You might compost and spend a little extra for wind-powered energy and contribute money to environmental causes and prioritize mitigating global warming as an issue when it comes time to vote and join marches and take part in activist organizations. Maybe you hold leadership positions in these organizations. You are nevertheless always nagged by the feeling that you would like to do more but don't know how. The feeling is vertiginous, a sharp drop into a well of doubt, and at the bottom—something you have trouble dwelling on—is the possibility that maybe there is nothing you, or anyone, can do.

It's too late. The feedback loops have already kicked in. There are too many sunk costs in fossil fuel–dependent infrastructures. Those with all the wealth and power rely on the burning of fossil fuels for their wealth and power, and they will not give up what they have no matter how bad things get. They don't want to share what they've gone out of their way to accumulate. The rich and powerful will choose fascism over democratic alternatives. Walls will get higher and more numerous, the growing ranks of the poor everywhere will suffer more, racial and ethnic differences will make it easier to ignore this suffering, and the police and military will become ever more merciless in the protection of property and the status quo. The ruling classes will act as they have always acted.

These scenarios often feel unavoidable to me—an already accomplished feature of the present world. In the midst of so much inevitability, my mind wants to turn to what is more manageable and concentrate on the regularity everyday life affords or at least promises to make possible. My mind might even take refuge in the idea that long after humans have gone extinct, life will go on and the planet will continue to turn on its axis. I feel deep sympathy for those who proclaim, "Burn it all down." Nothing seems salvageable anymore, every attempt at reform seems to shore up and strengthen corrupt institutions, and the very idea of the human itself seems flawed and in need of replacement or even abolishing.

I don't want to be dismissive of what might be too late to affect or to discount this position as overly negative. If anything, one of the weaknesses of environmentalist thinking has been that the worst-case scenarios it has been willing to focus on haven't been bad enough, and their likelihood has been underestimated, especially when they concern the making of government policy. Activists always fear that to focus on how catastrophic climate change is and how much worse it can become will be discouraging. They fear bad feelings.

The strength of this emotion leads some activists to insist that asking others to face such truly terrible possibilities too directly might prevent them from joining in or lead them to drop out. One example comes immediately to mind. David Wallace-Wells's *New York Magazine* article on climate change, which sought to depict the worst possible scenarios that can occur if emissions continue unabated and which became the most widely accessed article in the magazine's history, received a fiery response from many activists and scientists. The criticism both on social media and in online publications was so intense, mostly focused on how the article goes too far beyond what the science can positively verify, that the magazine published an annotated version to make explicit the scientific sources of its claims.[5] This same fear also seems to lead Sarah Jaquette Ray to recognize how awful the effects of climate change are—"Yes, *in general* climate change is contributing to a terrible sixth extinction"—while also leaving space to acknowledge, maybe even celebrate, how "overall societal well-being is as good as it's ever been."[6] It's bad, but it's not that bad. Let's be sure to calibrate your feelings properly.

The much greater problem facing climate activists, however, is the opposite of being overly pessimistic: the public's propensity not to be alarmed enough. In his account of the development of the climate change debate in the United States, the novelist and essayist Nathaniel Rich tells how the American scientist James Hansen famously announced during a Senate hearing in 1988 that climate change was already underway. Hansen wrote in his prepared remarks, "The greenhouse effect has been detected, and it is changing our climate *now*."[7] Many decades have passed since this sensational event, and the same announcement is still being actively debated, with many political leaders continuing to deny that global warming is something to worry about or, as is more and more the case, working hard to avoid talking about it altogether.

So much time has passed, and public discourse has become more degraded. Before Hansen's presentation at the U.S. Senate, there seems to have been wide agreement about the existence, causes, and dangers of fossil fuel emissions; afterward, the opposition hardened its stance and began to fund an aggressive program of sowing doubt about the science of climate change. "When it comes to the United States, which has not deigned to make any binding commitments whatsoever," Rich observes, "the dominant narrative for the last quarter century has concerned the unrestrained efforts of the fossil fuel industry, compounded by the ingratiating abetment of the Republican Party, to suppress scientific fact, confuse the public, and bribe politicians."[8] If anyone in 1988 had said that the public would be even more confused about the science of climate change in *their* far-off future than they were then, that person would undoubtedly have been criticized as overly pessimistic.

During decades of discursive sabotage, everyone concerned about the issue and capable of contributing anything substantive to the public discussion was stymied—and often demonized—by organized opposition. Basic facts were lied about, and a lot of money was spent on convincing the public that there was no reason to worry. Professional misinformation campaigns argued that scientists were divided about how bad climate change would get and how long it would be until it became something worrisome; in later years, the argument was upgraded to say that the science itself was flawed. Official denial thus became a blank check for the burning of as much oil, coal, and natural gas as possible to power incredible economic growth, most of which further concentrated wealth, exacerbated inequalities everywhere, and helped give rise to economic globalization and the construction of elaborate transnational supply chains.

There are many compelling reasons that you should feel an incandescent rage at this deliberate misinformation campaign and not be in a hurry to forgive those who enabled it. There have been, and are, many corporate and political leaders whose almost comical antisocial behavior makes them villains in the story of the present. You might respond that targeting them for punishment can neither recover the precious time that has already been lost nor do away with the enormous sunk costs invested in carbon-intensive infrastructures nor offer much guidance about how to proceed in the teeth of ever-harrowing challenges. I agree with these points. I do not, however, agree that culpability should not be a focal point of activism because it exacerbates division, makes finding commonality more difficult, ignores how everyone was somehow equally culpable, and therefore risks assigning too much blame to a few scapegoated players. The latter is the argument that the journalist David Wallace-Wells—who as an example of the dangers of focusing too much on the worst-case scenarios reveals himself unwilling to follow the full implications of his own thinking—puts forward when he writes, "The natural villains are the oil companies. But the impulse to assign them full responsibility is complicated by the fact that transportation and industry make up less than 40 percent of global emissions."[9]

"Less than 40 percent" is a lot of emissions! Any major reduction in this amount in the past four decades would have had a major impact on how much warming is currently being experienced. That the companies associated with this sector put so much effort into obscuring from public view what they fully understood, which severely circumscribed the action that was taken on limiting emissions and poses such a hurdle today, has done irreparable harm. The harm they have committed cannot be overstated. Their behavior deserves a full public airing: series of congressional hearings, breathless news coverage of corporate malfeasance, severe fines and individual criminal trials, demands to appropriate ill-gotten profits to mitigate a crisis these companies played such a major role in worsening. A full public hearing can also help restore confidence in elected leaders. By making the powerful who have behaved badly responsible for their bad behavior, a full public hearing can show that elected leaders are independent from corporate and personal interests and fully focused on serving the urgent needs of the public. Such a public hearing would also shore up attention, because those who care about this issue will feel more emboldened. Such a hearing cannot happen without their activism, and the meting out of culpability would mean their agency is waxing.

Perhaps it can't *always* be a focal point, but in the short term, attempts to remove bad actors from positions of power can help rivet attention because this gives audiences a greater sense of their power. Indeed, such attempts may be a prerequisite for moving on to what needs to be done; bad actors are bad precisely because they have been impediments to mitigation and adaptation efforts, and so long as they escape severe and highly visible public censure, they can continue to perform this role. In addition, censure can help set new norms for acceptable behavior, so that the spread of misinformation and deliberate lies are understood as the grave threats to everyone's well-being that they are. The removal of bad actors from positions of power is important work, and claims that everyone is somehow complicit fail to see how structurally imbalanced the debate about climate change has been, how this imbalance has been self-consciously perpetuated, and how it has aggravated the current crisis.

The problem Wallace-Wells seeks to diagnose is, then, founded not in an absence of worthwhile villains, as he claims, but rather in a situation in which their villainy does not easily register as villainy. If climate change isn't a big deal, as many believe, and if civility is more important to maintain than anger at government inaction, then the oil companies' lies about it can't be a big deal either. Their efforts to promote denial have thus paid off double, first, in preventing effective action to decrease fossil fuel use and, second, in blunting public anger at the executives who have promoted this denial.

Given this recent history and the effectiveness of misinformation campaigns, it is—yes—reasonable to feel overwhelmed by the topic. It's reasonable to feel that there are other, more immediate issues that you can pour yourself into, especially because, as severe as they are, it may seem possible to make a difference. When it comes to climate change, however, no such confidence can be justified, and you are left with effort without the benefit of expecting that anything will get better, even as you attract powerful scorn for caring too vocally. The more you think about climate change, the more powerless you might feel and the more diminished your agency might seem *given these circumstances*. In the midst of such uncertainty and strictures and so much doom and consequences, it's reasonable to refuse to give too much attention to what's happening to the planet you're living on. It's reasonable to give in and get along. It's reasonable to feel that nothing can be done, as individual human agency—and maybe even collective human agency—has so repeatedly been shown to be weak. It's reasonable to allow the forces of denial a total victory over the public discourse that surrounds climate change.

EVERYDAY-LIFE PROJECTS

There is no future point of no return, beyond which unchecked climate change will become catastrophic. *That* point has already passed. Conditions are already catastrophic. And the present is more and more dominated by the contours of this worsening catastrophe. What is possible now? Many who focus on this topic are struggling with this question—a search to find ways of living on a planet that is experiencing an ecological rupture that no human, and perhaps no living species, has ever witnessed before. As the editors of the aptly titled collection of essays *Arts of Living on a Damaged Planet: Ghosts and Monsters of the Anthropocene* recognize in their introduction, "living arrangements that took millions of years to put into place are being undone in the blink of an eye. The hubris of conquerors and corporations makes it uncertain what we can bequeath to our next generations, humans and not humans. The enormity of our dilemma leaves scientists, writers, artists, and scholars in shock."[10]

In a situation that causes so much shock, the parameters of reason itself need to be tested and expanded, and dismantled if necessary, so as to make possible alternative ways of living. Perhaps this is another way of saying what a character in Kim Stanley Robinson's climate change novel *Forty Signs of Rain* observes, "An excess of reason is itself a form of madness."[11] What is currently considered reasonable aids in climate change denial. So, while it's important to confront the worst-case scenarios head-on and take them seriously as likely possible outcomes, it's just as important to insist on the imagination of best-case scenarios, to stretch far to consider what can seem ever more remote, a human flourishing. Indeed, the most daring act of the imagination—more than a focus on how bad things are and how much worse they are likely to get, as daunting as these tasks are—might be to insist that good things are still possible; to posit courageous paths forward where sharing, collaboration, and greater democracy equal desirable futures; to imagine human agency as empowered to make the changes to the way people live their lives that are so urgently needed. To be daring is to recognize what the four coauthors of *A Planet to Win: Why We Need a Green New Deal* proclaim, "In the twenty-first century, all politics are climate politics."[12]

Sustaining attention to climate change in the everyday means living *without* the assumption of a predetermined future. It begins with believing that nothing about what is to come is fixed and that the range of what might happen in the next few years and decades and centuries is wider, more varied, and full of more surprises than is usually thought. No outcome is more likely than another, and between two extremes there is no probability that lies somewhere in a predictable middle. Imagine the bad and the good and everything in between with everything you know about climate change in mind. Make the range wide. And then make it wider. Your creativity is vital to the task. Tell yourself that any of these imagined futures is as possible as the next. The present becomes full of foreclosures and possibilities, a long hallway of diverging paths with destinations that cannot be known.

In the next few years and decades, literally anything can happen, as the first few months of 2020 have demonstrated. Wildfires consumed vast tracts of land in Australia and killed an unimaginably large number of animals living there, following on the heels of massive wildfires in Brazil, even as temperatures in Antarctica reached into the seventies Fahrenheit, and later Siberia broke records by reaching temperatures in the nineties Fahrenheit (on one day, it even broke a hundred degrees Fahrenheit). Meanwhile, as the fires raged and the ice melted, SARS-CoV-2 had already begun its expansion to the far corners of the human world—and Breonna Taylor and George Floyd were going about their lives, unaware that police officers would soon murder them, sparking mass protests in every U.S. state and in many countries around the world. The current decade, when the signal of climate change has decisively risen above the noise of weather variability and when much can be done to circumscribe the worst outcomes and prepare for the outcomes already baked into complex ecologies, provides a historic opportunity for anything to happen, even as so much will happen that the noise of the crises of everyday life threatens to drown out the ever-increasing loudness of climate change's signals. This is not the time to say that only the worst-case scenarios remain viable nor to dismiss them, for it matters so very much what humans do with their enormous collective powers during this crucial moment in history.

Even as I write these words, I worry that I'm being overly optimistic. The turn to making a wider set of possibilities than currently seems available must contend with the questions Curtis Marez poses: "Who can expect a future, who cannot, and why."[13] Is the claim I'm making justified? Am I grasping at straws? Being delusional? Focusing only on what's possible for some, at the expense of the many? I can't ignore these worries, but I need to understand them as conditioned by an ideological milieu that has for decades insisted the current world is the best it can be. Mark Fisher, who coined the phrase *capitalist realism*, defines it this way: "the widespread sense that not only is capitalism the only viable political and economic system, but also that it is now impossible even to *imagine* a coherent alternative to it."[14]

Not only has capitalism captured the whole genre of realism; it has also projected the contours of the present world to the far temporal horizon. The belief that human flourishing and desirable futures are possible reclaims realism as something wilder and potentially more conducive to a collaborative human and nonhuman well-being. To pay attention and to experiment with the forms such attention can take, as a rejection of capitalist realism, is to insist on the right to exist, and to continue existing, even in the midst of harrowing conditions, no matter how bad they get. To sustain attention is to insist that the lives of the most vulnerable in particular are worth living, even when surrounded by the message that only some lives are valuable. It is to make a way when there seems to be no way. It is to refuse to give up.

The difficulty of thinking the radical uncertainty of the present is why it's important to fight for as much control as possible over your reproductive rights; to seek out a mostly plant-based diet; to walk, bicycle, and use public transit; to compost and produce little waste; to participate in protests and demonstrations; to opt in to renewable energy use when available; to use reusable cups; and to annoy people around you by talking about what's happening to the planet. Do everything you think will help, both big and small. Be a pain in the ass and invite scorn. Be a climate killjoy. Be ironic. Be funny or be serious. Insist on your obligation to critique every facet of business as usual, and continually work to imagine alternatives, work-arounds, something better.

These activities may not in themselves have any meaningful impact on mitigation efforts, but they help nonetheless to keep the topic in mind, make new social collectivities possible, and act as the nucleus of whatever might emerge as vibrant public discourses that center on this topic. They help you to understand what you have control over and, just as important, what you are powerless to affect. The latter signals where you may want to work to expand your agency. These activists, then, aid in the making and remaking of civil society, a process already well underway in the work of numerous activist and community-based groups, founded on a recognition of how much the conditions of possibility for human existence have changed and how much the way people live their lives must change alongside such changed, and changing, conditions. They combine thinking with doing. They are part of a sustaining practice of everyday attention.

These activities are also what Andrew Epstein calls, in a magisterial study of postwar American poetry, "everyday-life projects," which he defines as "artificial, rule-bound, performative experiments that call for individuals undertaking the project to engage in certain activities, usually for a set amount of time, with the goal of channeling attention to one or more aspect of everyday experience."[15] People wear devices on their wrists that record how many steps they've taken, what their heart rates are, and how many stairs they've climbed. My own employer—not unproblematically (What can all that stored information be used for? What happens to all the electronic waste that's being produced?)—encourages employees to wear such devices so that, organized into groups, they can compete with each other for prizes. The hope is that greater awareness of these facts will lead employees to be more active, make them healthier, and lower healthcare costs.

Of course, people don't need this kind of prompting to share the minutiae of their lives. A variety of social media platforms allow them to record and analyze what they are doing, thinking, and eating on a day-to-day, or even hour-by-hour, basis. These are all everyday-life projects, which have proliferated in recent years—as is the young climate activist Greta Thunberg's voyage across the Atlantic in a solar-powered sailboat, which made headlines around the world.[16] Or some scientists' and academics' pledge to fly less.[17] Or the decision by two graduate students, David Rodriguez and J. Caity Swanson, whom I met at an environmental studies conference, to ride their bicycles from New York City to Detroit to share papers about the experience.[18]

On a trip from Boston to Washington, D.C., I chose to take the train. It was a long seven-hour ride—made longer by the United States' systemic disinvestment in its railway system. I'm not sure how much, if any, emissions were saved by taking the train over taking an airplane (certainly much less than if I had cycled), but it did feel like a way of being more mindful of the changes that are likely to be involved in a transition to a less carbon-intensive lifestyle. This was yet another example of an everyday-life project, in which performing some activities, even for short periods of time, serves as a way of molding attention around issues related to climate change. I was trying to live as if I were already in a postcarbon society or at least in a society more intent on lessening its carbon dependence and learning what such a life might look like.

Such activities build on experiments that writers and artists have long been engaged in. Henry David Thoreau's *Walden* is a notable early example of a writer engaged in this kind of project, and while other writers and artists have conducted similar kinds of experiments, postwar poetry has focused its considerable concentration on the everyday, which has in turn proved a formidable object to represent. Epstein's central argument, in fact, can best be summarized as follows: "The pursuit of the everyday in contemporary poetry often prompts an impatience with conventional modes of representation and generates restless innovations with poetic form."[19] This pursuit has been especially notable in the work of many contemporary poets. Novelists as well have worked hard to reimagine their form, to become less plot dependent, and to focus more on lyrical moments.

Careful reading of these literary texts can provide readers with ideas for engaging in their own everyday-life project that revolves around climate change. Such a project can, in turn, affect attention to this topic as a deliberate act and make it more difficult to turn away from its ramifications or the urgency it requires. Such sustaining of attention is essential to any effort to expand the imagination of what's possible. If coordinated state action and political leadership are what is most needed to mobilize massive efforts to change the way people consume energy, the sources of that energy, and the way they live their lives, such efforts will quickly falter and fall into acrimonious disagreements if there is no corresponding sense of alarm on the public's part. Indeed, it's difficult to imagine that such action and leadership will ever materialize unless a loud, querulous, buzzing public demands it.

Literature, I find, can be an essential aid in the attempt to think about climate change and everyday experiences together. The experience will not be the same for everyone, but for me it has been significant. I have tried, for instance, to walk, bike, and take public transportation as much as I can, taking advantage of the fact that I live in a densely populated city that doesn't always require driving to get around, and it has led me to relate to my surroundings differently. Walking is the slowest form of mobility on this list, and it's what I do most—and have done a lot for most of my adult life. In fact, I like walking because it is slow. It gives my mind time to wander and to process what I am sensing. I'm reminded of Walter Benjamin's hilarious observation in *The Arcades Project*: "In 1839, it was considered elegant to take a tortoise out walking. This gives us an idea of the tempo of flânerie in the arcades."[20]

The exaggeration of this image distills an important quality of the experience of walking, which is itself—as this quotation might suggest—a popular topic of literary meditation. The seeing and listening and feeling occur at a different tempo than when I'm driving down the same street, and indeed walking can feel painfully slow compared to how fast other aspects of contemporary life have become. There are other people but also buildings and trees and small animals scurrying under bushes—squirrels, rabbits, and chipmunks mostly, although I've also seen wild turkeys and, thankfully on rare occasions, a rat scurrying across a parking lot. Sparrows, robins, blue jays, cardinals, and finches, among other kinds of birds, hop and soar all around me, filling the air with their loud whistles. I see a dozen or more breeds of dogs being led around on leashes. The quality of the sunlight changes, season by season, day by day, and minute by minute. The air gets cold and then hot, humidity builds up and then dramatically releases, smells are constantly changing, and noises compete with each other to be heard. I observe differently when I walk. I have more time to let my thoughts wander.

Walking is intensely social, especially in the urban area where I live, because I have to share space with a lot of human and nonhuman activity. It's more mundanely social as well, in that I often run into people I know and sometimes people I haven't seen in a while. There is thus something communal in the way walking makes me more vulnerable and more open to my surroundings. There is, of course, the constant sound of cars and trucks. I curse their noise and the vile smells spewed by their hot engines on a daily basis. The people inside feel to me cocooned, oblivious of their surroundings and more likely to be contemptuous of whatever nuisance presents itself.

I fantasize about a utopia of no cars.

I was once on a crosswalk when an automobile screeched to a halt. The driver hadn't seen me and was about to yell at me for being in the way when she realized she knew me. She and I are in fact close friends. She apologized profusely, but it was clear to me that if she hadn't known me, no such apologies would have been forthcoming. Driving can make friends into strangers. Like her, when I drive, I'm a different person: less patient, more focused on getting where I'm going, mean to other drivers and pedestrians alike. The more I walk, the less I enjoy driving and the less I like who I am behind the wheel.

Now, walking, I'm vulnerable to the heat of the sun and the chill of the wind. If I can, I avoid going out on days when it's raining, making my activities sensitive to the limitations that the vagaries of weather can impose. Those vagaries are becoming more severe, more erratic. I'm aware of a coarsening tempo. My legs are often tired, and in the mornings they ache. My body has many limits, which I'm well aware of, especially as I get older, and walking makes me even more aware of them. On many days, I just don't feel like walking anywhere, and, eventually, a day may come when I won't be able to walk on my own. Of course, I might also just die before this happens. When I think of my own death, why do I imagine it so far into the future? Isn't this a kind of luxury afforded by who I am?

Against the liberal humanist claim that "we will all be disabled one day, if we live long enough," Jasbir Puar observes that this projection of a uniform future for all "is already built on an entitled hope and expectation for a certain longevity."[21] For many, many people, such a hope is cruel, and the expectation unfounded. This thought makes me more appreciative of the challenges of moving away from a way of life centered on the burning of fossil fuels. Nothing about such a transition is going to be easy, and the challenges are highly unevenly distributed. Too often, well-meaning people suggest otherwise, and they are perhaps fooling themselves as much as anyone else. Engaging in everyday-life projects that seek a less carbon-dependent lifestyle will soon disabuse anyone of such a comforting but misleading belief, even if the mind has to stretch to consider how one's experiences might be radically different from someone else's.

As I walk, especially on days with nice weather, my own mind tugs at whatever I've been reading, and I think about a phrase or an image that a poem, or a passage from a novel, or a quotation from a critical essay or work of nonfiction, has conjured for me. The literature affects my perception of my surroundings and leads me to reflect on everything I'm encountering differently. Lines from poems I've been reading come to mind. "I am so sorry, so, so sorry." "Global woman, waxy apple, record heat." "*Don't be afraid*, a child signs to a tree, a door." "Ppl like us." On some days, I think about how the present is all I have and how much I am grateful for it, no matter how tragic it might be. Other days, I think about what the same scenery will be like in a few years or a few decades or even a few centuries. Nothing seems as it is, given as if melted into amber, but rather everything appears to me in flux, each thing always in motion in time.

Often I think about how my experience of walking is shaped by who I am, a middle-aged Asian American cisgender able-bodied heterosexual man lucky enough to have a secure, well-paying job. How different the same experience would be if I were a woman, or of a different race, or gay, or transgender, or out of work, or younger, or older, or living in a place where mobility is severely circumscribed (like Gaza). How different the experience would be if I were in a wheelchair or had to lean on crutches or were blind or deaf or neurodivergent. And what if I lived elsewhere, in one of the many places in the world where walking is more conspicuous and the demographic more homogeneous? The experience could be less safe and less enjoyable—or maybe just nonexistent. I may be sensing things that I'm ignorant of now. I am undoubtedly privy to what others are excluded from.

I have to learn this lesson again and again. Not everyone can live the way I am choosing to live, in a way that allows me to think of the everyday as a project I can deliberately undertake. Everyday-life projects are not available to everyone, especially those who are already living a very low-carbon lifestyle because of their circumstances. And many people, too, are dependent on the technologies made possible by the use of fossil fuels. This does not mean I should not engage in such a project. If anything, it makes trying to be less dependent on fossil fuels more welcome, for it encourages me to reflect more on this lesson and to follow where its implications might lead me.

Here, too, literature seems capable of expanding what I can think about, allowing me to see and hear and feel with others what they see, hear, and feel. It makes me more aware of what I am shut off from and what I must strain to know. It reminds me, again and again, that the category of the human is leaky and profoundly exclusionary. By design, who is considered human is organized into hierarchies and gradients, and many are treated as if they are animals or objects or debris. Writers who come from groups that have been excluded in this way can speak back and highlight triumphs others may not be aware of. The African American poet Lucille Clifton proclaims:

come celebrate
with me that everyday
something has tried to kill me
and has failed.[22]

Here's an experience of the everyday that's different from mine, since I don't fear a murderous rage directed at me and lurking in the places where I walk. But maybe it's not all that different? Maybe there is something that's trying to kill me every day, and I'm just oblivious of it? There is certainly no shortage of examples of Asian Americans being targeted for violence.

Literature doesn't make me more empathic. It is, however, good to think with, acts as a prosthetic that extends the reach of my thoughts, makes possible a more varied encounter with the everyday. The everyday as a result becomes less familiar. It becomes, sometimes, frightening or threatening, oppressive even, and at other times literature offers an opportunity to struggle with such fears, to get to think about myself in relationship to my surroundings, to reconnect with others and to the physical world, to feel some semblance of what it means to be alive in a way that's not prepackaged for me (even if this literature itself *is* prepackaged, a commodity that's been sold to me for a profit). The everyday becomes an opportunity to value my life, to mourn what is changing all around me, and to think about changes that can be deliberately made to make life better for more people and the other living things with which they share this world.

"Sometimes," Jane Bennett observes, "ecohealth will require individuals and collectives to back off or ramp down their activeness, and sometimes it will call for grander, more dramatic and violent expenditures of human energy."[23] How to know when to back off and when to expend human energy? Literature helps me to think about this question as I make my way through my day, treating each day as an experiment in living, trying as best I can to use less fossil fuels, and the more I think of it, the more I'm convinced that now is the time for the mindful expansion and exertion of human agency.

PART II

BREATH

WHAT'S WRONG WITH NARRATIVE?

The Promises and Disappointments of Climate Fiction

THE CHIEF CONCERN OF RICHARD POWERS'S much-acclaimed novel *The Overstory* is one of the central concerns of this book: the relationship between attention and agency. This is why I'm using it to frame this chapter's discussion of *climate fiction*, a term I first came across in a *Guardian* article published several years ago. The article begins with a discussion of the freelance journalist Dan Bloom, who claims to have coined the shortened version *cli-fi*. It then goes on to describe the emergent genre as "novels setting out to warn readers of possible environmental nightmares to come."[1] What strikes me most about this definition is how it explicitly defines this fiction as focused on some future danger its narrative is intent on cautioning readers against. The catchy *cli-fi* emphasizes this focus on futurity, as it explicitly echoes the shortened version of *science fiction*, or *sci-fi*.

Having read most of the novels the article mentions and many more that have since been published that refer explicitly to climate change or focus overtly on related environmental problems, I find such a definition limiting. I am much more convinced by the argument that Heather Houser advances, that such fiction is part of a larger aesthetic practice focused on making sense of data, turning numbers into meaning, organizing information into classifications that illuminate and confound. She argues that artists "repurpose the data and methods of Eurowestern technoscience not to acquiesce to its ways of making sense of our world but to provide historical awareness of how that world has been made and, in some cases, to speculate on possibilities for making it otherwise."[2] Rather than imagining the dangers of climate change as something in the future, climate fiction situates the imbalances and extreme weather events in the present as part of ongoing processes of world building. It puts into narrative form what might otherwise seem a mass of unrelated events and facts. It engages an empirically based science in dialogue, seeking both to help amplify what this science is learning about the damage that's been done to the environment and to think through its assumptions to improve overall understanding about these damages.

The Overstory is a salient example of how climate fiction can do this by looking to the past as much as the future and highlighting foreclosed possibilities that might still be reactivated. The novel begins with a profusion of stories, a total of eight long vignettes taking up a third of its substantial length, which together emphasize the profusion of possibilities that have been foreclosed as it approaches the present. Each vignette focuses on a single character (except one that focuses on a couple). These characters are each associated with a different variety of tree, which the novel's publisher has—perhaps too literally—highlighted by putting a drawing of the relevant tree at the start of each vignette. This affinity leads the characters, following very divergent paths, to share an awareness of the dangers of deforestation before they pursue equally divergent responses to challenging these dangers. The novel thus focuses on the play of attention and agency. But as these characters become more politicized in the latter sections of the novel, and as the plot kicks in, some of them come together in ways that are obviously inadequate to the challenges they face, while others also flail in their attempts to fight the environmental damage that's being done.

Even though the novel itself is riveting, its narrative is disappointing. The central characters fail in the most obvious and predictable ways. They are unable to organize themselves and keep the momentum of their concerns going. They don't have any ideas for how to draw others in. If anything, they end the novel more powerless than when they began. The disappointment I feel in the way *The Overstory*'s plot unfolds makes me wonder if this disappointment points to an endemic weakness in climate fiction. Does narrative in general, because of some constitutional weaknesses, fail to deliver a story that can sustain attention on the topic of climate change and its many environmental, social, and cultural implications?

I address this question by thinking, first, about the way story and plot work in *The Overstory* and the reasons it might be inadequate for meeting the aesthetic challenges it confronts. I then turn to five concerns to be mindful of in fiction, foregrounded by the critical literature I am in conversation with in this chapter—a sensitivity to precarity, a wariness of progress, a rejection of mastery, an awareness of the slowness of different kinds of phenomena, and an acknowledgment of impurity. I roam freely in this section, drawing on numerous examples of print fiction to identify moments when these qualities come into play and to dramatize how much they can enrich readers' understanding of climate change. These examples aren't exhaustive but are meant to give a sense of the quantity and quality of this fiction. The chapter concludes by returning to *The Overstory* to consider how it both responds to these five concerns and falls short of what it seems to promise.

The organization of this chapter is meant to stress the ways in which climate lyricism (as both a making and an attending) draws readers of prose fiction into an encounter with the present, or what Powers refers to in the anecdote centered on Mimi Ma's childhood and young adulthood as "countless nows."[3] This is what I describe in the previous chapter as living *without* the assumption of a predetermined future. This chapter focuses on the novel and works to catalog the formal challenges confronting storytelling that explicitly focuses on climate change and related environmental issues. It works in concert with the next chapter, which focuses on the resources contemporary lyric poetry offers for the task of living with climate change.

A PROBLEM WITH PLOT

The first vignette in *The Overstory*'s opening section is a multigenerational tale of a family started by a Norwegian immigrant and an Irish immigrant in the latter half of the nineteenth century. They meet in Brooklyn and move to Iowa. Their children and grandchildren and great-grandchildren continue to live where they settled. One especially extraordinary passage sums up dozens of years of the family's living:

> The handiwork of heroin and Agent Orange that comes home with nephews from 'Nam. The hushed-up incest, the lingering alcoholism, a daughter's elopement with the high school English teacher. The cancers (breast, colon, lung), the heart disease, the degloving of a worker's fist in a grain auger, the car death of a cousin's child on prom night. The countless tons of chemicals with names like Rage, Roundup, and Firestorm, the

patented seeds engineered to produce sterile plants. . . . The generations of grudge, courage, forbearance, and surprise generosity: everything a human being might call *story* happens outside his photo's frame.[4]

In this passage an implicit distinction is made between story, where events happen without any apparent relationship to each other except succession in time, and plot, which the novelist E. M. Forster famously describes as "a narrative of events, the emphasis falling on causality." Plots do not, in other words, concern themselves only with what happened next but with why. A story, for Forster, is this: "The king died and then the queen died." A plot offers more explanation about the relationship between these two events: "The king died and the queen died of grief."[5] The latter offers clarity about causality but also simplifies. What did she die of? There is only one answer, grief. The former, which Forster argues is a less sophisticated form of narrative (which I believe is not necessarily the case), can leave open the possibility for more complex explanations of causation. What did she die of? The answer is unknown. It could be grief, but it could be something else, maybe old age, internal intrigue, or foreign invasion. Maybe a combination of causes. There is correlation, which shouldn't be confused with causation.

With this distinction in mind, it might be possible to say that the first vignette focuses on story. Meanwhile, its central conceit—that the men of the Hoehl family, for no good reason, take a monthly photograph of a chestnut tree that the patriarch planted when he first moved to Iowa—focuses on a nonhuman-centered plot. Even as the chestnut goes extinct across the East Coast, this one survives because it is isolated, growing in stature but unable to propagate because it is alone. Nicholas Hoehl, in particular, the last of the line of Hoehl men the reader meets, is mesmerized by the thousand photographs the male members of his family have taken of the tree: "Each picture on its own shows nothing but the tree he climbed so often he could do it blind. But flipped through, a Corinthian column of wood swells under his thumb, rousing itself and shaking free. Three-quarters of a century runs by in the time it takes to say grace."[6] The photographs reveal the tree's animation and in the process suggest a different experience of time than do the characters, who come and go like shadows in this first vignette. The tree itself seems to want something. It is motivated. There is causality in its growth.

Time compresses as readers move through the other opening vignettes of the novel. The second involves two generations; the third, an individual life, starting in early childhood; the fourth, the start of a romance that spans decades; the fifth, a few years of a young man confused about life; the eighth and final, a day in the life of a character who dies at the end of the vignette, only to come back to life moments later at the start of a new section of the novel. Vignettes six and seven break this pattern a little. The sixth focuses on a childhood accident that leaves a genius computer expert, Neely Mehta, confined to a wheelchair, moving from youth to adulthood. The seventh anecdote focuses on a dendrologist, Patricia Westerford, as she lives her life from childhood to grad school, from when her father, an "ag extension agent," drove his partially deaf daughter around the Ohio countryside, teaching her everything he knew about trees, to when her breakthrough research is rejected by her peers.[7] As suggested in the rough progression of these multiple narratives, however, the novel attempts to impose some kind of order on a profusion of story, where so much happens that readers are abuzz with a series of events without an apparent causal relationship to each other.

The other parts of the novel work to weave this unruly knot of lives into a single plot, as several (but not all) of these characters meet in the process of becoming politicized. They engage in ever more militant environmental activism until they turn to violence. I am not giving away anything worthwhile about the plot by pointing out that they prove to be inept militants, killing one of their own in an accident and dispersing to live their lives apart. Eventually the authorities catch up to one of them, and another is put in jail. The latter's sacrifice allows the others to remain free.

This is the plot of the novel, and it's not very satisfying. The characters' acts of violence come on suddenly and without much self-reflection, forcing a pattern to appear as a chain of causation in a way that is not fully earned. Their activities lead not to further collective action but to a retreat into individual and notably apolitical lives. Mimi Ma, for instance, turns herself into an unconventional therapist (she stares at her patients for hours without speaking) and ends up at a park in San Francisco, meditating on her life and its failings. Nicholas Hoehl creates enigmatic art in a forest with fallen trunks and gets help from some American Indians who happen to show up when he needs help and—in a very racially problematic way—mystically intuit what he's up to. The trunks are arranged to spell out the word "STILL." It's meant to be profound, but it feels as though the novel is trying too hard to say something meaningful at its end.

I must also admit that I would not be focusing on *The Overstory* if it did not have some Asian American characters. I do not appreciate being left out of the stories that I read and that are aggressively promoted to me by major book publishers, and I want not only to be represented but to be represented as part of a heterogeneous, historically mixed, culturally polyphonic clamor of humans that reflects social experience in the United States, and in many other countries, at the start of the twenty-first century. The inclusion of Mimi Ma and Neely Mehta in a large cast of characters who are all white feels like a small opening for me—as the reader—into the richness of this book, and everything it has to offer, even as the absence of central Black, Indigenous, Latinx, and Middle Eastern and North African characters is glaring and sorely felt. Such a lack makes me think hard about the challenges hindering the founding of necessary collectivities in a time driven to extremes by environmental rupture, given how this novel's impressively expansive imagination is so racially limited. Representation does not lead to such a founding but can contribute to it.

I am not alone in wondering whether the disappointment I feel about the ending of *The Overstory* is related to something more structural than the author's lack of personal imagination. The journalist David Wallace-Wells argues in *The Uninhabitable Planet: Life after Warming* that novels, films, and video games fail to represent climate change adequately because something about the topic itself resists narrative. He reasons that there's no obvious villain nor, for that matter, hero, and there's no resolution to whatever conflict can be eked out of such a situation. People might want to say that the big oil companies and their enablers are the villains, but Wallace-Wells insists this is a simplification (I disagree with this argument, as I discussed in the previous chapter), especially as such vilification focuses too much on the United States, where denial dominates in one political party, not both, and where "only two of the world's ten biggest oil companies" are headquartered.[8]

There is also the novelist Amitav Ghosh's well-known claim—prominently cited by Wallace-Wells and also discussed in the introduction—that novels are not well positioned to tackle the thorny narrative problems posed by climate change because they emerged to capture the regularity of bourgeois life. "In the pages of a novel," Ghosh observes, "an event that is only slightly improbable in real life . . . may seem wildly unlikely."[9] If so, a novel would have a hard time depicting the kind of wild weather-related events that are now becoming more and more commonplace, like a raging fire in California so large its smoke trails across the continent and fouls the air in Philadelphia and New York City, or fires in Australia that devastate more land and wildlife than scientists believed possible at one degree Celsius of warming above preindustrial levels.[10]

The critical discussion runs deeper still, adding to these formidable challenges. Some more prominent highlights include, but are not limited to, Rob Nixon's idea of "slow violence," or an environmental harm that takes years and decades to do its work and as a result defies average human attentiveness.

Human attentiveness has also become more attenuated: "In an age that venerates instant spectacle, slow violence is deficient in the recognizable special effects that fill movie theaters and boost ratings on TV."[11] Stacy Alaimo argues that even if it were possible, it would perhaps be unwise to slot what is happening to the Earth into familiar narrative forms founded on dominance: "The Anthropocene is no time for transcendent, definitive mappings, transparent knowledge systems, or confident epistemologies. Surely all those things got us into this predicament to begin with, where presumed mastery over an externalized 'nature' is all too triumphant, and yet also rebounds in unexpected, and usually unwanted ways."[12] Julietta Singh similarly challenges the idea that humans should strive for mastery: "Whether we desire mastery over a slave, an environment, or a body of texts, we are always returning to this primordial fracture—to the partial destruction of the object that the would-be master yearns to govern over completely."[13] The anthropologist Anna Lowenhaupt Tsing suggests that precarity, or "the condition of being vulnerable to others," is the "condition of our time." If so, she writes, "We can't rely on the status quo; everything is in flux, including our ability to survive. Thinking through precarity changes social analysis. A precarious world is a world without teleology."[14] Nor can anyone, according to the anthropologist Alexis Shotwell, appeal to a pristine past: "Being against purity means that there is no primordial state we might wish to go back to, no Eden we have desecrated, no pretoxic body we might uncover."[15] Not only are many available forms of storytelling ill equipped to imagine climate change, it would seem, but they replicate the very ways of knowing that have made the problem more possible and that obscure the kinds of literary forms that might emerge from the world as it is. Despite their differences, then, all of these arguments seem to share a common assumption: there's a problem with plot.

Of course, there are some dissenting opinions. Shelley Streeby, for instance, offers an explicit critique of Ghosh, writing, "People of color and Indigenous people use science fiction and other speculative genres to remember the past and imagine the futures that help us think critically about the present and connect climate change to social movements."[16] This kind of narrative, which looks both to the past and to the future to "think critically about the present," is similar to what Heather Houser seems to have in mind when she describes fiction's ability to act as an "artistic mediation of scientific information." As she goes on to observe, "Environmental understanding does not emerge from a vacuum of quantification but out of a cauldron mixing information, imagination, speculation, feeling, and even unknowing."[17] Together, the two critics seem to advise readers to look for minor perspectives and to think about how narratives work in relationship to science to make sense of all the data that have been collected about a changing climate.[18]

FIVE CONCERNS FOR CLIMATE FICTION

Many of the critics mentioned so far have helped me to form a vocabulary for thinking about what makes *The Overstory* disappointing for me. They have attuned me to five concerns in particular that are worth being mindful of when reading climate fiction. These are a sensitivity to precarity, wariness of progress, a rejection of mastery, an awareness of the slowness of different kinds of phenomena, and an acknowledgment of impurity. These concerns put constraints on the individual and on the ways readers think about human agency. In addition, they offer guidance for making sense of how narratives can effectively convey meaning about the ways in which the world is rapidly experiencing climactic change and the ways in which the consequences alter characters' understanding of their place in the world.

The presence of these concerns doesn't guarantee a work of fiction will be satisfying, but they offer some way to think about how narrative might aspire to capture an elusive phenomenon by reimagining the subjects of its storytelling. They also work against the argument that the forms currently available for storytelling are inadequate to the task of representing climate change, perhaps because they are locked into an investment in overvaluing the sovereign, self-possessed individual. Narrative might be, instead, highly plastic, capable of taking on many different forms. Climate fiction offers, then, experiments in such form taking that stretch and challenge the minds of its readers.

In laying out these concerns, I am following Houser again, this time in her thinking about artistic mediation as often organizing information into "classifications," or "narratives that repurpose techniques of natural history, including quantification, description, taxonomy, and precise illustration."[19] Taxonomy is how I've organized the qualities I want to spotlight because it mimics a narrative form that responds to a history of trying to make sense of the natural world by dividing these qualities into categories, finding commonalities in traits, and painting pictures that showcase these traits. Inevitably, as Houser points out, "what classification brings to the fore is its own limitations and failures; it occludes and invents as it strives for order."[20]

The following does exactly this, occluding and inventing while illustrating and uncovering what's already there, but in doing so I hope to foreground the kinds of aesthetic challenges contemporary fiction is responding to with remarkable self-consciousness and inventiveness. As much as I agree that classifications, both in natural history and in ethnography, have a checkered past and deserve critique, I do not think it's desirable to dispense with classification entirely. When I take walks, for instance, I frequently find myself wishing for greater access to a system of classification that could sharpen my attention to the flora around me. What are the names of the trees, plants, and flowers I am seeing? I regret not knowing more of them and not being knowledgeable in this way of their unique traits and needs, their provenances and chances for flourishing in ever more extreme weather conditions.

SENSITIVITY TO PRECARITY

This is an idea I gleaned mostly from Anna Lowenhaupt Tsing, but it is all too evidently a part of everyday experiences in the present, especially as jobs are becoming much more casualized, inequality widens as wealth becomes concentrated in fewer and fewer groups of people, and capital is locked up as wealth gets concentrated, preventing its productive investment in socially beneficial ways (such as education, health care, and infrastructure that is explicitly responsive to the need to mitigate and adapt to climate change) even as expenditures increase for the police and military. To be sensitive to precarity is to focus on an everyday marked by uncertainty about where the next paycheck will come from, whether there will be enough money to pay all the bills, and, more broadly, what disasters—both minor and major— might happen the next day and the day after that.

Such sensitivity posits that economic concerns are not separate from environmental ones. The treatment of minerals, vegetation, and animals as resources simply available for exploitation is intimately tied to the treatment of humans as sources of labor to be exploited. The fiction I've read in writing this book has made me more sensitive to the ways in which precarity has long been endemic to many people's experiences, especially for African Americans and other racial minorities. Jesmyn Ward's novel *Salvage the Bones*, for instance, captures the plight of a poor African American family living near the coast of Mississippi as they fail to prepare for Hurricane Katrina. I especially appreciate how this novel flips the generic expectations surrounding stories of natural disaster. Usually, such stories focus on the natural disaster itself and what follows, sometimes offering idyllic moments at the start of an idealized time before as a way to emphasize the destructiveness of what follows. Most of *Salvage the Bones* takes place before Katrina strikes, and the description of the storm and its aftermath is compressed into the final two chapters, suggesting in its loving and poignant descriptions of the struggles

Esch and her family face the ways in which natural disaster only compounds the precarity already endemic to their experiences of the everyday.

Cherie Dimaline's *The Marrow Thieves* also focuses on precarity. In this case, Indigenous youth are on the run in a world ravaged by climate change; everyone else has lost the capacity to dream and to stave off the madness that comes to the dreamless, who hunt these youth to extract whatever is in their marrow that allows them to continue dreaming. The centers where the extraction takes place are called schools, explicitly recalling the history of boarding schools in both Canada and the United States: "Soon, they needed too many bodies, and they turned to history to show them how to best keep us warehoused, how to best position the culling. That's when the new residential schools started growing up from the dirt like poisonous brick mushrooms."[21]

Even for those who are members of the middle class and of racial and ethnic majorities in their society, the dangers of extreme weather and political instability prove precarity making as well. In Megan Hunter's *The End We Start From*, a stripped-down narrative that tries to capture only the most basic facts of its story (and is therefore one of the least interesting of the examples I'm offering here), the unnamed middle-class narrator is forced to flee her comfortable London home and find refuge where she can when the flooding of the city ignites a civil war, suggesting how precarity expands to include even the well-off and socially accepted as environmental crises become more severe.

WARINESS OF PROGRESS

Progress as an idea tends to make sense of events, as they are presumed to move toward a specific goal. In the case of contemporary habits of storytelling, the goal of such a plot continues to be defined, as Lisa Lowe puts it, by ideas of "liberty, equality, reason, progress, and human rights," themselves already marked by a history of colonial expansion, exploitation, and racism.[22] Caution around such ideas is needed, as well as an attempt to retrain attention, focusing less on a horizon toward which all struggles should strive and more on a present that isn't necessarily much better than the past and on a future that isn't necessarily going to be better than the present. This doesn't mean that storytelling should abandon goals toward which its characters might work but rather that people must define these goals for themselves and have no guarantee they will attain them.

Such careful, conscious goal setting is what Priscilla Solis Ybarra has in mind when she writes about how Mexican American literature often posits

its own idea of the good life: "not too much but just enough, wealth measured by degrees of simplicity and community rather than material accumulation, a sense of respect for the dignity of the spirit and of the land all in one breath."[23] There is a notable absence in this description of what is desirable: an ultimate goal that all humanity somehow strives toward, defined by transcendence and dominance. *American War*, Omar El Akkad's tale of a climate change–afflicted United States divided by a second civil war, suggests this conflict is ending much as the first one did, with a defeated South that is determined to win the war after the war. As Viet Thanh Nguyen observes, "All wars are fought twice, the first time on the battlefield, and the second time in memory."[24] In El Akkad's novel, the South is on the path to victory in memory. History thus seems to repeat itself, as the novel explicitly asserts that the South had a similar victory in the first civil war, but by the end the outcome has exceeded expectations as a lab-engineered virus devastates the North after an act of terrorism, thus refusing any reader's hopes for a narrative of progress. Nevertheless, other people in this world have found a way to persevere and make a living on a planet severely damaged by past destruction.

Similarly, N. K. Jemisin's Broken Earth trilogy seems aware of how narratives of progress can easily get tripped up by their own ambitions. When the novels turn to the distant past, in the ruins of which the precarious present of these novels takes place, what brings ruin is the desire on the part of these earlier humans to harvest the very power of the Earth's core. This power promises eternal life and exploration into the far reaches of space, but, the narrator is careful to observe, this power would never have been enough: "The Earth's core is not limitless. Eventually, if it takes fifty thousand years, that resource will be exhausted, too. Then everything dies."[25] By placing its present millennia after the catastrophic event that upended such an aspiration, the trilogy shows how its characters have adapted to life on a planet that must suffer through periodic periods of geological and climatic upheaval. The expectation is built into the way they live, and they make do, even as those who are discriminated against continue to find ways to improve their society. This life seems somehow more desirable than the ideal of progress advocated by the ancients, whose aspirations ended up expelling the moon from the planet's orbit and upsetting the geological balance of the planet they live on.

Almost a tonic to a grasping for a mastery that can never be satisfied by the power it attains, Kim Stanley Robinson's *New York 2140*, which chronicles the efforts of several characters in a flooded Manhattan to rein in the financial industry, which is threatening the stable existence that those afflicted by climate catastrophes have carved out for themselves, concludes with a moment of both triumph (the characters succeed!) and humility. "So no, no, no, no!" the unnamed Citizen says, whose chorus-like observations punctuate this long novel: "Don't be naïve! There are no happy endings! Because there are no endings! And possibly there is no happiness either! Except perhaps in some odd chance moment, dawn in the clean washed street, midnight out on the river, or more likely in the regarding of some past time, some moment encased in a cyst of nostalgia, glimpsed in the rearview mirror as you fly away from it."[26] A similar sense of living among the ruins, rather than being tracked on the always forward-moving and preordained path of progress, pervades Pitchaya Sudbanthad's *Bangkok Wakes to Rain*, which contains an especially haunting description of an old capital city underwater. This part of its narrative is told from the perspective of three young people who somehow make a living on the recently expanded waters: "The elders talk wistfully of the olden days when the ocean was so bountiful that all they had to do was reach into a wave to hook a catch by its gills, but we only know of times where there are so many perches to catch and not enough in the sea."[27]

A REJECTION OF MASTERY

This idea builds on the work of Julietta Singh and Stacy Alaimo, who both insist on the need to resist mastery as a response to powerlessness. Alaimo, for instance, conjures a mesmerizing image of shells dissolving in acidifying oceans—a phenomenon caused by the oceans absorbing more and more atmospheric carbon dioxide.[28] Humans as well can imagine themselves like the shells, she argues, dissolving slowly in acid, which entails blurring boundaries between the human and the nonhuman. "It means dwelling in the dissolve," Alaimo writes, "a dangerous pleasure, a paradoxical ecodelic expansion and dissolution of the human, an aesthetic incitement to extend and connect with vulnerable creaturely life and with the inhuman, unfathomable expanses of the seas."[29]

Ted Chiang's novella *The Lifecycle of Software Objects*, which doesn't mention climate change but does focus on the differences between a virtual and a natural world, captures this sense of vulnerability in the fate of computer programs who have gained a high state of self-awareness and humanlike intelligence. When the purpose for which they were originally created comes to an end, and the platforms on which they exist become antiquated, they are in danger of going out of existence altogether because there's so little funding for their software to be updated so that they can exist on more advanced platforms: "Another two months go by. The user group's attempts at fundraising don't meet with such success; the charitably inclined are growing fatigued of hearing about natural endangered species, let alone artificial ones, and digients aren't nearly as photogenic as dolphins. The flow of donations has never arisen above a trickle."[30] Rather than suggesting transcendence and mastery over death, going digital is defined by Chiang as being ever vulnerable to change.

A similar sense of the vulnerability caused by a rejection of mastery ends Jeff VanderMeer's *Acceptance*, the final volume of his Southern Reach trilogy: "The world we are a part of now is difficult to accept, unimaginably difficult. I don't know if I accept everything even now. I don't know how I can. But acceptance moves past denial, and maybe there's defiance in that, too."[31] The rejection of mastery and the acknowledgment of vulnerability also punctures the end of Karen Thompson Walker's *The Age of Miracles*, in which the earth's rotation has inexplicably and very gradually slowed. By the end, all the characters in the novel have to contemplate a near future when life is no longer sustainable as one side of the planet fries and the other freezes: "We dipped our fingers into the wet cement, and we wrote the truest, simplest things we knew—our names, the date, and these words: *We were here.*"[32]

AWARENESS OF THE SLOWNESS OF PHENOMENA

This quality responds to Rob Nixon and his idea of slow violence. Such awareness requires being able to think with multiple scales of time, so that the slow is not assumed to be unchanging or unchangeable. In Powers's *The Overstory*, one of its many characters recalls reading a story about tiny aliens who come to visit Earth:

> Aliens land on Earth. They're little runts, as alien races go. But they metabolize like there's no tomorrow. They zip around like swarms of gnats, too fast to see—so fast that Earth seconds seem to them like years. To them, humans are nothing but sculptures of immobile meat. The foreigners try to communicate, but there's no reply. Finding no signs of intelligent life, they tuck into the frozen statues and start curing them like so much jerky, for the long ride home.[33]

In this analogy the readers are the aliens, and the apparently immobile humans are the trees. The aesthetic challenge Powers poses, then, is how to pay attention to the trees in their lively slowness.

One response to this challenge can be found in *The Sunlight Pilgrims*, Jenni Fagan's tender novel about a single man who joins a single woman and her transgender daughter in Scotland, waiting for the frigid weather to arrive as climate change triggers extreme cold in their part of the world. It takes patience to read this novel, as time dilates to match the feeling of expectancy that the creeping cold brings with it. By the end, time slows down, and what remains is the sense that waiting for an event and the event itself are indistinguishable: "Clouds drifting over his old, tired corneas, Constance curling into him as his eyes close too, just so tired, all of them, their bodies going into hibernation mode, just to rest here, like this, just for a few hours."[34] Another response can be found in Jenny Offill's *Weather*. Written in short, often-contextless bursts of prose, as if imitating the form of a tweet, it chronicles the life of a professional, middle-class white woman living in New York, carrying on with her day-to-day life, as the threat of climate change pervades her thoughts while remaining at a remove, something that is happening at a pace that does not match the pace of her daily concerns: "I listen to *Hell and High Water* on the way home. This one is about Deep Time. The geologist being interviewed speaks quickly, sweeping through millions and millions of years in a moment. The Age of Birds has passed, he says. Also of Reptiles. Also of Flowering Plants. Holocene was the name of our age. Holocene, which meant 'now.'"[35]

Both Fagan's and Offill's novels suggest a living with the slowness of climate change's temporality that is ultimately exhausting for their characters. They have no way to make sense of the different chronologies involved, and what happens is a winding down and learning to accept what they are powerless to change, much like the way Walker's *The Age of Miracles* ends, with characters accepting what they cannot change. Offill notes this feeling of exhaustion by ending her novel with the URL "www.obligatorynoteofhope .com."[36] The web address takes the reader to a note by the author and links to various inspirational figures and activist groups. But even as it does so, "obligatory" suggests what a chore this is. The author seems to feel she's not allowed to end the novel with a sense of the future that's overwhelming, in part because it takes the form of such enormous expanses of time.

Against such reluctant awareness of the slow, I find Ruth Ozeki's *A Tale for the Time Being* a welcome addition to this archive. This novel tells the story of a character named Ruth, who lives on an island off the coast of British Columbia in Canada. It's been weeks since the Tōhoku earthquake and tsunami devastated the Fukushima Prefecture in Japan, and a lot of its wreckage has made the voyage across the Pacific to land on the shore near Ruth's home. She finds a teenage girl's diary among the wreckage, and the novel moves between Ruth's reading of the diary and the story that's contained within it. Ruth herself is married to an environmental artist, Oliver, whose dialogue frames the novel's events in deep time:

Oliver wasn't worried. He took the long view. Anticipating the effects of global warming on the native trees, he was working to create a climate-change forest on a hundred acres of clear-cut, owned by a botanist friend. He planted a grove of ancient natives—metasequoia, giant sequoia, coast redwood, *Juglans*, *Ulmus*, and ginkgo—species that had been indigenous to the area during the Eocene Thermal Maximus, some 55 million years ago. "Imagine," he said. "Palms and alligators flourishing once again as far north as Alaska!"[37]

Even as the drama unfolds between Ruth and the teenager, who is pointedly named Nao (pronounced "Now"), the novel juxtaposes this drama against time imagined in millions of years. What is happening in the present and what will likely happen far into the future coexist. Human life is fast, but it is embedded in a much slower passage of time in which other living things, like the trees Oliver is planting, will survive. This much slower passage of time isn't unknowable or exhausting; it is simply a part of living as finite beings in (as far as anyone knows) an infinite universe.

ACKNOWLEDGING IMPURITY

While I try to emit as little carbon dioxide as possible in the way I lead my life, I am as guilty as anyone of living a carbon-intensive lifestyle. Although I try to eat a mostly plant-based diet, I have not succeeded in giving up the habit of eating meat. I like to travel, and flying is often unavoidable. I drive sometimes when I could walk, bike, or take public transportation because I feel tired, or because these other modes of transportation feel like such a hassle. I'm not as involved in political organizations as I feel I ought to be. It would, however, be counterproductive, not to mention exhausting, to feel shame (much less direct it at others) at the inability to lead a fully postcarbon life in a world still dominated by carbon. This is to seek purity where there is none. The problems such behavior is meant to counter are systemic, while the behavior is individualistic and also focused on consumer choice.

This means that something as intimate as food, which consumers might feel they have a great deal of control over, especially if they choose to be vegetarians or vegans, is inextricably connected to the food industry. As Alexis Shotwell observes, "If we orient toward eating as though we can personally exempt ourselves from ethical or physical ill-effects, we're engaging in a perpetually failing purity project."[38] A prominent character in *New York 2140* inveighs against a similar kind of purity project, suggesting how much the idea of purity pervades multiple kinds of discourses, after the polar bears she's trying to save by moving them to Antarctica are killed by radical activists who believe she is tainting that continent's pristine landscape. She responds, in an electronic announcement heard around the world, "We've been mixing things up for thousands of years now, poisoning some creatures and feeding others, and moving everything around. Ever since humans left Africa we've been doing that. So when people start to get upset about this, when they begin to insist on the purity of some place or some time, it makes me crazy. I can't stand it. It's a mongrel world, and whatever moment they want to hold on to, that was just one moment."[39] As if trying to see how "mongrel" such an impure world can get, Claire Vaye Watkins's *Gold Fame Citrus* imagines a future when drought in the western United States has created a massive and ever-widening sea of sand. Traveling there, the protagonist of the novel meets a charismatic cult leader who presents her with a field book he's written, classifying the new species of animals he's found in the "Amargosa Dune Sea." Although the field book proves an invention of his imagination, it offers a dizzying variety of animals, like the blue chupacabra, gravedigger ant, incandescent ant, land eel, vampire grackle, and, my favorite, dumbo hackrabbit—"easily identifiable by its enormous ears, which grow four to five times larger than the rabbit's body and serve as a cooling system in the extreme heat of the dune sea."[40]

This compendium of strange and unlikely life-forms recalls a similar moment of impurity in Karen Tei Yamashita's early novel *Through the Arc of the Rain Forest*, which I have written about elsewhere and believe to be an important predecessor of the many works of fiction I mention here.[41] Deep in the Brazilian Amazon, in an abandoned parking lot of military vehicles, new species form, such as mice "that had developed suction cups on their feet that allowed them to crawl up the slippery sides and bottoms of aircraft and cars" and birds that were "a cross between a vulture and a condor, that nested on propellers and pounced on the mice as they scurried out of exhaust pipes."[42]

ANOTHER PLOT IS POSSIBLE

In thinking about the kind of narratives these five qualities gesture toward, it's tempting to argue that plot as a chain of causation is somehow unable to capture the ways in which climate change itself actually comprises multiple phenomena with diffuse effects involving lots of actors (including nonhuman actors) and occurring at numerous scales of comprehension. It's an assemblage, something defined by entanglement and hybridity. It lacks obvious causation or occasion for struggle between a protagonist and a villain. It is unending in the stories it is a part of. If so, no neat resolution or solution is possible, only a becoming that defies any attempt at plot. Likewise, climate change will be addressed in multiple ways, and the most effective approaches to mitigation and adaptation will take numerous forms, will require enormous invention, and thus will comprise many stories where causation will not always be easy to track.

There would also be no end to the challenges it poses. At its best, *The Overstory* might teach its readers how to know trees as one way to imagine these challenges. Patricia Westerford observes, "In teaching us how to find their bait, trees taught us to see that the sky is blue. Our brains evolved to solve the forest. We've shaped and been shaped by forests longer than we've been *Homo sapiens*."[43] This attentiveness to the designs of other life-forms, which are always coevolving, is simultaneously a training in a specific reading practice, one that might spell trouble for the rigors of plot but might also enable other conventions of meaning making. Something is innately wrong, then, with a particular kind of narrative, one that centers on chains of causation that promise to lead to some kind of final destination. The actors in that kind of narrative are all sovereign, autonomous individuals who secure a quick return to some idealized past of natural homeostasis.

But as I think about this argument, I rebel against it. Maybe my disappointment with *The Overstory* results from the way it keeps trying to take readers to this conclusion. It seems to assert that human agency is always destructive and must be voluntarily given up somehow. Its most thrilling moments, in contrast, allow uncertainty to linger and remain unresolved. Against its central plot, then, which seems to lead inevitably to a recognition of the futility of organizing human agency to preserve what remains of the country's—and the world's—forests, I want to say that it's the first part of *The Overstory* that most astounds because it's full of stories, where this happens and then this happens. These stories suggest the possibility that other kinds of plots might develop, like the growth of the chestnut tree, "rousing itself and shaking free."[44] The latter parts similarly soar when passages get detained by moments of story that lose sight of the novel's overall plot and make space for alternative pathways to form. In such moments a potential is recovered that the events of the novel keep foreclosing.

Most notably, one of the final moments of the novel shows Westerford giving a talk, at the end of which she plans to kill herself (a scene I briefly discussed in the introduction). As she approaches the end, she thinks, "The single best thing you can do for the world. It occurs to her: The problem begins with the word *world*. It means two such opposite things. The real one we cannot see. The invented one we can't escape. She lifts the glass and hears her father read out loud: *Let me sing to you now, about how people turn into other things.*" The italicized words are from the start of Ovid's *Metamorphoses*. The quotation raises the possibility that humans are not frozen into a trajectory they have no ability to free themselves from. There is, in its place, ambiguity. The italicized words in this passage can refer at once to the ways in which Westerford will make herself into an "other thing" by killing herself and, as suggested by the doubt that has crept into her thinking, the ways in which she might decide not to go through with her plan after all. Immediately following this passage is a paragraph set off at both ends with a line skip, signaling its importance, which reads in part: "The speaker raises her glass, and the world splits. Down one branch, she lifts the glass to her lips, toasts the room—*To Tachigali versicolor* [a tree commonly known as the "suicide tree" because it flowers once before dying]—and drinks. Down another branch, this one, she shouts, 'Here's to unsuicide,' and flings the cup of swirling green over the gasping audience."[45]

The wording in the latter passage suggests that Westerford follows the latter path. The phrase "this one" stands out to indicate this is what happens. The earlier quotation, however, insists that the "real" world is one "we cannot see," while the "invented one" is something "we can't escape," suggesting that there is no access to knowing what actually happened in this moment. There is only invention. The world that splits is already an invented one, so that each branch leads to an equally invented outcome. There seems to be no access to "this one," where the referent is the actual world separate from our storytelling about it. This moment leaves readers stranded with narrative alone and without any access to a reality that exists outside its conventions of meaning making.

What happens? The plot may move in two very different directions, after all, and the chains of causation it relies on lead into futures readers cannot foresee. As a result, there is a subtle but noteworthy refusal to foreclose possibilities, deliberately leaving open the potential for something that has yet to be written. There is no mastery here, nor any assurance of a story following progress's ineluctable trajectory. There is, instead, a sense of the precarity of human existence, one immersed in a temporality that moves more slowly than can be perceived and is fated to stumble into the future without moral absolutes. There is always a choice to be made, which leaves space for the exercise of human agency. There are other moments like this one in the novel—subtle, so easy to miss—when it turns away from the demands of plot to focus on a moment in its characters' lives and lingers on details that both stun and encourage readers to look at the trees around them in a different way than they are likely accustomed to, potentially leading to alternative pathways than the ones they are entrenched in.

It can be challenging work spotting the pathways that are branching before the reader. About midway through, two of its central characters have become tree sitters, occupying an old-growth redwood they dub Mimas:

> The view cracks open his chest. Cloud, mountain, World Tree, and mist— all the tangled, rich stability of creation that gives rise to words to begin with—leave him stupid and speechless.... Through an opening in Mimas's crown, the tufted spires of nearby trunks swirled in the gauze of Chinese landscape. There's more substance to the grayish puffs than there is to the green-brown spikes poking through them. All around them spreads a phantasmagoric, Ordovician fairy tale. It's morning like the morning when life first came up on dry land.[46]

Reading this description of what these two see on their first morning high atop a tree that is destined to be cut down reminds me of the opening of Georg Lukács's *The Theory of the Novel*:

> Happy are those ages when the starry sky is the map of all possible paths— ages whose paths are illuminated by the light of the stars. Everything in such ages is new and yet familiar, full of adventure and yet their own. The world is wide and yet it is like home, for the fire that burns in the soul is of the same essential nature as the stars; the world and the self, the light and the fire, are sharply distinct, yet they never become permanent strangers to one another, for fire is the soul of all light and all fire clothes itself in light.[47]

Lukács's positing of an earlier prelapsarian time is surely a fairy tale, as is the view from Mimas, which *The Overstory* can't describe without some recourse to the exotic and mystical East ("the gauze of Chinese landscape"), and yet both speak profoundly to a felt sense of separation from the world.

I feel it keenly myself, this haunting idea, half formed and mostly inarticulate, that something is missing from contemporary life, that the "real" world is separate from the "invented" one, to use Westerford's phrasing. In this missing something's place is a perpetual longing for what has been lost. The feeling is nostalgic—a longing for home—and infused with troubling associations. This feeling is dangerous because it can lead to all sorts of reactionary politics, and it's very possible, maybe likely, that what is mourned hasn't ever existed.

But its strength suggests that contemporary invocations of entanglement and assemblage might be another way of saying that many people are feeling a sense of separation and isolation. Powers's novel contains numerous such moments when the wonder of what is observed seems to reflect back a being together that exists somehow beyond time and the boundaries that mark distinctions between the self and the world.

Even as I feel the attraction of this wonder, I also think of its invocation as a moment of branching possibilities. The invocation of wonder seems to call on readers to choose one path in particular, a condemnation of the present world as fallen and a return to some more pristine primordial state. It reverberates in Westerford's eloquent descriptions of nature's self-healing properties and the view from Mimas, as well as the ways in which humans seem always somehow to hinder such properties—without any attention to inequalities in their ranks and the ways in which capitalism feeds on such inequalities and on the extractivism all the characters in the novel must bear witness to. The very existence of humans is a danger to all life on the planet.

This position reminds me of the vision of natural renewal conjured by the journalist Alan Weisman in his popular book *The World without Us*, which vividly describes what would happen to many places if humans were to somehow magically disappear. It concludes with a call for a universal one-child policy that would give a shrinking population the "joy of watching the world daily become more wonderful."[48] Such a policy is premised on the belief that humans can have mastery over their societies and deliberately progress toward a universally acknowledged abstract good in a quick way. All it would take is a single generation. That good is a return to a pure state, one that leaves existing humans safer because they will have more access to the bounty of nature.

If climate fiction is to deliver on its many promises, it needs to challenge this way of thinking—premised on a view of the human as a single species that can act in concert with itself, never implementing population-control policies in ways that might be prejudiced or exclusionary, and that is incapable of performing important tasks that promote the robustness of the world's ecologies—by showing how it leads to further ruin. The vision of the good that climate fiction can offer instead, another pathway unexplored in *The Overstory*, is a living with climate change and the building of a shared human agency to realize the forms such a living can take. This work has no end, and there is no return to a fantastic pristine before.

WHERE ARE WE NOW?

Scalar Variance, Persistence, Swing, and David Bowie

DAYS AFTER DAVID BOWIE DIED, Pam Thurschwell recalls being awake at 5:00 a.m. and watching a recording of a crowd in Union Square in New York City. They were singing along to "Life on Mars." She feels sad for a lot of reasons, not least of which is that she grew up listening to his music and found in it possibilities that her life as "a 16-year-old overweight, grumpy suburban girl" rarely afforded. More than that, though, as she thinks back on his storied career, she concludes, "So much of his best work is set in futuristic landscapes that prefigure the rapid acceleration of the effects of climate change and late capital we live with today. Bowie might really be the first pop star of the Anthropocene." I hadn't thought of Bowie as having much to say about what humans are doing to their planet before reading this memorial. Thurschwell assures me, however, that I missed something essential about Bowie's music in all the years I've been listening to it. Maybe more than its deep investment in science fiction and willingness to consider how the future is less a line of progress and more full of the potential for capitalist ruin, what remains compelling about this music is how it suggests viable alternatives. As Thurschwell puts it, "If being young means holding on to the possibility that the future might turn out differently than the past or the present, then yes, we have to keep being young, even as we mourn and celebrate what Bowie meant to our own individual youths."[1]

To think of Bowie as "the first pop star of the Anthropocene" and in doing so to foreground the potential for a "future [that] might turn out differently" that his music contains, I need to continue thinking about the ways in which the lyric is intimately connected to a reimagining of the everyday as a refined attention to experiences that might otherwise seem hardly worth commenting on because they are so mundane. Maybe the mundane can then give way to something else, the exceptional and the extraordinary that is buried there, in the everyday. In this chapter I investigate this possibility further by drawing on the work of the poets Ed Roberson, Aimee Nezhukumatathil, M. NourbeSe Philip, Layli Long Soldier, and Li-Young Lee to distill three qualities of the revived lyric that have been helpful in making climate change available to my own quotidian sense of reality.

These poets exemplify the daring contemporary experimentation with the lyric that has suggestive environmental implications even if they don't always speak explicitly about this theme. In focusing on scalar variance, persistence, and swing, then, I have found they have changed my relationship to popular music, and to Bowie's music in particular. As Jahan Ramazani points out, "Song has long been conceived as poetry's closest generic kin."[2] At the same time, it's important to keep in mind that they are not perfectly in synchronicity with each other but different enough that there is frequent discordance and even rivalry. For poetry, in particular, there is the danger that it will be overshadowed by song, as illustrated by Bowie's outsize popularity. "In an age of hypersaturation by song," Ramazani continues, "poetry's more strenuous and difficult music must exist in an uneasy counterpart with the catchy tunes in our heads."[3] Even as I acknowledge the asymmetry in popularity between music and poetry, I believe lingering too much on this point unnecessarily pits the two modes against each other. Reading contemporary lyric poetry has led me to listen differently to Bowie's music, so that I hear more clearly the ways in which it has long sung about the environmental turmoil now associated with climate change.

SCALAR VARIANCE

Scale has figured large as a problem for many critics focused on the representation of climate change. Timothy Morton, for instance, coined the term *hyperobject* to get at the ways in which a phenomenon like climate change refuses familiar scales of reference. It is everywhere and at the same time impossible to touch or see immediately; it is occurring now, but its effects are measured by geological ages.[4] Seen from such a vantage point, as Timothy Clark elaborates, scale offers frames that inevitably reveal themselves to be inadequate, "running grave risks of being a simplification and even evasion."[5] And Dipesh Chakrabarty has argued that climate change challenges the writing of history because it "disconnects the future from the past by putting such a future beyond the grasp of historical sensibility."[6] Whatever scales historians have been using are being disrupted as historians are forced to make sense of an event that blurs the lines between human and nature, takes place in expanses of time measured by geological categories, and requires a focus on the human as one species among countless other life-forms.

If scale poses a problem for imagining climate change, the lyric is emerging as a way to imagine scale that enables thinking about space and time that is as variable as the phenomenon of climate change itself. Wai Chee Dimock gestures toward this quality of the lyric when she writes:

> I would like to argue against a strict separation between epic and lyric. Rather than aligning the former only with the macro and the latter with the micro, I would like to see these dimensional planes as up-and-down scalar variations that can be switched up and switched out of quite routinely, without too much fuss. Epic and lyric, in this view, are complementary registers, a functional duality allowing representational space to expand or contract as the need arises, to alternate when necessary between the technically bird's-eye view and the deliberately charged close-up.[7]

In this passage the lyric is asked to stand in for the close-up, a way of seeing the details and the minutiae and lingering over them. The usual brevity of the lyric accentuates this quality by making the reader more attentive to what is there in the poem. Brevity encourages rereading and repetition.

In my literal-minded way, Dimock's phrase "bird's-eye view" makes me think of the famous photograph "The Blue Marble," of the Earth in a vast darkness, captured by the Apollo 17 mission. Contrasted against the epic perspective of this photograph, the lyric would emphasize a more ground-level view of the planet. The two views are complementary, as if this photograph had such a high resolution I could zoom in and find an image of my street and of what was happening there at the moment this photograph was shot. The epic (which tends now to be associated with prose fiction and narrative) and the lyric are thus less distinct than critical discussions about them assume. When they are seen as sharing this tug of perspective, it's also possible to see how together they provide an important versatility in terms of scale. Perhaps, then, the boundaries between poetry and prose are porous and held in place by assumptions that haven't served readers well.

Of course, this idea of zooming in on a picture and seeing ever finer details "without too much fuss" comes to mind easily because it builds on an already familiar model: Google Earth. Go to this widely accessed website, and you will find an image of the planet suspended in space. Click on the planet and move the cursor, and you can control its orbit and orientation. Center on a place you are interested in, such as downtown Chicago along the shores of Lake Michigan, and you can double-click to zoom in. The screen fills with more details—of the Americas, then of the Midwest, then of highways and the city. Eventually you can make out individual buildings and houses, as well as trees, until the image becomes pixelated and obviously a digital model. The illusion of perceptual mastery is broken at this point, and the viewer is reminded that what is being looked at is not the Earth itself.

I choose the example of Chicago because it recalls how Google Earth was inspired by the short animated film *Powers of Ten*, created by the famous midcentury designers Charles and Ray Eames and funded by IBM in 1977 (and itself inspired by the earlier, less polished film *Cosmic Zoom*, directed by Eva Szasz, and the book *Cosmic View: The Universe in 40 Jumps*, by Kees Boeke). The film begins with an image of a heterosexual couple picnicking on the shores of Lake Michigan. A square measuring one meter on each side frames the man as he lies down and falls asleep; the woman, who is outside the frame, is sitting and reading a book. Each second, the square grows by a power of ten, so that it captures more and more space in its frame. It eventually zooms out to contain all the known galaxies in its frame until there is a vast emptiness, before zooming rapidly back to its starting place. The woman is now asleep as well, which suggests subtly that time has passed since the film's journey began. Then the square narrows to represent a smaller area by a factor of ten, continuing until it reaches the subatomic level.

According to Derek Woods, this film "is an aesthetic event comparable to the first image of the earth from space. Though much less discussed, the Eameses' film represents all known scales of the universe in one continuous zoom, expressing a space-age cosmology. Images that many had by then seen in textbooks and magazines seem sutured together in a single, virtual shot."[8] What seems seamless, however, hides from view "the jump that should exist at the edge of each still image," so that what seems like a smooth motion is actually a series of images collected in a modernist collage; even the scene of the picnic was shot in Los Angeles and not Chicago. Scholars of scale, like Woods, call this illusion the "zoom effect." This effect is dramatized by Google

Earth and makes possible a way of thinking of scale that sees little difference between the microscopic, the mesoscopic, and the macroscopic.[9] *Powers of Ten* centers this effect on Paul Bruhwiler, the white Swiss designer whose body is the starting place of the film. The film situates Etsu Garfias, an Eames staffer, physically outside the frame of this starting place. Thus, both the known universe and its subatomic inverse are measured by the figure of a single white man, while a woman (who seems to me Asian American, although I haven't been able to verify this) is casually but firmly sidelined.

This way of thinking of scale, according to Woods, should be contrasted with "scalar variance," or "the observation that things happen differently at different scales due to physical constraints upon becoming."[10] It's obviously physically impossible for a camera to zoom in and out of an image in the way *Powers of Ten* does, and even Google Earth relies on enormous and varied sets of data, so much so that it, too, might be thought of as an aesthetic experiment in modernist collage. Here the contemporary lyric has something interesting to offer, as it suggests it's possible for people to attain a vantage point where they can rise above their lowliest analogies to look down at what otherwise wouldn't be visible. Hyperobjects are no barriers to such perception.

As Lynn Keller observes of the work of Ed Roberson, "His poems suggest that humans move through the world perceiving in a kind of constantly shifting scalar kaleidoscope. Roberson . . . implies that apprehending Anthropocene scales is only an extension of an adjustment that, however astonishing, has long been part of the human tool kit."[11] If Keller is right, Roberson shows that people's perceptions can easily adjust to changes in scale at the spatial level. As Roberson puts it in "A Low Bank of Cloud," found in his evocatively titled book *To See the Earth before the End of the World*:

> As if the surface we are seeing
>   drops   the more seeing is added
>
>   while we feel the stories as well as our height
> from which to see.[12]

Roberson invites his readers to imagine themselves high above the clouds, on an ascending airplane. The higher they go, the more the land shrinks below them, and they can see more of it. A vast panorama opens up through the tiny porthole of the passenger window. The speaker has little trouble understanding what they are seeing or their own relationship to it. They are in motion, and the world changes perspective. They see more of the land even as they see fewer details.

What about at the level of time? Aimee Nezhukumatathil's poem "Dream Caused by the Flight of a Bee around a Pomegranate One Second before Waking Up," a meditation on the Salvador Dalí painting by the same name, seems to offer an answer. It begins:

In one second, three hundred fifty slices of pizza
are eaten somewhere on this earth. A heart beats just once.

These two facts, juxtaposed in these two lines and further emphasized through the use of enjambment, suggest how the multitude of humanity is able to consume an impressive sum in a very short period of time even though as lone individuals their lives are tethered to a much slower beat. The poem continues by evoking some dreamlike images and describing the scene in Dalí's painting before ending with more comparisons:

In twenty-four
microseconds, a stick of dynamite will explode after
its fuse burned down. Houseflies flick their wings once
every three milliseconds. Even that fly is long gone

to the other side of the yard in the time it took to write flick.
Giant tortoises and compact discs last one hundred years.
In one million years, Los Angeles will move forty kilometers
north because of plate tectonics. A spaceship zooming along

at the speed of light would not yet reach the halfway point
to the Andromeda galaxy. One billion years: one ocean born.
The time it takes for the last waxy smudge of me to stop loving
you. Only at the bottom do you find anything about a bee.[13]

Everything about these final three stanzas speaks to a present that operates at different scales of time: microseconds, milliseconds, millions of years, a billion years. The humans at the center of this poem are radically decentered, so that writing as a measurement of time is too slow to capture the quickness of the common fly. Their great city, Los Angeles, turns out to be built on plates that are always moving, but the motion can't be perceived by its residents because it is too slow. Meanwhile, their consumer products, like the already largely antiquated compact disc, will survive long after those who made them have perished. The slowness of the compact disc's survival is also measured by the life span of the notoriously slow-moving, and largely endangered, giant tortoise, which suggests both longevity and the prospect of mass extinctions to come—if not the mass extinctions already taking place. Thus, when the poem finishes by turning out to be a surprisingly conventional love poem, boasting of a love that exists beyond conceivable frames of human time and extends to the outermost time of a billion years, or the time it takes for "one ocean" to be "born," it ends on an unavoidably humorous note. The love it boasts of is epically impossible in its longevity.

It's important that the poem is so interested in time in particular, even as it comments on a static painting that might lead more easily to spatial metaphors, because so much of climate change is understood in terms of time. David Farrier, in his study of contemporary poetry and environmental discourses, insists on this focus on temporality when he points out that humans have always lived with deep time. Their very existence is defined by "a debt owed to the long history in which nonlife shaped the conditions for life to flourish." People become more intimate with this fact when they use fossil fuels, themselves the accumulated matter of past lives lived across vast expanses of time. In addition, the matter that industries are actively engaged in producing—such as "ballpoint pens, smartphones, plastic bottles, artificial knee joints and heart valves, fiber-optic cables, contact lenses, Styrofoam cups, plastic banknotes" (and compact discs)—will exist long into the future, enduring on and on, perhaps in the same way that the fossils dug up from the ground have endured.[14]

Go to any store or mall, and look at the many items on display. Many, if not most, of these items will continue to exist long after whoever purchases them will have thrown them out. Their very presence in the store is a reminder not only of what existed, in the deep past, but what will continue to exist, in the deep future. People are surrounded in their daily lives, among the ordinary objects that fill them, by artifacts of a temporally multiscalar present. Objects are not just what they are in the moment when consumers stop to purchase them but come from somewhere and go somewhere. Objects are never just one thing, outside of time, but are in transit in a never-ending time. A poem like Nezhukumatathil's works hard to capture such scalar variance and reminds its readers to pay attention to how time works in multiple temporalities. This is also something music does, with its tempos and beats. Music is, after all, one way to mark time. In the graphic narrative *Asterios Polyp*, by David Mazzucchelli, the eponymous character meets an African American composer who explains that a sheet of music is "a record of time passing in a certain way." He points to a bar of music on a framed sheet hanging on the wall and says, "This one, for example, represents about thirteen seconds, while this one is about, about four and a half minutes."[15]

In contemporary lyric poetry, time is not only captured in its variant temporalities—as in Nezhukumatathil's poem—but intensified as attention to an estranged present. Such poems are not as preoccupied by a past event they are seeking to narrate or a future event they seek to anticipate as they are focused on the present, in a way that makes the present enduring. One especially memorable example of this focus on a present that bends ordinary ideas of temporality is Christina Sharpe's use of "residence time." This concept comes up in a discussion of M. NourbeSe Philip's long poem *Zong!*, which focuses on the 1781 throwing overboard of over 130 enslaved Africans in an attempt to collect insurance on the loss of what the ship's officers considered cargo. While trying to understand what happened to their bodies and the bodies of other Africans thrown overboard into the Atlantic during the Middle Passage, Sharpe asked a colleague in the Earth Studies Department of her school, "What happened to the components of their bodies in salt water?"[16] The answer she received is that bodies are eaten and the organisms that eat them are eaten in turn. The bodies thus enter a cycle that goes on and on; *residence time* refers to how long this cycle lasts. "Human blood is salty," the colleague points out, "and sodium . . . has a residence time of 260 million years." Recalling this conversation, Sharpe observes, "We, Black people, exist in the residence time of the wake, a time in which 'everything is now. It is all now.'"[17]

This nowness of the slave trade—like the "constant nows" of Mima Ma's growing up in Richard Powers's *The Overstory* or the now of Nao in Ruth Ozeki's *A Tale for the Time Being* (discussed in the previous chapter)—is reflected in Philip's poems, which are all composed from words found in the legal case report associated with *Gregson v. Gilbert*. This is a record of the court's decision adjudicating the claims of the plaintiff, the insurers who did not want to award payment to the owners of the slave ship *Zong*. Philip deliberately tears the words in this legal document apart, trying to find in its dry language, which does not acknowledge the lost lives as the loss of life (thinking of them rather as goods), something that exists beyond story. As she puts it, "I murder the text . . . create semantic mayhem, until my hands bloodied, for so much killing and cutting, reach into the stinking, eviscerated innards, and like some seer, sangoma, or prophet who, having sacrificed an animal for signs and portents of a new life, or simply life, reads the untold story that tells itself by not telling."[18] This "semantic mayhem" results in a form that remakes her understanding of the lyric as something that exists beyond language:

"Seems I was trying to put my own meaning on the words and that doesn't work. Have to let them offer themselves up. Have found a batch of rough ones at the back and they move but they move more towards the lyric and less towards language."[19] This contrast appears again later in her reflections on the writing of these poems: "Found these latter poems a struggle—as if having to work harder to resist my meaning—more lyric."[20]

The "more lyric" the poems in *Zong!* become, the more they seem to evade familiar forms of verse, which the earlier poems more or less adhered to. What results is a spatializing of words and word fragments that molecularizes language on the page, making it scatter in the way an object might scatter in water. Consider, for instance, this excerpt from an early poem in the book, in the section entitled "Os" ("bone," as translated from the Latin):

                        is was
    is
            should be
                    or
            have been
                is there.[21]

This poem exemplifies persistence in the way it focuses attention on an existing that is determinedly an "is there" that does not give way easily to a "should be" or "have been." The later poems in the book become more difficult to decipher and suggest that the only way to read them is visually. They seem to defy pronouncement:

    ce my no   nce queen of the ni
            ger the sea   ble o
        ne nig   *ra afra*
            sa   *d*[22]

And yet, as difficult as it is to imagine reading such poetry aloud, Philip's discussion of how these poems came to be emphasizes their innate vocality. The lyric signifies sounds that exist independent of language, a kind of cry insisting on an existence that has been denied but can't be quieted and continues still. As Sonya Posmentier points out, this cry does not come from one speaker but from "the multiple voices in the poem. . . . [I]t concatenates and collects the voices of others."[23]

A similar kind of persistent present is evoked at the start of Layli Long Soldier's collection of poems *Whereas*:

Now
make room in the mouth
for grassesgrassesgrasses[24]

Only later in the book is the reader told of Andrew Myrick, a trader who

is famous for his refusal to provide
credit to Dakota people by saying, "If they are hungry, let them eat grass."

Long Soldier goes on to write:

When settlers and traders were killed during the Sioux Uprising, one of
the first to be executed by the Dakota was Andrew Myrick.

When Myrick's body was found,

his mouth was stuffed with grass.

I am inclined to call this act by the Dakota warriors a poem.[25]

The uprising occurred in 1862, but as Long Soldier suggests, it continues into
the present, the word "grass" lingering as a physical taste in the mouth (which
is emphatically what is happening "now," the very first word of the book,
which is presented on a line all by itself), the attitude expressed by Myrick,
so common, itself an act of cruelty and violence, and the ways in which such
violence is mirrored back, so that it becomes a kind of expression. Speech
becomes physical violence, especially in the way it deprives people of food
when they are starving, and violence becomes speech, in the way stuffing a
mouth full of grass makes a comment. This is obviously not a form of residence time, but perhaps it can be called *grass time*.

Such persistence enables the lyric to train the attention on what is there, an
event that it turns into an event by the sheer force of its attentiveness. Let me
give one more example. Li-Young Lee's "The Cleaving" starts with a speaker
gazing at a Chinatown butcher and reflecting on the similarity of their faces:

He gossips like my grandmother, this man
with my face, and I could stand
amused all afternoon
in the Hon Kee Grocery,
amid hanging meats he
chops.

The poem continues to detail what the speaker sees, including the meats on
display, the face of the butcher, the motion of the butcher's body and the

noise he makes while at work, and the many thoughts the speaker is having as he watches—about ancestry, about eating, about the body's functioning, about the language used to describe the body. Near its end, the poem reflects on the violence that is often required to keep the body alive:

> No easy thing, violence.
> One of its names? Change. Change
> resides in the embrace
> of the effaced and the effacer,
> in the covenant of the opened and the openers;
> the axe accomplishes it on the soul's axis.
> What then may I do
> but cleave to what cleaves me.
> I kiss the blade and eat my meat.[26]

All of this happens in a single moment, no longer than the time it takes for the speaker to give his order, taste a sample, and wait to pay. The speaker doesn't even complete his transaction, so the poem focuses on an even briefer moment than the fullness of this encounter would entail. And yet this moment is fixed by the poem's descriptiveness and the speaker's musings. The latter invite the reader to consider the meaning of the scene and the many connections—among body, consumption, and race—that make such a moment possible. In doing so, the poem turns what would otherwise be a brief and easily forgotten encounter into an event worthy of sustained attention. The moment doesn't end in the poem and as a result asks the reader to imagine it as still ongoing, a taste of violence in the mouth like the taste of grass in Long Soldier's poems.

And, like the way Philip violently reaches into a legal document and extracts what is buried but still singing behind its words, Lee foregrounds the violence of a moment that is everyday and ordinary, a visit to the butcher. The moment both cuts the speaker and clings to him, both cleaving and cleaving, and he takes the result of the violence of this moment into himself by making a kiss and consuming. This passage does not speak about the refusal of violence but about the recognition that it is part of his daily existence, an embrace of the cost of living in terms of the sacrifice of other lives. The reader can't forget the violence of eating meat. Such an invitation is only possible because of what I'm tempted to call *butcher time*, so as to line up alongside grass time and residence time. In such varied ideas of temporality, the lyric evokes different ways of apprehending a here *and* a now that is available for careful scrutiny and thought. *Persistence* names a lyric experience of time that focuses on a moment turned into an event and invites thought about how that event remains a part of the now.

SWING

Despite the persistence of a moment that the lyric lyricizes, there is also an important play of rhythm. The lyric continues to share with its etymological cousin *lyrics* a deep interest in music and sound, and indeed much of what it depicts depends on music and sound to arrest attention. The poet Robert Pinsky has gone so far as to say, in describing ordinary speech, "It is almost as if we sing to one another all day."[27] His point is that poetry distills and amplifies music that is already there in everyday speech. Derek Attridge, whose extensive study of poetic rhythm informs Jonathan Culler's understanding of the importance of the aural in lyric poetry, is a strong advocate of listening carefully to the beats that emerge in metered verse, as if he were taking Pinsky's point literally.[28]

According to Attridge, beats do not always correspond to stressed syllables, although they often do; instead, they correspond to a sound pattern, especially in the popular poetic forms that are most in alignment with musical forms. These forms comprise lines that contain four beats. These lines are repeated four times, so that they form a quatrain. There are thus

> four groups of four beats, producing a very familiar and insistently regular rhythm. This is the most common of all the possible rhythmic patterns, if every kind of verse is taken into account. It is the basis of most modern popular music, including rock and rap, of most folk, broadside, and industrial ballads from the Middle Ages to the twentieth century, of most hymns, of most nursery rhymes, of a great deal of printed poetry. Its popularity is not limited to the English language, either; there is evidence of its use in a number of European and non-European languages, especially in children's verse.[29]

In the United States (and elsewhere in the English-speaking world?), children are taught the alphabet to the music of "Twinkle, Twinkle, Little Star," which has a very pronounced four-by-four structure.

Before I read this description, I puzzled over the refrain in "Under Pressure," the powerful duet sung by Freddie Mercury, the lead singer of Queen, and David Bowie.[30] The phrase "This is our last dance" has always confused me because it doesn't fit the thematic concerns of the song, which focuses primarily on the ways in which the rush and acceleration of modern life put people under enormous stress. As is typical of popular songs, the lyrics suggest that love can help alleviate this stress. But if so, why then introduce at the end the almost apocalyptic image of a "last dance"? If the listener pays attention to the beats in this refrain, what is revealed are the ways in which it breaks down Attridge's four-by-four formation to its most basic elements:

```
/  /  x  /   /
This is our last dance
B  B     B   B
```

In this scansion, "/" refers to a stressed and *x* to an unstressed syllable. Under this line are *B*s for the beats. The unstressed syllable in the middle of this line gives a heightened pause, breaking the rhythm into two perfect half lines. In recorded versions of this song, Mercury and Bowie can be heard taking an exaggerated pause at "our," so that there is a conspicuous taking in of breath. The line is repeated in the song, and then the four-beat pattern is repeated in the words "This is ourselves under pressure / under pressure" with a long caesura between the two instances of "under pressure" filled by the song's famous musical refrain. These lyrics can easily be lineated into a quatrain:

This is our last dance
This is our last dance
This is ourselves
Under pressure, under pressure

Notice that the third line does not have an unstressed syllable, while the fourth line has a comma in the middle to allow for a pause and therefore maintains the same rhythm as in the first two lines. The third line thus breaks the pattern the most and as a result calls attention to how the third beat of the line is "our," which gives what was unstressed a new emphasis. That the refrain "This is our last dance" is a thematic outlier in this song while integral to its rhythm suggests to me that it only makes sense in the song if you listen to the beats and not just to the words. If you pay attention to the beats— which isn't difficult to do because this is a catchy song that I easily find myself listening to several times in a row and even humming for the rest of the day—the word that lingers most from this phrasing is not "last" or "pressure" but "our," a shared condition, the fact of having something in common with others. When I listen to this song now, I can't help but hear the way in which Mercury's and Bowie's voices harmonize on an elongated "*our*-selves."

This rhythm, which is a notable feature of many lyric poems written in stressed meter *and* in most of the popular forms Attridge mentions, is what

I consider *swing*. Attridge doesn't pause to define this term, but he uses it to describe how the lines of William Blake's "Never Seek to Tell Thy Love," when read "aloud, letting their individual rhythm emerge," will "develop a swing of their own. A different impulse of rhythmicality emerges to mesh with that of the language itself, and perhaps even alter it." A short while later, Attridge connects this "impulse of rhythmicality" to the beat:

> We say that a stretch of language has beats when, on hearing it or reading it aloud, we sense an impulse to move at regularly occurring places—to bring down the hand, to nod the head, to tap the foot. The oldest meaning of "beat" is "striking repeatedly," and its later use in discussion of music and poetry still carries something of that sense of repeated physical action. What was discussed as the "swing" of the Blake lines quoted earlier is the effects of the beats that emerge when we read it.[31]

I have had to get technical in trying to distill the meaning of swing because it is a shaping of time that everyone senses at an intuitive level as part of the way language works. As such, it is difficult to gain the necessary distance to analyze it and make sense of the way it works in an explicit manner, and in doing so to call attention to how powerful a force it is. Swing operates not at the level of sense or meaning but at the level of pattern, which is etched deep into the conscious mind so that it may be remembered as a hum that makes listeners aware of how their movement through time is accompanied by its own patterning. Swing demands a physical response, a tapping toe or a swivel of the head or even the full body in corresponding rhythmic motion, and this physical responsiveness indicates more than anything else that the listener is in its grasp. Swing is a partner to patterns, and as such the motions it conjures can reflect when patterns start to go awry, when they lose their shape and begin to erode, as in the present. Who can say anymore when any of the seasons end and begin? What kind of swing is possible when you can't even rely on the seasons to tell you what time of the year you're in? Because of climate change, are the years losing their swing?

In asking these questions, I find myself thinking of the song "Under Pressure" as profoundly environmental in its preoccupations. It focuses on the stress caused by contemporary life under capitalism, as the demands of work increase and threaten those who can't keep up with being put out "on the street." What the song sings about, and sings against, is what Margaret Ronda focuses on as the Great Acceleration, a primarily post–World War II "dramatic scaling-up . . . of the intensified extractivist and expansionist strategies of global capitalism in the twentieth century and now twenty-first century."[32]

The Great Acceleration thus names for Ronda the speedups and casualization of work, the focus on efficiency, the building of global supply chains, and the ramping up of fossil fuel use that has intensified the problem of climate change. Half of the carbon dioxide that's been put into the atmosphere by human activity has been put there in the past thirty years.[33] If swing measures tempo, the swing of "Under Pressure" marks an ever-quickening beat and an ever-accelerating maddening pace, against which the astounding scream Mercury lets out near the middle of the song makes a bold protest.

THE LYRICS OF "WHERE ARE WE NOW?"

Throughout "Where Are We Now?," a song released just three years before his death, David Bowie repeats the refrain "walking the dead."[34] It's an enigmatic phrase. Who is doing the walking? Is the dead a thing that can be walked? Where is the dead being walked to? A literal understanding of this phrase won't work. Despite its high figurativeness, it's not difficult to intuit that mortality is on the singer's mind. As a contemplation of death, the song is remarkable for another reason: how it captures a kind of unspooling of time. The singer is "a man lost in time." The question that is also the song's title, which appears twice in the song, references this sense of being lost. In each instance, the question "Where are we now?" is repeated, with the emphasis first on "where" and then on "are." "Where" might thus refer to a place but can refer to a state of being as well. The "are" suggests the passage of time, as in, How is where we *are* now related to where we were or where we have been? How did we get from then to now and from there to here? How do we define, much less live in, the here and now? How does our past relate to our present, and where is it leading us?

The persistence of such unasked questions is strengthened by the song's allusions to specific places in Berlin and the ways in which these figure the divisions of the Cold War and the dramatic events that occurred after the Berlin Wall came down. When scholars think about the present, 1989 poses itself as a possible marker for the start of the contemporary, or what Amy Hungerford describes as "whatever comes after modernization."[35] Francis Fukuyama famously thought the year and the event signaled the end of history and the final triumph of liberalism, although he has since moderated this claim.[36] For someone like me who was still a young person when the Berlin Wall came down, that event is memorable but distant. Little about that symbolic moment felt germane to my own immediate existence, and in any case there have been, as Jodi Kim argues, many "ends" to the Cold War.[37]

I have no personal connection to the city of Berlin, and what I remember as an equally momentous political movement of that era was the fight against apartheid in South Africa. Several other events that have punctuated the beginning of the current century have also felt to me momentous and world altering: the fall of the Twin Towers; Hurricane Katrina; the Indian Ocean tsunami; the housing-market crash; the Haitian earthquake; Fukushima; the Syrian Civil War; Brexit and the 2016 U.S. presidential election; Hurricane Maria and Typhoon Haiyan and Cyclone Amphan; the flooding of Venice two years in a row; the fires in the North American West, Australia, and Brazil; the COVID-19 pandemic; and all that has happened since. Each feels like a catastrophe that was as catastrophic as the one before, and their cumulative force makes me brace for what is to come. I have no doubt that worse is coming, and will have come by the time what I'm writing finds print.

In this fraught moment, the question that animates Bowie's song resonates beyond the scalar specificity of a looming death and his memories of a time lived in tense geopolitical confrontation. It rings with force in the present, quizzing its listeners about a moment that leaves us feeling lost, unmoored, and full of trepidation. The repetition that song lyrics depend on heightens this sense of haunting. *Where* are we now? Catastrophes blossom around us, institutions are buckling and are on the verge of imploding, political leaders seem determined to take us down destructive paths, inequalities widen and in their widening produce more and more suffering. Where *are* we now? It is almost impossible to find examples of contemporary storytelling that don't project this mood into a future full of more of the same, so much so that every dystopic narrative feels like an exaggerated version of the dystopic worlds we are currently inhabiting. With each passing year, the exaggeration feels less exaggerated.

And yet, despite this kind of worrying, the song ends in a way that is soothing and hopeful. It seems to promise that whatever happens, something endures. I'll repeat the last words in full here:

As long as there's sun
As long as there's sun
As long as there's rain
As long as there's rain
As long as there's fire
As long as there's fire
As long as there's me
As long as there's you

The me and the you, invoked so strongly in so many lyric poems, are mixed up with something more elemental, forming an ecology that allows any one person to continue existing in the continued existence of another in the same way that sun is equal to sun, rain to rain, and fire to fire. There is, in these lyrics, a democratic substitutability between "me" and "you."[38] For Bowie, as for the lyric poem as it is currently being reinvented by so many talented poets, the emphasis remains focused on what *we* have in common—the space between me and you, which also includes the nonhuman. Even if I, whoever I am, were to die, you, whoever you are, would continue to live in a world of sun, rain, and fire. Together, we persist, swinging in a present that defies the passage of time and requires variant scales of reference for sense making.

PART III

URGENCY

THE SCALE OF THE EVERYDAY, PART 1

The Keeling Curve, Frank O'Hara, and Bernadette Mayer

THE KEELING CURVE REFERS to one of the most famous, if not the most famous, data collection and visualization projects of the post–World War II era. Named after Charles David Keeling, the scientist responsible for overseeing the project, it is a meticulous record of increasing carbon concentrations in the atmosphere begun in 1958 atop Mauna Loa on the big island of Hawai'i. Record keeping continues into the present, although Keeling himself passed away in 2005. The graph forms a rough seesaw pattern that moves steadily upward on a standard *x-y* graph. Scientists believe carbon dioxide concentrations averaged about 280 parts per million (ppm) before the start of the Industrial Revolution. When the project began, the average was about 315 ppm. By 2019 concentrations were consistently over 410 ppm. In the 1960s, the rate of increase was approximately 0.6 ppm per year; by the start of this century, the rate had increased to approximately 2 ppm per year, making a steeper gradient as the curve approaches the present. In other words, as figure 7.1 shows, the fast emission of carbon after the middle of the century got faster at the end of the century.[1]

In the documentary *An Inconvenient Truth*, Al Gore recalls his famous undergraduate professor Roger Revelle, who originally came up with the idea of measuring carbon dioxide concentrations in the atmosphere, explaining

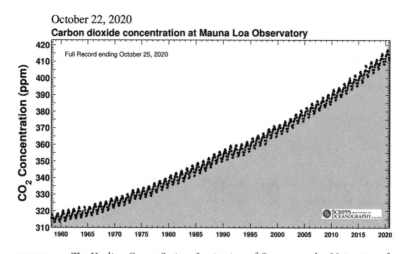

October 22, 2020
Carbon dioxide concentration at Mauna Loa Observatory

Full Record ending October 25, 2020

FIGURE 7.1 The Keeling Curve. Scripps Institution of Oceanography, University of California, San Diego (keelingcurve.ucsd.edu).

that because most of the Earth's landmass is north of the equator, when the northern hemisphere is tilted toward the sun, lush vegetation soaks in carbon dioxide. When it is tilted away, less carbon dioxide is absorbed. Hence, carbon dioxide concentrations peak in May and reach their nadir in September. Gore comments, "It's as if the entire Earth takes a big breath in and out once each year," a graceful, phenomenological image that depends for its effectiveness on anthropomorphizing the planet.[2] The difference between May and September is subtle and would not have been detectable if Keeling hadn't developed a method that could measure carbon dioxide concentrations in the air with a precision of 0.5 ppm.[3] More significant, of course, is the quickening increase of carbon in the atmosphere, now reaching a steady peak that hasn't been seen for hundreds of millions of years.

In this chapter and the next, I want to consider what the Keeling Curve means for ideas of the everyday. Because it tracks carbon dioxide concentrations in the atmosphere on a daily basis, it can be called another everyday-life project that seeks to find creative ways of keeping track, and making sense, of what happens in daily activities that, because they are daily, often get lost to consciousness. It might also be thought of as an *aggregator* everyday-life project, in the sense that it doesn't track the activities of individuals, which the original term applies to, but the activities of all humans on the planet, some obviously more than others. It is, therefore, a ceaseless reminder of what industrial activity is doing to the very chemical composition of the Earth's atmosphere.

The Keeling Curve is a record of the past half century, the passage of time measured in parts per million rather than years. It is a marker of political futility as well, for nothing anyone has done has altered its fundamental trajectory. Every year, there is more carbon in the air than the previous year, and it keeps going up without any indication of when it might stop. It is, finally, the ultimate arbiter of the effectiveness of responses to climate change, for effectivity must be measured by whether this curve rises less steeply, until it flatlines and in the future somehow bends down.

What happens, then, if the everyday is measured in terms of how much additional carbon dioxide has been put into the atmosphere? Does the experience of the everyday lose its sense of ordinariness or enter a temporality different from what it is usually associated with? In addressing these questions in this chapter, I consider the conditions in which the Keeling Curve was produced and what it has to say about the present moment and its refraction through what Sianne Ngai calls the "zany." I draw on Frank O'Hara's breezy postwar poems in *Lunch Poems* (319 ppm), which was published just before his untimely death and helped to establish his formidable—and growing— literary reputation, and Bernadette Mayer's long poem *Midwinter Day* (340 ppm), which chronicles the poet's journey through a single, uneventful day that happened to coincide with the winter equinox in Lenox, Massachusetts, as a way to make sense of how aesthetic experiments can respond in indirect ways to their times. There are no subheadings in what follows, which I hope will break up the rhythm of the earlier chapters and introduce a sense of urgency by imitating the continuity of the Keeling Curve itself.

This discussion leads me, in the next chapter, to contrast the work of these poets with more recent poetic accounts of everyday experiences, particularly in Ada Limón's *The Carrying* (407 ppm), Tommy Pico's *Nature Poem* (405 ppm), and Solmaz Sharif's *Look* (402 ppm), where the everyday can't be described as breezy or uneventful. It is, instead, full of portentous meaning requiring strenuous thought. In the progression of these chapters, there's a noticeable quickening of tempo and a more sober tone in the poems I consider.

Foregrounding the Keeling Curve in this chapter and the next thus suggests how the environmental consequences of more greenhouse gases in the atmosphere have subtly, but noticeably and with greater prominence, been altering the conditions of possibility on which experiences of the everyday rely. Increasing emissions are not the only factor in such alterations, of course, but it would be a mistake to argue that their impact is negligible. Perhaps just as important, most of these emissions have occurred after World War II as scientific advances allowed massive changes to the world's economies and systems of extraction, production, and distribution, of which the Keeling Curve itself is a part.

In other words, the Keeling Curve might not exist if it weren't for the conjunction of a number of historical factors that have contributed greatly to global warming. The first is the Cold War, which continued the military investment in geophysical research and in meteorology, in particular, that began during the war. As the historian Spencer Weart observes, "Military officers recognized that they needed to understand almost everything about the environments in which they operated, from the ocean depths to the top of the atmosphere. In view of the complex interconnectedness of all things geophysical, the military services were ready to sponsor many kinds of research."[4] A second is the development of artificial nitrogen, essential to the process Keeling developed for extracting carbon from his air samples. Nitrogen itself was first artificially made during wartime as an important ingredient in munitions manufacturing, but in the postwar era it continued to be produced as an essential ingredient in fertilizer. The creation of artificial nitrogen is largely responsible for the green revolution, when food production increased to keep pace with a fast-growing population.[5] A third is the establishment of the National Oceanic and Atmospheric Administration's observatory at Mauna Loa, which is unavoidably embedded in a longer history of U.S. expansion into the Pacific and its establishment of sovereignty over the Hawaiian Islands. This history flared into view recently over the proposed installation of the Thirty Meter Telescope (TMT) atop Mauna Kea, "a mountain of major cultural and ecological significance." Construction "was blocked by hundreds and then thousands of protectors, who would not allow the construction of the TMT to desecrate this sacred place."[6]

All of these factors are part of the Great Acceleration, which began after World War II. Margaret Ronda describes this phenomenon: it is "characterized by metabolic rifts occurring at a global scale, from the sharp spike in CO_2 emissions and the disturbances of the nitrogen cycle to massive biodiversity loss and ocean acidification. While many of the broad-based environmental changes occurring in the Great Acceleration precede 1945, they undergo a dramatic scaling-up in the post-1945 era, a direct result of the intensified extractivist and expansionist strategies of global capitalism in the twentieth and now twenty-first century."[7] During this period, the Cold War heated up in proxy battles around the planet and then was lost by the Soviet Union as the United States ramped up its military arsenal; massive infrastructure projects made the world feel smaller as automobile and air travel became more commonplace; advances in computing technology gained speed and sophistication at exponential rates; and supply-chain capitalism was pioneered by Japan and adopted by the other industrialized nations, which improved efficiency and limited liability even as it depended more and more on far-flung production and assembly.

All of these events, and many more that could have been mentioned here, point to increases in scale and speed. They are the major contributors to climate change and a host of related environmental concerns and reflect as well how much experiences of the everyday have become more frantic, conflict prone, and unequal. In thinking about the Great Acceleration, I find it difficult not to think about Sianne Ngai's ambitious argument in *Our Aesthetic Categories: Zany, Cute, Interesting* (392 ppm), in which the terms named in the subtitle are the aesthetic categories that have replaced the beautiful and the sublime, which were the focus of aesthetics in the past. Such a cultural transformation was enabled, Ngai reasons, by late capitalism's inflation of the importance of efficiency, information, and the commodity. *The zany* refers to the acceleration of production that, for instance, performance reviews in the workplace are meant to encourage; *the interesting* refers to the way information itself, as it becomes ever more plentiful, operates at lower levels of affective response (a raised eyebrow or a laugh out loud rather than a feeling of amazement); and *the cute* refers to many items on sale at the store in the guise of adorable smallness and relatability.

When I focus on contemporary poetry, I am turning to an instance of the cute. The short lyric poem in particular stands in for the much larger failures of the avant-garde; its poetic output is exactly like the cute in its smallness, vulnerability, and deformations. Imagine, for instance, a Hello Kitty squishy toy with its large eyes and no mouth, so diminutive it can easily be held in the palm of your hand, and the satisfaction of being able to squeeze it tightly in your fist only to release it and watch it expand slowly and in irregular ways until it bounces back to its original plush shape. These are qualities of the cute, which poetry has come to share throughout the course of the twentieth century as it spoke to smaller and smaller audiences, became contained in the cultural institutions that largely kept it funded, and proclaimed often-outsize ambitions that rarely, if ever, came to fruition. "We can thus see," Ngai writes, "why cuteness might be explicitly mobilized by the poetic avant-garde as a meditation on its own restricted agency, as well as on the fetishization of its texts."[8]

Frank O'Hara's *Lunch Poems* exemplifies the cuteness of postwar American avant-garde poetry. Its very size is provocatively small, measuring a diminutive five inches by four inches. From the front, the book looks just like a square greeting card you can buy at a store, which you have to pay extra postage to send by mail (even as I describe this once common greeting card, I feel dated, as greeting cards themselves seem an increasingly old-fashioned way of marking an occasion with others—how fast things go out of date during the Great Acceleration). From the side, it presents a narrow profile, suggesting brevity. It's easily held in the hand, and reading it feels a lot like reading a pamphlet someone might hand you on the street or in a doctor's office, warning you of the dangers of a life lived in sin or of a sexually transmitted disease. The covers fold easily, even in one hand, and bounce back when the hand is relaxed, uncannily like a squishy toy. The experience of reading the poems in this volume, as opposed to those in *The Collected Poems of Frank O'Hara*, which strives to emphasize the monumentality of O'Hara's total accomplishments as a poet, is unique in that it seems to go out of its way to convey an affect that's very similar to Ngai's notion of the cute.

The poems themselves range from a few lines to, at the longest, a few pages. The cadence is irregular but rhythmic, like the patterns speech might form for someone who is just trying to describe how his day went. This is to say that the poems are conversational. The very first poem in the volume, "Music," begins with the speaker talking to the reader about places around New York City as if the reader is already familiar with them, suggesting the kind of intimacy that comes from a shared landscape:

> If I rest for a moment near The Equestrian
> Pausing for a liver sausage sandwich in the Mayflower
> Shoppe,
> that angel seems to be leading the horse into
> Bergdorf's
> and I am naked as a table cloth, my nerves humming.
> Close to the fear of war and the stars which have disappeared.
> I have in my hand only 25¢, it's so meaningless to eat![9]

The Equestrian statue, Mayflower Donuts, and the Bergdorf Goodman department store make appearances in the first three lines, with "Shoppe" and "Bergdorf's" set off at the end of the line to give them greater emphasis. These are fairly well-known Manhattan icons, all located on Fifth Avenue in Midtown, and speak in a surprisingly compact way about the past (the Equestrian statue is more commonly known as the Sherman statue and commemorates William Sherman's march through the South in the Civil War), about immigration (Mayflower Donuts is a chain founded by a Russian Jewish immigrant who invented an automatic doughnut-making machine and might have been the first to shorten *doughnut* to *donut*), and about consumerism (the famed department store Bergdorf Goodman).

That he's going to eat a "liver sausage sandwich" at the Mayflower seems significant as well, as the liverwurst sandwich, as it's more commonly known today, was a dish brought to the United States from eastern and central Europe. It seems to have been popular right after World War II, which invites speculation about how the popularity of a sandwich made with organ meat might reflect the deprivations of wartime, when fresh meat would have been relatively rare and expensive. The sandwich couldn't, however, ever have been thought of as anything but food for a common meal, something to be eaten in a hurry and often rather than something expensive that one rarely could get and that was therefore special. This suggests, then, that the explicit choice of sandwich is meant to situate the speaker in a very ordinary situation, on an ordinary day.

It would be inaccurate to say, however, that this poem is only grounded in the imagination of the ordinary as somehow merely a matter of empirical observation, of what it was like to be in a specific time and place, for such apparent empiricism is undermined right away by an image that's difficult to decipher. Contrasting with the homeness of a "liver sausage sandwich," there is the enigmatic and incongruous image of an "angel" with a "horse" going into a department store. I can't read this poem without pausing over this third line and feeling confused. Perhaps the angel and horse were part of an elaborate display that the department store was mounting? Perhaps he imagined it? Perhaps it's supposed to be metaphoric for something unseen?

Next, the speaker expresses the sense of vulnerability that this moment seems to give him, a flash of interior reflection that the lyric in particular is strongly associated with, but this moment is not allowed to remain inward dwelling, for the next line turns outward, to a suggestive historical context where war seems possible. (But what possible war? After the poem ends, the year it was composed is listed—the same year that the Korean War ended.) The fear that war conjures is amplified by the image of the stars disappearing, which again is enigmatic and unexplained. The moment the poem conjures seems to take place midday, so how could the stars have been seen to begin with? Are the stars a metaphor for a loss of wonder or points of reference to locate oneself by? The final line of the quoted passage definitively returns the reader to a concrete and noticeably mundane problem: not having enough money in his pocket to get the sandwich he looked forward to buying.

A lot of different stimuli are juxtaposed, then, like the experience of standing on a busy city street corner. There's the public monument, the stores, the consumer items for sale (including food), perhaps a newsstand with headlines discussing war nearby, and an occasional sight that can't easily be explained. I find it especially interesting that when the speaker turns inward, to acknowledge a feeling of vulnerability at all the stimuli surrounding him, the feeling is compared to "a table cloth," which could easily have come to mind because he was standing near a restaurant with elaborately set tables on display to entice potential diners. There is, then, something highly material about this poem, for it draws on what the speaker can see and sense and uses these to construct a self who experiences this moment.

"Music" is typical of the poems found in *Lunch Poems* in that it works by making a lot of references to sensory stimuli that would have likely been available to O'Hara living in New York City, which he does not explain in any way (as if assuming the reader will just know what he is talking about), and by heaping on contrasts between the profound and the profane, between introspection and action, between being somewhere specific and thinking about faraway topics. Repeatedly, the poems emphasize that the speaker is just going about an average day. "A Step Away from Them" begins:

> It's my lunch hour, so I go
> for a walk among the hum-colored
> cabs.[10]

The speaker can make profound observations, touching on painful histories, such as in "Naphtha":

> we owe a debt to the Iroquois
> and to Duke Ellington
> for playing in the buildings when they are built
> we don't do much ourselves
> but fuck and think
> of the haunting Métro
> and the one who didn't show up there[11]

At such moments, O'Hara sounds as if he's worried about the triviality of the everyday and the takeover of attention by consumer society. At the same time, he seems to resist such thinking, as when he follows these lines with an internal monologue, the "I" and the "you" working hard between shifting, unnamed antecedents:

how can you
you were made in the image of god
I was not
I was made in the image of a sissy truck-driver.[12]

Or when O'Hara concludes "Steps" with this celebration of wasting time and indulging too much in minor vices:

oh god it's wonderful
to get out of bed
and drink too much coffee
and smoke too many cigarettes
and love you so much.[13]

The concluding line is sentimental and familiar, and yet because it follows a morning of pleasurable excess, it gains something original and joyous. The whole poem sees in modern life something to hold up for admiration. This is very much in line with how Jasper Bernes characterizes O'Hara's ambitions, to think of "lyric modalities" as not distancing and escaping "from the mercenary exchanges and exacting labors of the workaday world" but more precisely as taking "place among and through them, allowing for meaningful human interaction, erotic and otherwise."[14] There's also "Poem (Lana Turner Has Collapsed)," which is simply about the speaker's love of the actor Lana Turner and his concern that she fell down in public. The poem revels in the speaker's immersion in popular culture and his psychic investment in celebrities.

In these latter moments, O'Hara participates in an emerging culture of the cute and its commingling with consumer culture. And just like the cute, O'Hara knows how to transfix a gaze and encourages lingering in a culture that otherwise prompts constant distraction and busyness. The cute is, in other words, valuable to late capitalism for precisely this reason. It knows how to draw a look and hold it. The cute also draws power from, as Ngai puts it, "the desire for an ever more intimate, ever more sensuous relation to objects already regarded as familiar and unthreatening," and for this reason "cuteness is not just an aestheticization but an eroticization of powerlessness, evoking tenderness for 'small things' but also, sometimes, a desire to belittle or diminish them further."[15] There is in the cute's promise of intimacy a troubling aggression, both toward the object (in "the desire to belittle or diminish") and, just as important, *from* the object. The word *cute* comes from *acute*, which "suggests mental alertness, keenness, and quickness."[16] These qualities are certainly evident in all of O'Hara's poems. In the reversal of meaning suggested by this etymology, there remains the threat that what is adored might, like a puppy dressed up too much and squeezed too sharply, snap back with a sharp bite.

Take, for example, the most humorous and antiserious poem in the book, "Poem (Wouldn't It Be Funny)," which asks the reader to consider a creator ("The Finger") making humans unable to "shit" except "once a week." This setup is followed by this profane punch line:

> all week long we'd get fatter
> and fatter and then on Sunday morning
> while everyone's in church
>
> ploop!17

This poem is deliberately short—it is in fact just a simple joke—and makes use of vulgarity, "shit," while ending with a word that performs the gross sound someone's shit would make if it were to come out all at once. Its compactness and refusal to be taken seriously are a manifestation of the cute, but so is its irreverence, and its going out of its way to make sure this image is contrasted to allusions to organized religion ("on Sunday morning"). The poem might elicit a laugh, but it might just as easily elicit disgust. This example of the cute is also acute.

At the risk of belaboring this point, let me turn to one last example from *Lunch Poems*. This comes from another humorous poem that is designed explicitly to offend middle-class conventions and religious pieties. Entitled "Ave Maria," it is an apostrophe addressed to the "Mothers of America" and encourages them to send their kids to the movies, where they might meet a stranger with whom they might have their first sexual encounter.[18] This poem is clearly meant not only as a joke but as a pointed condemnation of attitudes that imprison children at home and make them fearful of going out and meeting strangers in the name of protecting their innocence (which is always racially coded). It conjures a common fear of what might happen to children and suggests that not allowing children to take risks and encouraging them to consider all strangers as potentially predatory—what I was taught in grade school as "stranger danger"—has its own steep costs. It leads them to

> hanging around the yard
> or up in their room
> hating you.19

This is a very courageous poem, one that risks severe social censure then and now.

As perceptive as these poems are, however, none of them has anything to say about the environment. It's an assumed background, so solidly there that there's nothing to say. It might be midwinter and cold, it might be raining and snowing all mixed up together, or the sun might be out and the sky blue. Such observations are all the attention the environment merits, and so it might be safe to say that when carbon dioxide concentrations in the atmosphere average 319 ppm, as they did when this book was first published, the environment could easily, and perhaps safely (although this is an ideologically contentious claim, as concentrations were already creeping up beyond the average baseline of the Holocene), be allowed to be a minimalist setting that didn't warrant any comment, no matter how much you were paying attention to the minutiae of the everyday.

And yet it's possible to find in O'Hara's short poems—and their association with the small, vulnerable, and deformed as well as their ability to be biting—an adept skill in arresting attention and so perhaps a template for how to prolong contemplation of an everyday that can be so easily overlooked. Going to get a liver sausage sandwich and discovering you don't have enough money to purchase it might bring down your day, but how do you focus on it for a long time and consider how it shapes your sense of the whole world around you? This is something O'Hara was able to capture. I wonder if such a focus on a single persistent moment can offer one way around the impasse that discussions about climate change and storytelling have found in fiction's heavy investment in plot. That is, I wonder if reading the kind of poetry O'Hara wrote can train readers to linger over the moment and to savor experiences of the everyday that greet them on the most familiar street corner.

It is certain, in any case, that attention to postwar American poetry, which shares so many traits with the cute, offers a sharp contrast with the zany, which Ngai understands as an aesthetics that responds to the demand for work speedups. The demand reflects the preoccupation with improving efficiency, and hence aiding the all-consuming need for economic growth. Ngai observes, "Zaniness is essentially the experience of an agent confronted by—and endangered by—too many things coming at her at once."[20] While it is often portrayed as playful, it actually refers to work that gets pushed to extremes, so that play and work get mixed up:

> In all its appearances across the *longue durée* of a modernity never entirely identical or reducible to capitalism but driven primarily by its contradictory

logic of incessant expansion, and perhaps most conspicuously since the last half of the twentieth century, it is this cross-coupling of play and work—one marked by an increasing extraction of surplus value from affect and subjectivity, in particular—that provides the best explanation for the contradictory mix of affects that makes the zany what it is.[21]

The zany elicits laughter but also a sense of breathless exhaustion, frantic movement, a swirl of activity that doesn't allow time for deliberation or reflection. The laughter is always uneasy. Indeed, the very focus on doing stuff as quickly as possible creates "a sense of character as nothing but a series of projects and activities," which makes this description of the zany so resonant in the present.[22] While Ngai hesitates to make too strong a historical claim, it seems (to me, at least) reasonable to argue that the "cross-coupling of play and work" has become exponentially more pronounced during the Great Acceleration, as the "logic of incessant expansion" has been carried to its own extreme.

I can't help but think of conversations with my students, who often talk about how stressed out they feel by the demands of study, work, family, and a future that (understandably!) fills them with anxiety. They pay a lot to attend college and are filled, partly as a result, with a sense of what they call FOMO, or the fear of missing out. They sign up for too many activities and spend their days running back and forth between them while trying to cram social interaction and study into the small gaps that remain. Often they can't do it all, and so they end up disappointing people who are counting on them, drop activities they overexuberantly committed to earlier in the academic year, and struggle in class. They stretch the resources of the school's counseling center and get prescribed medication and are sent to the hospital for an array of mental disorders in heightened numbers. They drink too much, probably take drugs (both legal and illegal), and burn out emotionally long before graduation day comes along. Their lives are zany, which is to say funny if it weren't so painfully serious—and many of these students come from wealthy families. Imagine the much steeper challenges facing students from working-class backgrounds.

In similar ways, the Keeling Curve itself is zany. Its zigzagging back and forth throughout the past several decades suggests less the dignified inhale and exhale of Revelle's and Gore's imagination and more a comic movement. The curve's upward trajectory points to the quickening of a tempo, so that the comic movement itself is getting faster, its back-and-forth motion speeding up at ever-increasing rates like a dance reaching its end, the musicians sawing comically away to a beat that gets faster and faster and leaves the dancers swirling and breathless and waiting for the song to end. Or maybe there are no musicians, and what the curve represents is a Saint Vitus's dance (now known as Sydenham's chorea), a rare neurological disorder that leads to jerky and involuntary bodily movements. I first saw reference to it in *Walden*, where Henry David Thoreau writes, "We have the Saint Vitus' dance, and cannot possibly keep our heads still."[23] The zany figures a collapsing of the humorous into the serious, a commingling of laughter and unease.

My sense is that O'Hara's poems participate fully in a fast-moving, swirling modernity, but the tempo that dominates isn't all that fast. Readers could be forgiven for wondering if the speaker of these poems ever works, for work never makes an appearance in them. It's clear he has a job (and one that makes him fully participatory in the global promotion of abstract art in the name of capitalism), but work is always implied, and the focus is on what happens outside of the workplace; the emphasis of the book's title is obviously focused on lunch as a midday reprieve, a moment of leisure or at least frenetic activity freed from the strictures of labor, which is what O'Hara most focused on in his poetry. The situation is different in Bernadette Mayer's *Midwinter Day*, where work dominates—both the work of being a poet and that of being a mother and wife. As Andrew Epstein observes, one of the greatest contributions Mayer's writings make to postwar American poetry's interest in the everyday, of which O'Hara is an outstanding example, is the addressing of "a broader absence," which is "the lack of a viable tradition of women's writing, in general, about pregnancy, childbirth, and being a mother."[24]

Divided into six parts, *Midwinter Day* can be read as a single poetic meditation on the speaker's journey from dreams to morning, midday, late afternoon, evening, and night, all of which takes place on December 22, the winter solstice. Its mix of prose and verse pushes the definition of what forms a poem can take, signaling its participation in an avant-garde experimenting with the boundaries of received literary forms; in doing so, its form reflects the mental state of the speaker at different moments in her day. Part 1, which recalls the dream Mayer was having before the day begins, is one of the longest sections of the book and is written in a verse form that jams incongruous images next to each other, reflecting a dreamlike space, but as it reaches its end and day approaches, the stanzas look like inverted paragraphs, where the first line is the only line not indented. The final two pages grow more verse-like again, as if the speaker is struggling to sleep a little longer and resisting the need to awaken:

Don't take what I say too seriously
Or too lightly,
       I'm sorry,
            Nevermind
I was just playing around, I'm trying to find
What I guess I'd rather not know consciously[25]

The following section, part 2, is the shortest one in the book and contains discrete paragraphs written in prose. But the prose is difficult to read, with a strong rhythm that distracts from the content of what is being described, so that it can be a challenge to keep focused on the facts of what's happening. The family has woken up and is eating breakfast and getting ready for the day: "On eggs or ordinary toothpaste, fantastic pigeons who always live above us murmuring fly, it looks right at us, but hit the roof to rest where there's a space between the bricks before they fly out again, one is all white."[26] The sentences in this section are run-ons and can't seem to describe what's happening with easily discernible sense. They convey the disorientation of sleep inertia, as if everyone is struggling to shake off sleep, and of rushing, trying to do all the things that need to be done in a compressed amount of time.

This sense of being in a rush doesn't dissipate in the rest of the book and in some parts only grows stronger, especially in part 3, when the speaker takes her two young daughters into town. Sometimes the speaker lists what she sees, like all the stores in town or the titles of all the books for sale at the bookstore she visits, which might evoke Ngai's aesthetic category of the interesting (a point I don't feel inclined to consider more because the very idea of the interesting is itself only mildly interesting). Her mind is always wandering, drifting between the urgent tasks she has to perform, thoughts about her past, reflections on books she's reading or has read recently, and the history of literature, especially in Massachusetts. In part 4 the tug of these different kinds of thoughts feels most strained by her duties as a mother. The family is back home, the youngest is napping, the husband is in his study, and she has to take care of the oldest, who is still very young. She prepares a meal as soon as they come home, makes sure the youngest is comfortable, and reads to the oldest. Each line of the discrete paragraphs that make up this section begins with a description of what she is doing but is followed by where her thoughts have drifted off to.

Maybe this description of the events *Midwinter Day* recalls and the way it uses different literary forms to convey the speaker's conflicted mental state as she experiences these events is enough to suggest that the book is an example of Ngai's zany. If so, then it's worth focusing on the last section, when the kids are asleep and she and her husband (who is also a poet) can focus most on their writing. Here, when her body finally gets to be in repose, the book is written in a recognizable verse form, the lines short and carefully calibrated to focus attention on the cadences of her thought, and the meter is more regular. She is less concerned with what she is doing or what is happening around her and more concentrated on her ambitions as a writer. As her thoughts progress, they focus on literature and its relationship to the greater world. She thinks about famous women writers, who are important to her because they offer a precedent for the writing she's doing, and she thinks about different kinds of creative outlets that are matched, in their variety, only by the new technologies that are springing up around her. Much like the lists in an earlier section, there is a list of the creative outlets she's thinking about ("New image painting, silkscreen collage and watercolors," and so forth, for another eighteen lines) and, immediately afterward, a list of technological innovations ("Adrenalin, air conditioning, a satellite of Pluto," and so forth, for another extraordinary thirty-nine lines).[27] These lists feel like a catalog of the Great Acceleration and its intensification of human activity and ingenuity.

Amid this hectic flow of making in all of its forms, from the creative to the scientific, the speaker reflects on her personal life and how much, despite the strains it puts on her, she values being married and being a mother as well as a writer. Her husband goes out to do an unspecified errand, and she writes:

> While you're out love is stored
> In intensest hours, this cave of it,
> We go too fast,
> Switched from the speed of variegated love
> Writing's married and fallen in with family,
> Though it's more exhausting to love to write
> Then to pursue what might have been described
> About the past as being fast,
> Sometimes we feel like
> Fools, lunatics, paranoid hermits having manic flights
> With nothing to come of it[28]

When I read these lines, I think most about the gender imbalance in the relationship between the speaker and her husband, whom she addresses throughout the book in an intimate second-person "you." This makes the reader the recipient of all of her thoughts, as well as a part of them, but at the same time it puts the reader at a remove from the domestic concerns that demand so much of her time. The distance between the "you" and "I" feels as if it might be posing a question: What do the two have in common? The husband does little to help around the house, and even when the speaker makes and serves the meal for the family after her return from town with the kids, the husband does not eat with them but takes the meal to a separate room. So how much of the feeling of going "too fast" belongs to a "we," and how much of it is the strain put on the speaker as a wife and mother who is responsible for all the childcare, cooking, and other family-related matters?

If there's something zany about *Midwinter Day*, in its many harried hurried moments and crowded thoughts, part of the cause is how the demands of the family fall on the female speaker. But just as important, the book recognizes the ways in which the hurry is itself constitutive of the times they occupy. The lists suggest the accumulation of stuff and activities, while the demand is always there that they do something productive with their time. Simultaneously, as poets, the husband and wife struggle with a high level of economic precarity:

We don't even want to be famous but we do
                                  hope to survive.[29]

Perhaps because Mayer is willing to foreground what it means for her to go about her day as not only a writer but also a wife and mother, there is extra sensitivity to the ways in which work itself is an ever-present demand that contributes to the sense of life's activities having sped up, and continuing to speed up, a zany motion that leaves the speaker feeling as if she's on

                    manic flights
With nothing to come of it.

By the last two pages, however, it becomes clear that the speaker doesn't believe nothing has come of her day or her intense thinking about it. The poem concludes, "Something is discovered." What? She is watching television and learning about the trouble that the shah of Iran is facing as popular revolt threatens to end his rule—before, as readers now know, Ayatollah Khomeini solidifies his power and establishes an Islamic republic in the country. This leads her to think:

We wait to see what happens
We hope it's not a war or suffering
And that the women will shake off the veil
In the myriad future of our still

Revolutionary munificent dreams, our lust
For surprise benefitting us like the sun
Like the supplicating weather we fear
May suddenly change from what it is
To another ice age but not before
The climate warms undetectably
Forcing us all to move to the moon[30]

As it turns out, her fears about what will happen in Iran are justified—there will be a war (with Iraq) and a lot of suffering, and women will have to wear a veil (the question of what this signifies is a complex one that feminism in particular will struggle with in the years to come).

Just as noteworthy, however, these musings turn to the climate. While it's not clear why she worries about an ice age, there is nevertheless a sense that something momentous is happening in the background that, in a moment of late-night retrospection, can finally be considered. Even at about 331 ppm (the average carbon dioxide concentration in the atmosphere in 1978, the year in which the day Mayer chronicles occurred), there's already awareness that something once stable is slipping and that this can lead to catastrophes of planetary significance. The speaker advises:

Keep in touch with what's happening,
                                    wonder
At nature, emergencies, extreme heat,
Cold and unassailable new beauty,
                                    births
Unusual time exposures of earth,
Intercourse, sex, copulating, fucking[31]

There is, in this final admonition, a demand for the kind of attentiveness that *Midwinter Day* itself performs, and at the end of this attentiveness is recognition that the domestic and mundane activities it recalls are connected to events happening in far-flung places (like Iran); to the history of literature and creative expression more generally, as well as the history of scientific discovery and technological innovations; to the developments in the town where she lives, which is connected to the larger world through commerce and trade; and to the body and its sexuality. The long poem ends with this ecological vision, emphasized perhaps by the fact that the day the poem records so carefully occurs on the winter solstice, when the planet's axis tilts the northern hemisphere to its furthest point away from the sun.

It's the shortest day and longest night of the year where she lives, and also the moment when the days are about to get longer and the nights shorter. The focus on this day, then, encourages thinking about the planet, the ecological processes that depend on its predictable motion, and the ways in which this motion seems to promise the durability of seasonal changes. Thinking planetarily thus encourages being mindful of how one process is related to another and can't be thought of as apart without affecting the working of the whole. Mayer suggests that to contemplate such interrelatedness, the reader needs to pull the mind away from the flow of incessant activities and the demands of everyday life to consider a single day that might recede into the ones before and after. Such attentiveness is how Mayer, at least, tries to "keep in touch with what's happening."

The problem is, at lower concentrations of carbon dioxide in the atmosphere, when the effects of global warming are still hard to distinguish from the noise of weather variability ("The climate warms undetectably"), it's challenging to keep in touch in this way, as both O'Hara and Mayer illustrate. Their focus on the everyday, scrupulous and attentive and discerning, leads to obliviousness or belated concern with regard to the environment. In Mayer's *Midwinter Day*, in particular, when the signal is starting to become louder, environmental concerns connected to the climate are registered but simultaneously lost in the loud hum of other concerns. Waiting in the future, just in the United States alone, are James Hansen's testimony before the U.S. Congress in 1988 announcing that global warming had already begun; the massive heat wave in 1995 that killed 739 people in Chicago; the destruction of the Gulf Coast, including New Orleans, when Hurricane Katrina struck in 2005; and the massive flooding of New York City when Hurricane Sandy made landfall in 2012. Marking time in the background of these events is the steady rise of carbon dioxide concentrations, ticking 350 ppm, 359 ppm, 379 ppm, and 392 ppm.

THE SCALE OF THE EVERYDAY, PART 2

Ada Limón, Tommy Pico, and Solmaz Sharif

I WISH I COULD SAY THAT there has been a significant shift in the way people talk about global warming over the past three decades as the scientific evidence has mounted. This shift would have taken the form of a fast-expanding awareness that would have made it difficult, if not impossible, to describe everyday experiences without thinking about how these experiences were affected by a fast-changing climate. Imagine a direct correlation between rising concentrations of carbon dioxide in the atmosphere and a clamoring of speech about the problems this signifies. There would be so much speech, now, that you couldn't stop thinking about climate change. You would walk down the sidewalk and see all the cars driving by. You would have been repeatedly told each car is emitting pollutants that will remain in the atmosphere for centuries. Inevitably, you would wonder, how much does a single drive add to the upward drift of the Keeling Curve?[1]

Go to the airport in this other world and marvel at the lingering glamor of traveling by air: the wide-open atriums and long corridors, the bustling shops and restaurants (no matter what time of day you're traveling, you can see someone sitting at a bar enjoying a drink), the flight attendants in their sharp matching uniforms watching over you as you fly through the sky. How much is this trip costing the environment? How much worse is flying for global warming than driving? Look at all the bright lights of the city and suburbs, the streetlamps that stay on all night long down endless stretches of road. How much of the electricity powering this light is produced by burning coal and natural gas?

It's also possible, in this other world, that such questions would be asked more frequently but that there would be fewer occasions for asking them, because more discourse would have led to less driving and more fuel efficiency, fewer flights, a severe decline in coal use, a nonexistent natural gas industry, and an already maturing infrastructure powered by renewable energy. Maybe electronic boards would be everywhere, giving live updates of where the curve is at right now (and everyone would know what the Keeling Curve is). Public service announcements would punctuate your social media timeline, reminding you to turn off lights in empty rooms and lower your air-conditioning setting. "Let's reverse the curve!" would flash across the jumbotron in bright neon lettering during basketball games. When you stepped outside, there would be solar panels on every roof within sight. In every alleyway behind every restaurant, there would be a separate bin for compost. Meat would be eaten sparingly. There would be no controversy about whether or not climate change is happening and what is causing it. The fiercest debates would be about the use of nuclear energy. People, more aware of the problem wherever they looked, would have readily accepted policies that directly impacted the way they lead their lives. They might even have demanded these policies, overcoming industry recalcitrance and disinformation campaigns. They would feel enabled, powerful, full of agency and purpose.

There's no simple cause and effect. Just because people talk more about climate change doesn't necessarily mean they are more amenable to such policies. Their desire for such policies also wouldn't necessarily translate to their leaders proposing them, nor does speech guarantee anything about the kind of policies that would be enacted. Such policies could become co-opted to protect the wealthy and the status quo. It's difficult to say what would have happened if any organized policy designed to slow down the emission of greenhouse gases had been enacted, because any counterfactual exercise is always a form of speculation—and, even as speculation, what I have just described is surely far from ideal. At the same time, it's difficult to imagine coordinated, effective action at the scales necessary to affect the Keeling Curve taking place without sustained popular attention. Without sustained popular attention, efforts to develop publics where policy could be debated would also be stymied.

Of course, nothing close to what I describe has happened. People have rarely, if ever, talked about climate change in everyday circumstances, and this continues today. As a result, I have no idea what goes on in other people's minds, whether they ever give thought to how their daily routines depend on emissions that are accumulating dangerous gases in the air all around them. My own thoughts don't always linger on this subject, despite my best efforts. There isn't a lot of encouragement for them to linger there. Cars, air travel, streetlights, and so on are a continual part of the background and don't require a lot of my attention. It's all like the sound my refrigerator makes. I have to be very still and listen deliberately to hear it. Meanwhile, the radio is on loud, there is street construction out my window, and my phone keeps buzzing with messages. In the midst of so much noise, what kind of boost can the signals of climate change get, so that attention begins to match the urgency of the problem?

In thinking about this question, I find it useful to turn to contemporary poetry once again. The work of Ada Limón, Tommy Pico, and Solmaz Sharif in particular seems to offer acute observations of the everyday. Limón's poems are perhaps the most traditional and familiar, as in her most recent book, *The Carrying* (407 parts per million [ppm]). They are compact and take full advantage of their form to train attention on a specific event—how the speaker is trying to get pregnant and failing; how animals, plant life, and human life are connected to each other; and how the misfortune of animals cause her emotional pain. Pico's poetry is more fluid. Each of the books he has published—*IRL* (402 ppm), *Nature Poem* (405 ppm), *Junk* (407 ppm), and *Feed* (415 ppm)—can be thought of as a long poem. And while each is written in a different style (the first in short lines and nonexistent stanzas, the second in more varying lines and more distinct grouping of words that resemble stanzas, the third in a series of unrhymed couplets, and the fourth in a scramble of forms that's difficult to generalize about), they feel as if they are spoken by the same speaker, repeatedly returning to the themes of gay urban life, Indigenous ancestry, and environmental breakdown. Their length enables the speaker to elaborate, wander off topic, and return suddenly with sharp insights. Unlike Limón and Pico, Sharif in *Look* (402 ppm) doesn't seem all that interested in environmental concerns, and yet her poetry is bold in asking the reader to look at the ways in which language disguises violence, especially the kind inflicted by the state in the Middle East and other far-flung places. She thus interrogates the language of the everyday and calls attention to how it has already become militarized. The language of her poems is likewise fragmented, and often difficult to comprehend, but in a way that makes reassembling their order back into meaningfulness a work of paying renewed attention to an everyday that would otherwise fade from mind.

The poetry of these three poets is sharply different from Frank O'Hara's and Bernadette Mayer's, which I admire very much but which seems to belong to another era, when carbon dioxide and other greenhouse gas concentrations were significantly lower in the atmosphere and environmental concerns less obviously pressing—especially for those like O'Hara and Mayer, who were white and middle class and who benefited from an enormous amount of social and cultural capital. The more contemporary poems feel to me more contemporary precisely because they seek to express how harsh the present has become and is becoming. While formally they still very much respond to the poetry that came before, socially they seek to make sense of a present that's undisguisedly dystopic and less forgiving of fanciful indulgences.

Some of the changes that seem to be happening to these poets as their careers develop suggest that they are responding to what I think of as *the social*. In using this term, I am taking my cue from Margaret Ronda and Lindsay Turner, who write, "To investigate the *social* forms of poetry . . . raises questions about the kinds of historical thinking that unfolds in and through the formal processes of a particular text, and the extent to which these processes might creatively reconfigure the dominant social forms of their present. In this sense, form might be understood as an enactment of struggle and contradiction rather than an embodiment of achieved order or closure."[2] If so, the poems I look at in this chapter provide specific social occasions for thinking about how environmental concerns can impinge on thinking about struggle and contradiction. These poets write from specific nonwhite perspectives (Mexican American, Kumeyaay, and Iranian American), which complicates their relationship to the forms they have inherited. As a result, their poetry self-consciously critiques common ways of talking—about reproduction, about nature, about danger—and in the process seeks to find alternative ways to describe the everyday.

I

Ada Limón never uses the word *climate change* in *The Carrying*, but there's a sense in many of her poems that careful attention is being paid to the ways in which the speaker's experience of the everyday is being transformed by its effects. Take the poem "The Vulture & the Body": the speaker is going to a "fertility clinic" and sees along the way "five dead animals" lying on the side of the road. After seeing the last of these animals, she recalls:

> I say something
>
> to myself that's between a prayer and a curse—how dare we live
>
> on this earth.[3]

I found this moment breathtaking. It might seem a typical misanthropic statement, the kind that comes easily to some people's lips when talking about climate change, that is, the sentiment that the world would be better without humans in it, which feels to me like its own kind of denial, for climate change is explicitly a problem for humans because it threatens human well-being—and it's impossible, at least for me, to imagine any kind of human well-being that isn't accompanied by the flourishing of other species. To say the world would be better without humans leaves open the possibility that it would be ethically permissible to allow many humans to die, as their absence would enable greater nonhuman flourishing—a suggestion that, beyond its obviously monstrous wish for mass death, allows eugenic thinking to come into play, as some groups of humans might be seen as more disposable than others. And yet the misanthropy of the question the speaker poses in this quotation is belied by the fact that she is on her way to a fertility clinic and is eager to get pregnant.

The question "how dare we live / on this earth" is thus addressed to her own desire to have a child and the ethical consequences of doing so at a time when so much seems to be uncertain and unraveling. The dead animals become symbolic of this uncertainty and unraveling, especially in the ways in which they are personified. The raccoon she first sees is lying on its back with its paws facing the sky,

> like he's going to catch whatever bullshit load
> falls on him next.

Then a deceased coyote is described as a "trickster no longer," while the three deer she sees at the end of her trip are "all staggered but together."[4] Although no longer alive, the animal remains seem nevertheless still lively, occupying the murky boundaries between the human and the animal and between the animate and the inanimate. They have strong opinions about what's happened to them, they are quick-witted and fleet thinkers, and they are social beings that have sought each other's company even as death has separated them.

She senses during this trip that there's a profound connection between the death of the animals on the side of the road and her own desire to get pregnant. In sensing such a connection, she is not alone. The adult whispers are getting louder, suggesting perhaps that in discourses about reproduction, which are so problematically linked to thinking of the future, a language is developing for thinking about the consequences of a human-caused changing climate. Some of my students, all women, have said these words to me: "Imagine having a child now." "I'd like to have a child, but I worry it's unethical to bring a new person into this world." "I just don't see what kind of future any child, much less my own, will have." Another student told me that all of her friends majoring in environmental studies or biology have said they plan not to have children.

Writers, too, are typing essays on the subject. Elizabeth Bruenig in the *Washington Post* wonders, "Even if one assumes that having a child won't contribute to the problem—that our progeny will take seriously the creeping catastrophe their parents didn't—it still seems likely that today's youths will be faced with a world vastly and unpredictably altered. Why put them through it?" (Her answer is, because "life is good. Life itself is good.")[5] Maggie Astor for the *New York Times* interviewed "more than a dozen people ages 18 to 43" and found climate change loomed large in their thinking. "Some worry about the quality of life children born today will have as shorelines flood, wildfires rage and extreme weather becomes more common," she reports. "Others are acutely aware that having a child is one of the costliest actions they can take environmentally."[6] The ethicist Christine Overall concludes, "If we have a responsibility to limit our consumption and our environmental footprint, then surely we also have a responsibility to limit the birth of new human beings who will otherwise contribute both to that consumption and to the despoliation of our planetary home."[7]

In the poem the speaker wants to explore this connection further, giving shape to the misgivings that these other women are trying to give voice to, but is frustrated by the lack of opportunity to do so. When she meets her doctor, the doctor is efficient and dismissive, his interaction ending like "quicksilver." As Limón puts it, "I'm left to pull my panties up like a big girl," which suggests how she feels both infantilized and abandoned by this encounter. There's something plaintive about this phrase—so graphic and ordinary and yet enigmatic (what does the phrase "like a big girl" mean?)— that suggests being left alone with one's body, especially as a woman, to figure out how to make sense of "struggle and contradiction" (as Ronda and Turner put it). The speaker seems to turn to the doctor as a figure of authority who might help to resolve these tensions, but he is unavailable, and she is left with a question:

> What if, instead of carrying
>
> a child, I am supposed to carry grief?[8]

The question is never explicitly addressed to the topic of climate change, but the poem conjures a sense of occupying a world where the human and the animal are entangled. Their fortunes seem equally intertwined, so that the poem ends with her driving in the opposite direction on the same road she came on and observing:

> The great black scavenger flies parallel now, each of us speeding,
> intently and driven, toward what we've been taught to do with death.[9]

Such entanglement is dangerous, because the fate of animals and other non-human living creatures is foreshadowed in this poem in the figure of the dead animals on the side of the road. What has happened to the animals might very well happen to many humans, as other humans might be like the vulture, scavengers of what their deaths leave behind.

A similar sense of entanglement is invoked in a later poem in *The Carrying*, "On a Lamppost Long Ago," which conjures a list of "things that are disappearing: fishes, birds, bees, trees, flowers, bees," and adds, "languages too":

> In the time it takes to say *I love you*, or move in with someone
> or admit to the child I'm carrying, all the intricate words
> of a language become extinct.[10]

A lot is happening in this opening. There's the paralleling of mass extinction—what the journalist Elizabeth Kolbert calls "the sixth extinction," contextualizing the mass death of life-forms on Earth that is happening now in the deep history of life on the planet, which has witnessed similar events only five times before—to the loss of language diversity, which again intertwines the human and the animal (as well as other living things).[11] Indeed, language loss is explicitly conflated with extinction, which is itself tangentially related to climate change. There's the attempt to understand the speed of all of this loss, the ways in which the extinction of languages is taking place at an incredibly fast rate. Since language loss is equated with species loss, the poem also asks readers to consider how quickly the living things around them are disappearing. There's the news as well that the speaker is pregnant, so that again pregnancy is figured as connected to losses occurring in the world all around the speaker. This connection is further emphasized in the poem when it's revealed that the speaker's father-in-law suffers from Alzheimer's.

The later poems in *The Carrying* are suffused with the sense of loss that comes with the loss of the child the speaker has been carrying. What happened to the pregnancy is never revealed; only the feeling of absence remains. "Carrying," which gives the volume its title, describes a cold November day in Kentucky, where the speaker lives, and imagines "any / mare worth her salt" at this time "carrying the next / potential stakes winner." The parallel between animals and humans is broken, however, when she notes, "How my own body" is "empty / clean of secrets."[12] "Mastering" recalls a meeting with an old male friend, who goes on about the pleasures of parenthood, which leaves her hurt and angry:

> I want him to notice what he said, how a woman might feel agony,
> emptiness, how he's lucky it's me he said it to because I won't
> vaporize him.[13]

"Sway" recalls the speaker's need to put plants in her ground, and her anticipation of the return of her husband, who's been away on a trip: "And by god, I will throw my body toward him." The speaker continues:

> I don't know how to make medicine, or cure what's scarring
> this planet, but I know that last night, the train came roaring
>
> right as I needed it.[14]

And "After the Fire" speaks of crying "so hard / that there'd be nothing left in you," with the crying itself compared to "the wind" that "shakes the tree in a storm" (so that, again, there remain something human and something else, this time more elemental than a living thing), but, paradoxically, this sense of loss sustains the speaker:

> Funny thing about grief, its hold
> is so bright and determined like a flame,
> like something almost worth living for.[15]

These later poems most made me want to write about *The Carrying*, for they speak to the resolve to continue finding meaning in a world full of loss. The figure of the child is obviously a figure of futurity, so the loss of a pregnancy, as painful as it is for the speaker, figures in these poems as the loss of a sense of what there is to look forward to. The future is empty of its usual meaning and the conventions that mark such well-trod ground, and in its place there is a desire to fill the present with reasons to continue. These poems thus ask a set of vexed and difficult-to-answer questions. How do you live on amid loss? How do you keep going when everything seems to be unraveling? How do you not give up?

II

Limón offers only a handful of poems in *The Carrying* that address her race and ethnicity. This is not because she doesn't think this topic is important. As she makes clear in a poem published in an earlier volume, it matters a lot to her. "Prickly Pear and Fist Cuffs," a prose poem, begins, "My older brother says he doesn't consider himself Latino anymore and I understand what he means." Later she recalls being in a bar in Tennessee where someone jokes, "*At least I didn't say wetback*," and she thinks, "And I don't care what he says. My brother would have gone down swinging and fought off every redneck whitey in the room."[16] Maybe class and upbringing have made the speaker of this poem feel only an attenuated relationship to other Latinx people, but at the same time it's also clear that disruptions in everyday social encounters, or racial microaggressions, have a way of reaffirming how others think about her within these kinds of racial framework. The focus on this moment is reminiscent of Claudia Rankine's poetry, including the use of prose that helps to reaffirm the sense that there is something prosaic, or commonplace, about the ways in which race can suddenly disrupt social occasions. Such moments are sharp reminders that others never stop thinking of her as a Mexican, Latina, and "wetback." And at such moments, there's a strong desire to fight back, to assert a connection that helps her to refuse to be the object of such racist thinking.

But in the few poems where Limón references her race and ethnicity, there's also the sense that to focus too much on this topic is to be defined by it and forced into a narrow relationship to what her poetry can be about. The most salient example that leads me to this conclusion is the poem "The Contract Says: We'd Like the Conversation to Be Bilingual." The long explanatory title already makes clear how explicit such expectations are—that as a Mexican American poet she must write poems about Mexican Americans. It begins:

When you come, bring your brown-
ness so we can be sure to please

the funders.

The poem goes on to make just as explicit the thinking that often goes into invitations to the speaker to speak at public events. The inviters want her to perform her difference, which must not be too emotionally disruptive ("Will you tell us stories that make / us uncomfortable, but not complicit?") and at the same time must mark her social distance from an assumed white, middle-class audience ("Don't read us the ones where you / are just like us").[17]

The frustrations expressed in this poem feel familiar, as many Asian American writers I have read and talked to have expressed similar frustrations with the ways in which their racial and ethnic identity prescribes audience expectations about what they will write about. Many such writers refuse to be called an Asian American writer or avoid discussing how their race might affect what they write, exactly because they don't want to be pigeonholed as a writer who always and only writes *about* racial identity. Monica Youn observes, in a poem that mimics and satirizes forms of academic discourse:

> Revealing a racial marker in a poem is like revealing a gun in a story or like revealing a nipple in a dance.
>
> After such a revelation, the poem is *about* race, the story is *about* the gun, the dance is *about* the body of the dancer—it is no longer considered a dance at all and is subject to regulation.
>
> Topics that have this gravitational quality of *about*ness are known as "hot button" topics, such as race, violence, or sex.[18]

Dorothy Wang has argued that "*about*ness" is especially pronounced in poetry circles, as "minority" and poetry are thought of by critics as "intrinsically opposed—content versus form, sociological versus literary, and so forth." As a result, "minority poetry is often seen as belonging more properly to the provenance of cultural studies or ethnic studies."[19] The more commercial, mainstream "lyric" poetry tends to be most focused on treating works by nonwhite poets as ethnographic writings, interesting only for their content and the window into the lives of Others they might provide. It is this kind of expectation that Youn's poem calls explicit attention to and that Limón writes against.

At the same time, it's important to recognize how the avant-garde, which has tended to define itself against the commercial properties of the lyric, tends to ignore all questions about race, "even when the poet makes clear that racialized/ethnic identity is not a trivial concern in the work."[20] This exclusion has led Cathy Park Hong, poetry editor for the *New Republic*, to write a poetry manifesto, which begins, "To encounter the history of avant-garde poetry is to encounter a racist tradition," and ends, "The avant-garde has become pet-rified, enamored by its own past, and therefore forever insular and forever looking backwards. Fuck the avant-garde. We must hew our own path."[21] Rachel Greenwald Smith points out that at the time Hong's manifesto was made public, the avant-garde itself was thought to have died out, replaced by a more conciliatory and less antagonistic aesthetics welcoming differences of every kind. The prominence of Hong's call to "fuck the avant-garde," then, calls attention to the ways in which the avant-garde's demise was overstated.

Its renewed relevance, in turn, Smith continues, calls attention to both the rise of demagoguery, which tends "to encourage violence from those who feel as if they are representatives of a given society's dominant group—those who feel representative of 'the people,'" and the urgent demands of a left that speaks, through the manifesto (itself an important form for the avant-garde), "as if they have been shut out of the very definition of 'the people.'"[22] Speaking out against the avant-garde might then be a return of the avant-garde, but, if so, the return must be understood as with a difference, one that sees the ways in which this poetic movement's continued relevance is tied to demagoguery. There is, then, not one avant-garde but two, moving in polar and antagonistic directions, and the side focused on those who are excluded speaks more directly against a moment that seems dominated by the violent reclamationist rhetoric of white supremacy. If this is the case, it would be clarifying to find another name for this side—not the avant-garde as such (which, honestly, can't wither away quickly enough) but something else, which I've been calling the *revived lyric*.

A similar critique of an ignorance of race and a willingness to compromise with demagoguery can also be made of climate change discourses. There are the mainstream lyricists who speak about the beauty of nature and the avant-garde who speak about catastrophes and mass deaths that are starting to occur. In both camps, there has been a slow and muted discussion of race and of the ways in which the history of conquest, imperialism, and enslavement shapes who is suffering the most now and who will remain the most vulnerable in the near future. Sounding a lot like Wang and Hong, Kathryn Yusoff writes, "The Anthropocene might seem to offer a dystopic future that laments the end of the world, but imperialism and ongoing (settler) colonialisms have been ending worlds for as long as they have been in existence. The Anthropocene as a politically infused geology and scientific/popular discourse is just now noticing the extinction it has chosen to continually overlook in the making of its modernity and freedom."[23] The Anthropocene is a term I avoid, in the same way I avoid the term *avant-garde*, because it tends to universalize a topic without thinking about the many differences that constitute its subject matter.

Tommy Pico is interesting to read within this context because his poetry seems to fill the joint between these two kinds of critique—on the one side, that of the history of poetry and, on the other side, that of climate change discourses—and in particular shows how both of these discourses depend still on a racist tradition of imagining nature. Pico's first book, *IRL*, is often playful and fun, but the second, *Nature Poem*, is more discordant and angry. The third, *Junk*, is largely resigned, although all are infused with a profound sense of humor, and the fourth, *Feed*, is more outward focused and less concerned with the speaker's internal struggles. Pico himself has likened this affective progression to the stages of a romantic relationship: from the first flirty moments to its difficult middle, sad end, and sober acceptance.[24] If so, it's noteworthy that the middle is tumultuous, which suggests that it mirrors a social that's ever more toxic. Pico's verse, then, seems to be responding to this toxicity in a direct, engaged way as his career advances, making use of his poetic persona Teebs to consider how being queer and Kumeyaay affects his understanding of current events, everyday encounters with other people, and awareness of environmental crises. *Nature Poem* is most directly concerned with the last of this list and deserves special attention because it is so self-consciously aware of how the available literary forms cannot quite capture the particularity of Teebs's concern about the environment.

The very first page conjures familiar ways of talking about crisis and the environment. There is distance and a sense of the cosmos such distance conjures:

The stars are dying

like always, and far away.

There is also the insistence that such distance can be conflated, so what seems far away is actually right here:

But also close, like the sea stars on the Pacific coast. There little
arms lesion and knot and pull away

the insides spill into the oceans. Massive deaths.

This juxtaposition thus presents scalar variance to the reader, so that while the universe itself is a distant abstraction, the damages being wrought to the biosphere are immediately threatening to everyone, and everything, that is alive. There is in this again (as in Límon) an emphasis on human and animal entanglement. But the speaker refuses to keep this focus going, instead deliberately breaking up the elegiac mood it creates to swing attention around to something more mundane:

> Anemones n shit. Sand crabs n shit. Fleas. There are seagulls
> overhead. Ugh I swore to myself I would never write a nature poem.[25]

This is a deflation of the conventionally lyric and a demand to speak in a way that's closer to how people speak in ordinary occasions.

On the second page Teebs announces, in a way that's already becoming a refrain:

> I can't write a nature poem
> bc it's fodder for the noble savage
> narrative. I wd slap a tree across the face,
> I say to my audience.[26]

It might thus seem as if the central tension of this book-length poem will be the impossibility of an Indigenous person writing about nature without falling into the many ways in which Indigeneity has been made to stand for nature itself. The very concept of nature, as many critics have critiqued, is itself problematic for the way it separates humans from their surroundings, making the latter a domain for picturesque contemplation and nostalgic melancholy only when the idea of a landscape untainted by human activity is perceived as lost and irretrievable, and for the way it conflates the surroundings with people who aren't quite human, especially Native Americans, who are subject to a brutalizing idealism.

The poem swerves from this topic to focus on the ways in which poetic form itself recapitulates exactly this way of thinking. More than halfway into the book, the speaker returns to the claim that he can't write a nature poem, commenting:

> why shd I give a fuck abt
>
> "poetry"? It's a container
>
> for words like *whilst* and *hither* and *tamp*. It conducts something of
> *permanent* and *universal* interest.

Following this are a series of irreverent images meant to speak to more immediate concerns. There is a "NDN drag queen" and the speaker wanting to "give a wedgie to sacred mountain" and then strolling "into the china shop of grammar" to "shout LET'S TRASH / THIS DUMP." The defiance of these images is undermined by the ways in which the speaker is also unwilling to perform such defiant acts too openly. After the last shout, he says, "then gingerly slip out." Perhaps the most succinct critique of tired poetic forms is this apostrophe, near the end of this page: "Get in, loser—we're touring landscapes of the interior."[27]

Or again, a few pages later, the speaker introduces a poem: "Here is a short, peaceful, pastoral lyric." What follows is not a careful distillation of natural beauty but a straightforward description of environmental degradation:

Crappy water
Shoots thru purgatory creek
On its way to the Colorado River.

The reader is never meant to take these terse lines seriously as an imagist poem, the form it most seems to copy, and this point is redoubled when the Environmental Protection Agency says in response, *"My bad,"* to which Nature responds, *"Fuck you too."*[28] The overwhelming tone of this poem, which is shot through with these kinds of moments, is mockery. It refuses to take seriously what already takes itself too seriously, seeing in such earnestness something too easily commodified and susceptible to the conflation of Indigeneity with nature. The lyric verse and the kind of avant-garde poetry that has followed are presented by Pico as unable to capture an experience of the everyday that can speak about how nature runs through this experience. To speak of nature is to find oneself "in the Hall of / South American Peoples in the American Museum of Natural History"; it is to be, for an American Indian, the object of a conversation that says:

it's horrible how their culture was destroyed

as if in some reckless storm

but thank god we were able to save some of these artifacts.[29]

Maybe the most haunting, and troubling, moment in this long poem comes at its end, when it concludes, "The air is clear, and all across Instagram—peeps are posting pics of the sunset."[30] This line foregrounds the ways in which perceptions of nature are unavoidably mediated, seen through both a technology of representation and an eagerness to use this technology for self-aggrandizement. This moment seems to have anticipated the ways in which (mostly white) people with large Instagram accounts have taken pictures of themselves in the midst of flowers blooming in Lake Elsinore. Heavy rains in the region in early 2019, possibly connected to the cycling of drought and sudden rains that Southern California has been experiencing (itself probably connected to climate change), led to what news outlets have called a "super bloom," the flowering of bright red poppies in the desert. Eager to capitalize on this spectacle, people had been destroying the flowers, trampling on and even rolling in them to get the perfect picture that would get the most likes.[31]

III

"Let's be clear, I hate nature—hate its *guts*," Teebs tells his audience. But then more quietly, to himself, he says, "*I don't hate nature at all*. Places have thoughts—hills have backs that love being stroked by our eyes. The river gobbles down its tract as a metaphor but also abt its day. The bluffs purr when we put down blankets at the downturn of the sun and laugh at a couple on a obvi OkCupid date."[32]

IV

In a transcribed speech published in the *Guardian*, the novelist, essayist, and political activist Arundhati Roy talks about the ways in which the poorest of the poor who had fought most actively for important environmental issues in India were hunted by the government and accused of being the nation's greatest security threat. Now, Roy observes, climate change is understood as "the world's single greatest security challenge." With this ironic change in focus, something else happens: "The vocabulary around it is becoming militarized." The enemies are likely to remain the same. The poor who are its immediate victims "will become the 'enemies' in the new war without end." The language of a climate *emergency* lends urgency to this view, as well, as it enables and excuses all sorts of behavior that seems necessary.[33] This observation is sharp and needs urgent attention, for it suggests how much talk about a topic like climate change reflects a culture saturated by war making, which is itself informed by a past history of talking about colonial expansion.

This kind of discourse is what Pico seems to have in mind when, for instance, *Nature Poem* turns to the possibility of finding other life-forms in the galaxy: "Nature asks aren't I curious abt the landscape of exoplanets." The speaker of the poem replies, "It's hard for me to imagine curiosity as anything more than a pretext for colonialism." The language that's commonly used to describe space exploration is, as this poem succinctly observes, the very same language used in the past to talk about the European expansion into the Americas and elsewhere. Indeed, Teebs is explicit that this language does not have anything specific to say about space exploration as such but is rather a metaphor that is always talking about something else: "I thought we all understood planets are metaphors." What is this something else? "NDN teens have the highest rate of suicide of any population group in America. A white man can massacre 9 black ppl in a church and be fed Burger King by the cops afterwards. A presidential candidate gains a platform by saying Mexican immigrants are murderers and rapists."[34] The language of curiosity and exploration speaks to a desire for even more expansion and conquest, further exploitation of the rich resources elsewhere in the solar system, and a desire as well to turn attention away from the mundane problems here on this planet and in this country: the racism directed against Indigenous peoples, the police's tolerance of white supremacy, and the normalization of violent anti-immigrant sentiments.

But it's not necessary to look to the future to see how this language, as metaphor, perpetuates a colonial way of thinking. The same language shapes the U.S. war on terror, which has greatly aided the militarization of everyday life in the United States itself. This war, fought in actual far-flung places across the Middle East, South Asia, and Africa, is part of the "forever war," which Ronak Kapadia describes as "a fantasy sense of temporal perpetuity in wartime's violence in the dystopian here and now that likewise mimics the uninterrupted and limitless spree of US global war-making across the long twentieth century." What motivates this fantasy is the desire "for total planetary control across all the combat domains: land, sea, air, space, outer space, and cyberspace."[35] Such war making, then, is about dominance not only over territory and other peoples but over the planet itself. It is a form of seeking mastery, an imperial kind of human agency that dovetails with the industrial destruction of the environment.

And given its "total" nature, the military cannot help but seep into other kinds of discourses. Solmaz Sharif's poems in *Look* address one such seepage by exploring the conflation of the everyday and the military. They do so, most notably, by drawing on the U.S. Department of Defense's *Dictionary of Military and Associated Terms*, which the note at the end of the volume tells readers is "a supplement to standard English dictionaries (e.g., Merriam-Webster)."[36] This document is updated constantly, so it's noteworthy that the word *drone* appears in the 2007 version but not in the 2015 version. Sharif observes, "It is likely 'drone' was removed from the dictionary since understanding of the term has fully entered English vernacular; in other words, the military definition is no longer a *supplement* to the English language, but the

English language itself."[37] The everyday and the military are thus increasingly becoming coconstituted as the specialized language of the latter becomes part of a common vernacular, which also helps to popularize the perspective of the military. Militarization, then, can be understood not only as a building up of soldiers and weapons of death but as a way of understanding the world. U.S. leaders can thus talk about a war on poverty, a war on drugs, and a war on terror. It's not difficult to imagine, as Roy argues, that the next link in this metonymic chain is a "war on climate change."

This last possibility does not come up anywhere in *Look*, but Sharif nevertheless is obviously aware of the ways in which military language manipulates and alters perception of everyday experiences. The very title conflates a common word with something more specialized. An epigraph tells the reader that the term *look* refers to "mine warfare." It is "a period during which a mine circuit is receptive of an influence." This definition conjures a moment of danger, when a signal can set off an explosion and another signal can prevent an explosion from happening. The poems that follow weave between similar moments of danger and other moments when danger can't be avoided.

The early poems in the volume also focus on a specialized military language, always presented in all caps, and its adjacency to familiar domestic scenes. For instance:

PINPOINT TARGET   one lit desk lamp
                   and a nightgown walking past the window[38]

The adjacent terms aren't always as benign as these, however. They are frequently threatening and horrific, easily commingling with the more mundane and reassuring. The next poem offers a longer list of words opposite the military term "LAY," starting with "down" and "to sleep then" and progressing to

in a shroud
in a crib
on top of car
chained to a bumper.

The associations become increasingly more disturbing as the reader goes down this list, especially as the location is specified as "in the Tigris" and "under water boiled from smart bombs." What might have seemed close by to a reader in the United States is now far away, located in a geographic zone marked by the invasion of Iraq and the continuing war on terror. The associations end by asking the reader to take the view of those at the receiving end of invasion and war,

on a cot
under a tent
still holding your breath
beneath dining table
beneath five stories
in a hole.[39]

The later poems continue this juxtaposition, collapsing military language with images of working- and middle-class domesticity in the United States; violence in the Middle East, especially in Iran and Iraq; and personal memories of migration. In "Master Film," the speaker is a child living with her mother in Alabama while the father lives elsewhere,

in Poughkeepsie, lifting lumber in Rochester, thirtysomething
and pages of albums killed,
entire rows of classrooms
disappeared.

The speaker's only connection to her father is mediated by technology, a video of him looking at pictures of her and her mother. A friend asks the father in the video, "*How do you feel when you see Solmaz?*" The poem ends, "Can you please look away I don't want you to see my baba cry."[40]

Migration and separation are preceded by allusions to a war that killed many of the father's schoolmates. There's a series of imaginary letters to someone imprisoned in Guantánamo, each letter heavily redacted so that words and whole phrases are left out of sentences that communicate concern for the addressee and the dull details of the writer's life:

Dear Salim,

At the store, they brought
　　　　already, bruised on the
but still juicy. I pitted sour
　　　　all day, the newspaper
went　　　with their juice. I save you
jars of preserves for your return.[41]

The letters are never signed, suggesting that the sender's identity is redacted. The gaps ask the reader to consider what is allowed to be said and what is censored.

It's not clear in this example, as in the other poems in the "Dear Salim" series, what is being censored and why. How can the name of the fruit the author found at the store be a threat to security? What news, if any, is the detainee allowed to hear? Even as such large questions are evoked, the contents of the poem are decidedly domestic, focused on food preparation, as well as optimistically caretaking—the writer is anticipating Salim's return.

The last part of the volume consists mainly of a longer poem entitled "Personal Effects," which makes juxtaposition an even more pronounced feature of this book's formal arrangement. There is the speaker's first-person account of looking at a photograph on her desk of her uncle; a second-person address to the uncle, who died during the Iran-Iraq War; and factual accounts of major events associated with this war. Throughout, the specialized military language, which had receded into the background in the middle poems of the volume, returns, framing what the speaker can say of her own thoughts about her uncle and the war and, at the same time, commenting on this language and its inadequacies. The speaker is more direct than in the earlier poems in offering a critique of this language:

> Daily I sit
> with the language
> they've made
>
> of our language
>
> to NEUTRALIZE
> the CAPABILITY of LOW DOLLAR VALUE ITEMS
> like you.
>
> You are what is referred to as
> a "CASUALTY."[42]

At this moment the reader is confronted by the euphemistic nature of military language. And as this language is widely adopted in more common speech— "the language / they've made // of our language"—the militarization of the imagination is revealed in this passage to be the work of interpretive denial. There's no refusal to admit that the uncle has lost his life, but the language removes responsibility for this loss of life from those who use this language and, in the process, works to imagine this life as not a major loss. Its value, measured in dollars, does not amount to much.

V

The title poem of Sharif's volume, "Look," takes the form of an official resolution—similar to the conclusion of Layli Long Soldier's *Whereas*. A series of "whereas" clauses make explicit the occasion for the statements to come and attempt to establish a set of commonly agreed-upon facts. One of these clauses is this one:

> Whereas it could take as long as 16 seconds between the trigger pulled in Las Vegas and the Hellfire missile landing in Mazar-e-Sharif, after which they will ask *Did we hit a child? No. A dog. They will answer themselves.*

Following these clauses are four short statements that the poem commits to. These are

Let it matter what we call a thing.
Let it be the exquisite face for at least 16 seconds.
Let me LOOK at you.
Let me LOOK at you in a light that takes years to get here.

In these statements, there's an explicit attention to a shortness of time. The "LOOK" refers again to a moment when a mine might go off or not, while "16 seconds" recalls the time between the pulling of a trigger and the landing of a missile fired from a drone. Both images convey the sense that, for many who are at the receiving end of such military violence, there are only brief moments in which their lives can take place. Life occurs in the "16 seconds" and in the "LOOK," the former incapable of delivering the precision that drone warfare has promised, while the latter suggests some reprieve is possible. Perhaps the mine won't go off. Perhaps it might be possible to live instead in a more expansive time frame, marked not by the trigger and the pin but by the vastness of space itself, referenced by the "light that takes years to get here."

Such contingencies of time, and the scalar variance the imagination of such contingencies depends on, reflect not only a militarized present marked by the war on terror but, increasingly, a militarized present marked by growing anxiety and fear about the environmental impacts of global warming as the Keeling Curve continues its steep climb. Maybe the "16 seconds" and the "LOOK" are another way of measuring time, in addition to the measured concentration of atmospheric carbon dioxide. If so, who will be the targets of a remobilization of rhetoric and euphemism? Who will be seen as the enemies who must be eliminated?

The pervasive use of drones, which Sharif's poem explicitly references, may solidify a pact between the U.S. military and the U.S. citizenry. This pact promises that, as J. D. Schnepf observes, "the burden of living under drones falls disproportionately on those who live beyond the territorial boundaries of the United States." Meanwhile, the use of drones within these boundaries has become domesticated; U.S. citizens have "the privilege of experiencing a drone hovering above their homes and bodies as a pleasure."[43] How, then, in a regime of nationalist pacts and hardened borders, will drones and other technologies, many of them still under development, be mobilized to protect an "us" against a "them," or a privileged few, who will somehow find a way to wage, but never win, a war on climate change against the many others who will be both victims and avatars of climate change and therefore the very nemesis against which this war will be fought?

VI

A brief coda to these two linked chapters: in contemplating the work of Límon, Pico, and Sharif, I find myself thinking that Sianne Ngai is not entirely correct in arguing that the cute, the interesting, and the zany are the present's dominant aesthetic categories.[44] While they are prominent and do much to capture salient aspects of a present that seems ever more organized toward the production of profit through extraction, exploitation of labor, the externalization of costs through environmental pollution, and ceaseless economic growth, I'm struck by how difficult it is to read the poems discussed in this chapter in particular without conjuring the older aesthetic categories of the sublime and beautiful.

Perhaps these older aesthetic categories haven't gone away but endure, supplemented by newer aesthetic categories but nevertheless framing an understanding of the present that fills me, at least, with a profound sense of intimidation at the sheer enormity of the transformations human activity is wreaking on the planet and a profound appreciation for what endures despite such transformations. The Earth remains full of the sublime and beautiful, bound together in inextricable ways. As Sharif writes, conjuring both terror and admiration for human perseverance and tender acts of love:

: we have learned to sing a child calm in a bomb shelter
: I am singing to her still[45]

The singing is a form of shared agency, shaped by the courage to persist in the midst of others' ruin making.

THE GLOBAL NOVEL
IMAGINES THE AFTERLIFE

George Saunders, J. M. Coetzee, and Han Kang

I INVITE YOU TO SIT for a moment with the following fact, which I've already alluded to but which I feel deserves repeating: "More than half of the carbon exhaled into the atmosphere by the burning of fossil fuels has been emitted in just the past three decades."[1] This is an extraordinary figure. It dramatizes how global warming is a fast-moving, and accelerating, phenomenon. The effects of all of this pollution will almost certainly last for centuries, if not millennia. But the emphasis on deep time that is part of a lot of contemporary discourses about the environment can take attention away from the fact that what matters for everyone you know is time imagined in vastly shallower terms.[2]

So, what has been happening in the past thirty years that coincides with this massive acceleration of emissions? I already mentioned some of the major events that have occurred during this period in earlier chapters, but major phenomena that I want to emphasize in particular are the rise of globalization, the neoliberalism that has abetted it, and the increase in policing and military action that accompanied it. The rule of Ronald Reagan and Margaret Thatcher ended around the same time as the fall of the Berlin Wall in 1989, but they, along with Deng Xiaoping, swept ideological innovations modeled after experiments conducted in Chile and Argentina a decade earlier into the mainstream in their countries and around the world, leaving a sweeping legacy behind them. These innovations, if the sociologist David Harvey is to be believed, continue into the present: "From these several epicentres, revolutionary impulses seemingly spread and reverberated to remake the world around us in a totally different image."[3] The word *globalization* entered the popular lexicon alongside these innovations, and with it flourished the promise of what Anna Lowenhaupt Tsing calls "supply-chain capitalism." The promise was that globalization would produce enormous wealth and lift the poorest countries in the world out of abject poverty. At the same time, it "allowed lead corporations to let go of their commitment to controlling labor. Standardizing labor required education and regularized jobs, thus connecting profits and progress. In supply chains, in contrast, goods gathered from many arrangements can lead to profits for the lead firm; commitments to jobs, education, and well-being are no longer even rhetorically necessary."[4]

The rise of the global novel cannot be separated from these other phenomena, for it, too, is a recent artifact, an idea that has come into being only in the past three decades. The word *global* connects its growing salience to globalization, while the word *novel*, of course, means "new," so that as a form the novel boasts of its ability to change with the times and remake itself as needed. In this emphasis on the new, it might be possible as well to hear faint echoes of the new embedded in neoliberalism. The global novel thus seems to shadow global capital, flowing freely across borders, tracking through centers of accumulated wealth, promising to bring greater representation to areas of the world that have been largely ignored by the metropole's culture industries. This means that the novel might be defined by the very kind of flexibility that is associated with globalization.

Also like globalization, these claims made on behalf of the global novel, regarding its ability to reinvent itself and to travel freely, do not match reality. The global novel—at least in the narrow sense I'm defining it here—is an industrial product that markets to readers in English-speaking countries (as well as countries speaking other European languages) an idea of being able to travel without restrictions across every conceivable kind of border and to dip here and there into other people's lives. But the global novel doesn't travel everywhere, and certainly not in equal numbers. Moreover, only a few prominent authors are eligible to act as expert guides, and they are anchored to specific national experiences.

When I add translation to the mix of concerns associated with the global novel, it's possible to see how further restricted this form is. Only a small fraction of any national literature is ever translated into English (about 6 percent of non-English literary works), and English itself remains a language that matters a lot for the sale of books and their international prestige.[5] Nasia Anam highlights this point when she observes, with regard to the growing popularity of something called the "Global Anglophone" in U.S. literature departments, "It evades the more politically thorny issues of translation or area studies training that a job in Comparative or World Literature might. That the new term specifies *Anglophone* literature has the convenient effect of removing the need for non-English language training. It also brings the U.S., Canada, Australia, and Ireland back into the fold without automatically necessitating an anticolonial perspective."[6]

When I turn to the novels of George Saunders, J. M Coetzee, and Han Kang, I find myself thinking of how their international renown is associated with a culture industry enmeshed in a global network of extraction, production, marketing, and waste making. This network has played no small part in the fast worsening of climate change. These are associations that terms like *the global novel* and *the global Anglophone* seek to minimize, even as they favor English-speaking, white authors from the world's metropoles, as illustrated by the list of authors I'm focusing on in this chapter (with its two white male authors from English-speaking countries). There's something suspect about the traveling fame of these literary works. Or, as I want to insist, to pay attention to how these literary works travel along such networks is to acknowledge a neutral statement about the conditions in which these writers create and get read. It is about how *all* writers create and get read. As Sarah Brouillette states, "Autonomous authorship is socially mediated; or, autonomy is a function and a mode of sociality."[7]

There is, in this analysis, a call to recognize limits. Novelists aren't free from constraints but must instead work with these constraints to try to say something meaningful to their readers. And sometimes—maybe most of the time—novelists can't find a large readership, or they fail to say something as meaningful as they'd like. The constraints are binding, and it seems important to recognize their power. This tension between constraint and creativity, however, interests me with regard to the ways in which *Lincoln in the Bardo*, *Elizabeth Costello*, and *Human Acts* are each in their unique ways preoccupied by the afterlife. The afterlife itself, as an imaginary construct, depends so much on acknowledging what is obviously the greatest constraint any person must live with, their inevitable death, and then exceeding it in an act of creative daring. It's no wonder that often the afterlife becomes an occasion for reflecting on questions of aesthetics and politics, for its positing a sentient existence beyond death gives it a perspective that allows for sharp critical thought about how life itself is organized by humans.

The imagination of the afterlife in these novels forces their readers to reckon with death and the finitude it demarcates. I can't stress this point enough. More and more, for humans, living in the present means an awareness of mass death. If the predictions about the impacts of climate change are accurate (if anything, they seem to me to be too conservative), you must prepare for exactly this, the end of human life in numbers the human species has never before encountered. The causes will likely be extreme weather events, such as hurricanes, wildfires, and droughts, and the spread of pathogens borne along vectors of warmer weather, as well as draconian responses to the suffering and unrest that follow. There has already been a heavy investment in the military, and the militarization of the police, which the end of the previous chapter touched on, and this investment is surely a by-product of neoliberalism. While never small, this investment remains more important than ever. As governments retracted from offering social services to their citizens and other residents and enacted more and more austerity measures, they have had to use force to protect businesses and keep the discontented in line. As demonstrated most saliently by the recent U.S. response to the COVID-19 pandemic, which led to more than 575,000 deaths in this country alone (with over 3 million deaths worldwide) by the end of April 2021, neoliberal-led governments often fail to enact the most basic measures to protect their residents from preventable death.

Even this emphasis on the deaths to come, as alarming as it is, minimizes this concern too much, since it projects the problem into the future and therefore distracts from the deaths that have already occurred and are occurring now. Just as important, the focus on death overlooks the ways in which many populations suffer from debilitating limits on their bodies—from physical disabilities experienced individually to social incapacity that inhibits mobility, impairs cognitive abilities, and shortens life expectancies. Many people infected with COVID-19 have struggled for many months with acute symptoms, and it's not clear what the longer-lasting consequences to their health may be. Debility is also often the effect of the use of force, which is focused less on the taking of life and more on the incapacitation of the living.

What might novels like the ones I focus on, then, tell readers about their relationship to death and debility and to life with death's expanding presence? In addressing this question, this chapter highlights two meanings of the afterlife: the imaginary life of the spirit that goes beyond death to what might follow and the equally imaginary life of the people left behind by the dead, who must find a way to keep living despite the dead's painful absence and the many uncounted hardships the living incur.

CONTEMPLATING NECROPOLITICS

The writer Roy Scranton had a breakout moment with the publication of an op-ed in the *New York Times* entitled "Learning How to Die in the Anthropocene." His point was simple, but many seem to have misinterpreted it. He argues that climate change is now a reality his readers must learn to accept. The question is not "whether global warming exists or how we might stop it, but how are we going to deal with it." When his readers turn to this latter question, he writes, they are confronted not only with the urgency of thinking in terms of security, food, energy, and a "way of life" but with large philosophical questions that revolve around death. As he puts it, "In the epoch of the Anthropocene, the question of individual mortality—'What does *my life* mean in the face of death?'—is universalized and framed in scales that boggle the imagination. What does human existence mean against 100,000 years of climate change? What does one life mean in the face of species death or the collapse of global civilization? How do we make meaningful choices in the shadow of our inevitable end?"[8]

Perhaps the most prominent figure to engage with this argument is the legal scholar Jedediah Purdy, who dismisses it at the start of his book on politics and the Anthropocene as merely being about "composing one's feelings into the proper existential attitude." In contrast, Purdy wants his book "to be worth reading."[9] This kind of hostile response seems to be elicited by the belief that Scranton advocates a Miss Lucy–like attitude toward climate change that leads inevitably to a fatalism that proclaims: it is too late; there's nothing to be done but find a way to live with dignity in the time people have left. But this is actually not what he argues. He writes that people must accept that their "way of life" cannot last, that it is already being unavoidably changed by a planetary phenomenon unlike any the human species has ever experienced. If you accept this premise, then you have to come to terms with the death of a certain way of life—as well as the death of many actual human beings—to enable new ways of living to emerge. In a more recent essay, Scranton writes, "We each have our allotted span of years on the planet, some more, some less, and then return to the nothing from which we came. Learning to accept this simple fact is a difficult, lifelong task, but it's the first step in understanding that the self isn't a unique, isolated thing at all but a product of generations enmeshed in a world, a transmaterialization of stellar dust, the expression of a vibrant, buzzing universe, a future and a past."[10] What do I lose when I die? What remains? What persists?

For critics working with ideas about biopower and biopolitics, Scranton's position should strike them as a reasonable critique of a political order founded on its ability to promote life—even if Scranton is also prone to conjuring unnecessarily large scales of time. What is most dreaded in such a political order is death itself, which signals the limits of its powers and therefore must be shunted off to the side, out of sight, an embarrassment that does not deserve to be discussed, or it must see death as what furthers the cause of life. Death is never conquered, but it is ignored or instrumentalized for the sake of life itself. So death counts, which so often follow natural disasters and which have become a feature of how the progression of the COVID-19 pandemic is reported, are not just attempts to reckon with the enormity of a tragedy but also a way of not having to engage this enormity. The fact of death is not refuted, but its meaning is displaced to numbers that grant distance and control over the management of life.

Death signals the opposite of mastery and of the colonial projects that such mastery is an inextricable part of; it signifies, in Michel Foucault's famous words, "power's limit" and "the moment that escapes it."[11] In thinking through Foucault's idea of biopolitics, especially as presented in one of his Collège de France lectures, Achille Mbembe calls attention to how a politics of life itself is founded on *necropolitics*, a determination of who must die so as to make live. He rejects Foucault's focus on biopower as "insufficient to account for contemporary forms of subjugation of life to the power of death." Far from being overshadowed by biopower's focus on making live, the sovereign right to kill is now exercised at unimaginable scales of destruction, and "weapons are deployed in the interest of maximum destruction of persons and the creation of *death-worlds*, new and unique forms of social existence in which vast populations are subjected to conditions of life conferring upon them the status of *living dead*."[12]

As Julietta Singh observes about mastery in particular, "To be characterized as the master of a language, or a literary tradition, or an instrument, for instance, is widely understood to be laudable. Yet as a pursuit, mastery invariably and relentlessly reaches toward the indiscriminate control over something—whether human or inhuman, animal or inanimate."[13] And as Lisa Marie Cacho insists, in the United States, "the war on terror far exceeded the biopolitical objectives of regulating and regularizing populations" by insisting that it is the "United States' right to determine who may survive and who *must* die, to exert the power to let live and *make* die." Such an exercise of power is possible only because of a perceived "threat to human existence."[14] From these perspectives, there is something politically troubling, in the good sense, about an argument like Scranton's, which insists that his readers pay attention to death and confront head-on their individual and collective finitude.

But this argument is also limited in that it fails to take into account not only the deaths that are here and to come but also what happens to those who survive. The worsening effects of climate change pose grave challenges to the living and make living itself marked by impairments that a focus on necropolitics overlooks. Indeed, the deliberate causing of injuries that do not kill may be one way in which power is exercised, so that populations that might rise up in revolt are sapped of their means to do so. There is, in short, a taking away or weakening of agency as a means of control. Jasbir Puar makes this point forcefully:

> Maiming is a practice that escapes definition within both legal and biopolitical or necropolitical frameworks because it does not proceed through making live, making die, letting live, or letting die. My reframing adds a critical axis to the four quadrants, insisting that debilitation—indeed, deliberate maiming—is not merely another version of slow death or of death-in-life or of a modulation on the spectrum of life to death. Rather, it is a status unto itself, a status that triangulates the hierarchies of living and dying that are standardly deployed in theorizations of biopolitics.[15]

Think, for instance, of the ready availability and wide use of "less lethal" weapons by many police forces around the world. Tasers, rubber bullets, tear gas, pepper spray, water cannons, and sound cannons (or Long Range Acoustic Devices) are not designed to kill but to incapacitate. They shoot volts of electricity into the body, tear through muscle and bone, overwhelm the eyes and mouth and skin, fling the body across space, and pierce the ears to such a degree that permanent hearing loss can occur. Neither a focus on life nor a focus on death can explain the short-term and long-term effects of such weapons of control, as they are focused on disabling their targets. They can kill, but death is not why they were manufactured. In Gaza as well, as Puar details, the Israeli authorities enforce numerous checkpoints that severely impair mobility, assure that infrastructure crumbles, impede access to much-needed supplies for hospitals, and severely regulate digital communications, as well as target the bodies of protesters and insurgents for long-lasting damage.

It was predicted, Puar observes, that by 2020 Gaza would be uninhabitable, which is odd to consider now that that date has passed. What purpose does such a prediction serve? "The year 2020 functions as a perverse apocalyptic timeline," she writes, "that is all too familiar to us now, largely through the predictive algorithms mapping for us the demise of the planet due to climate change. The prehensive is narrative produced as if this is a thing that is happening to us, when indeed, we made it happen."[16] There is, in this analysis, the recognition that the power of human agency is often hidden as a way to elude culpability for an effect that has been caused deliberately, even as the language itself seeks to debilitate in that it works to produce the same effects that bodily injury and impairment intend. Namely, the use of the *prehensive*, or what has been adapted for grasping (as in a prehensile tail), in storytelling focuses on the weakening of an agency that can put up resistance to power and the status quo, because it makes an outcome seem moved by forces that can't be understood, its ends inevitable, and human actors powerless to make demands of any kind.

TRANSITIONS

Both George Saunders's *Lincoln in the Bardo* and J. M. Coetzee's *Elizabeth Costello* are written in English, and they have more in common with each other than with Han Kang's *Human Acts*. They also follow their characters to a liminal state, in which their spirits are stalled between life and whatever might follow, and in the process offer occasion to question the meaning of life and death itself. The former is a historical drama set during the U.S. Civil War, when the President Abraham Lincoln's son, Willie Lincoln, has died and is interred at the Georgetown cemetery. There he encounters other spirits who reflect on their deaths and their inability to move on to whatever is next. Similarly, Coetzee's novel, a collection of shorter narratives centered on a famous fictional author from Australia, ends with its titular character in a square in front of a mysterious gate after her death. She must pass through it, but before she can, she has to complete a final writing assignment, a statement about her beliefs.

Lincoln in the Bardo is a familiar narrative about grief written in an innovative way. Almost as if mimicking the forms of social media, which are themselves reminiscent of avant-garde poetry, what is emphasized throughout is brevity, juxtaposition, and polyvocality. Saunders seems to recognize the constraints he operates under, and he foregrounds them in the same way the many contemporary poets discussed in this book have foregrounded constraint in their intense formal experiments. There is never just one person speaking, nor is any single character held up as an authority figure. Meaning is made in the spaces between characters, who often speak past each other as much as they do to one other. In addition to several invented characters, there are excerpts from historical documents, such as Elizabeth Keckley's "Behind the Scenes or Thirty Years a Slave and Four Years in the White House," Margaret Leech's "Reveille in Washington, 1860–1865," and Dorothy Meserve Kunhardt and Philip B. Kunhardt Jr.'s "Twenty Days" (Dorothy Meserve Kunhardt is most known today as the author of the children's book *Pat the Bunny*).[17] History and invention are thus mixed up, so that the story about a child who perishes in the first year of the Civil War and remains tethered to the earth in a Buddhist *bardo* feels taut with contemporary significance. Especially at a time when, in the United States, there is growing uncertainty about the future of the country's political structures, the novel promises to illuminate present-day concerns by shedding light on the past.

The novel is not concerned with deep time but with a way of thinking of time that does not imagine its passage as a succession of unrelated moments. The past matters and persists into the present, as ghostly as the ghosts it focuses on:

> Kneeling there, it seemed he could not resist opening the box one last time.
> the reverend everly thomas.
>
> He opened it; looked in; sighed.
> roger bevins iii
>
> Reached in, tenderly rearranged the forelock.
> hans vollman
>
> Made a slight adjustment to the pale crossed hands.
> roger bevins iii
>
> The lad cried out from the roof.
> hans vollman
>
> We had forgotten about him entirely.
> roger bevins iii[18]

The people named here are prominent characters in the novel, whose observations provide the most direct insight into Willie's suffering as a spirit newly parted from his body. While they often get caught up in their own struggles and offer occasional farcical distractions, they observe in this passage the president entering his son's crypt to take one last look at his body. There's a gentleness in the scene that marks the difficulty of grief, with the president's grief suggestively the affective tie that knots Willie to his current state of limbo. At the center of the narrative the novel depicts, then, is the drama of having to let go of the dead so as to pick up the struggles of the living. Such a drama would be difficult to enact under any circumstance, but in the midst of a war in which the forces Lincoln commands have suffered early defeats, the urgency to get on with this task is immense. There is no time for Lincoln to grieve for his son. He must let go and turn his attention to urgent matters of public importance.

I love the way this story demands of its readers attention to the same urgent matters. That is, *Lincoln at the Bardo* connects a deeply private concern, the death of a child, to a larger story of civic responsibility. It thus turns away from the private and the individual toward the public and the collective. The novel provides a visceral sense of the stakes involved in the struggle the president endures with the help of quotations from historical documents:

> As the dead piled up in unimaginable numbers and sorrow was added to sorrow, a nation that had known little of sacrifice blamed Lincoln for a dithering mismanagement of the war effort.—LARRY TAGG, *The Unpopular Mr. Lincoln: The Story of America's Most Reviled President*

> The President is an idiot.—GEORGE B. MCCLELLAN, *The Civil War Papers of George B. McClellan*

> Vain, weak, puerile, hypocritical, without manners, without social grace, and as he talks to you, punches his fists under your rib.—SHERRAND CLEMENS in CARL SANDBURG, *The War Years*

> Evidently a person of inferior cast of character, wholly unequal to the crisis.—EDWARD EVERETT in ALLAN NEVINS, *The Emergence of Lincoln: Prologue to the Civil War, 1859–1861*

The quotations are often shorter than the elaborate citations.[19] This ratio emphasizes the historical authority of these comments—they reflect what was actually said!—and contributes to the sense that a pervasive official attitude against the president had developed during this period: he was viewed as someone who was failing to master the situation he found himself in. The president is debilitated by grief.

The public occasion of an individual's grief is further accentuated by the fact that the spirits surrounding Willie are literally in denial about their own deaths. They do not want to admit what has happened to them and cling to the semblance of life that being in the bardo provides. Even at the end, some spirits rejoice in the maintenance of their denial and their continual survival in a place that is neither fully alive nor fully dead. They cling to their shadowy existence as a form of life, with life understood as the supreme good, while the other spirits have moved on. These other spirits have, in other words, overcome their denial about what is happening to them and are *able* to move on, much as Scranton writes that his readers must learn to do when confronted by the deadliness of climate change. You and I, then, to follow this way of thinking further, must accept that a way of life that is, for instance, dependent on air travel, the ready availability of consumer goods, cheap meat, access to clean water, and even fresh air, is coming to an end, and what follows is, as yet, unknown. Indeed, this way of life is already dead, but those living don't realize it yet. Unless they realize it and overcome their implicatory denial, they won't be able to find ways to compensate for what they can no longer do with ease. The present is, in other words, a kind of bardo.

Likewise, Elizabeth Costello in Coetzee's novel is also stuck, unable to move on. Unlike the spirits in Saunders's novel, however, she understands she has died. What prevents her from moving on? Partly, it's a failure of the imagination. As she notes angrily, the world, or the illusion of the world, that she finds herself inhabiting is a literary cliché: it resembles a square in a small northern Italian or Austro-Hungarian town, and the predicament she confronts is notably Kafkaesque: "The wall, the gate, the sentry, are straight out of Kafka. So is the demand for a confession, so is the courtroom with the dozing bailiff and the panel of old men in their crows' robes pretending to pay attention while she thrashes about in the toils of her own words. Kafka, but only the superficies of Kafka; Kafka reduced and flattened to a parody."[20] For Costello, what remains after death is not a spirit divorced from its body but the literary itself, which is dead from overuse and familiar allusion. Literature is all she has left, and if she is to free herself from it, for it feels like a trap, she must ironically write something that will convince the judges to let her go. Unfortunately, she can't. She is stuck in this world. Even when she tries to imagine what might lie beyond the gates, she sees "nothing but a desert of sand and stone, to infinity. It is her first vision in a long while, and she does not trust it, does not trust in particular the anagram GOD-DOG. *Too literary*, she thinks again. A curse on literature!"[21]

This focus on the literary also makes more earthly matters somehow beside the point. During her first meeting with the judges, one asks her about her opinion of the Tasmanians. When she responds with a confused generality, he continues, "I mean the old Tasmanians, the ones who were exterminated. Do you have special opinions about them?" The other judges are confused as well, so he turns to them to elaborate, "Atrocities take place. . . . Violations of innocent children. The extermination of whole people. What does she think about such matters? Does she have no beliefs to guide her?" Something about this exchange elevates the absurdity of the situation Costello finds herself in toward the farcical. The whole exchange is played for laughs. As a result, her feeling of outrage at being subjected to this line of questioning is granted greater validity. She thinks, "The extermination of the old Tasmanians by her countrymen, her ancestors. Is that, finally, what lies behind this hearing, this trial: the question of historical guilt?"[22]

Rather than address this question, Costello turns to her role as a writer. She was and perhaps remains, she says, a mere secretary, whose duty is to listen to the voices of the invisible and to transcribe what they say faithfully. She's ready to write about the plight of the Tasmanians as well as of children, but also of those who have inflicted atrocities on them. "I am open to all voices," she says, "not just the voices of the murdered and the violated." When asked whether she makes no distinction, then, between these two groups, she responds, "Do you think the guilty do not suffer too? . . . Do you think they do not call out from their flames? *Do not forget me!*—that is what they cry. What kind of conscience is it that will disregard a cry of such moral agony?"[23] This feels to me like one of the most extreme contemporary claims in favor of authorial autonomy. Writers write only the truth, uninhibited by other considerations, and can be judged only by their fidelity to this truth. The truth itself seems somehow to stand outside of the social and as such evades any need to grapple with thorny questions of responsibility or reparations.

If so, Costello's fate suggests that such fidelity to the idea of authorial autonomy leads to a literary cliché. She is trapped in a world of imaginative world making, limited in scope and conscience, where everything presented lacks context and historical meaningfulness. There are only allegorical symbols that don't allegorize anything. She is stuck and is unlikely ever to get out. And what is outside? It is just an abstraction, as there's no evidence in the novel that what lies beyond the gate is preferable to where she is. It turns out that the claim she has long made about herself, as an accomplished and celebrated writer, does not mean much. She is ordinary and common. When she asks the guard, in a fit of frustration, "Do you see many people like me, people in my situation?," he responds angrily, "All the time. . . . We see people like you all the time."[24]

I'm tempted to say that this particular imagination of the afterlife is a critique of the conventions of the global novel as an industrial product, with its lineage traceable to early twentieth-century Eurocentric ideas of world literature (especially, and obviously, Franz Kafka), its privileging of the author as somehow free of constraints, and the focus on profound abstract problems that transcend mere historical concerns like climate change. Sometimes the very idea of the literary can be a profound impairment.

THE DECEASED BODY'S CORPOREALITY

Both Saunders's and Coetzee's novels imagine the afterlife as a transitional state between actually living and what follows (although I leave the possibility open in my reading of *Elizabeth Costello* that the afterlife it imagines is actually a permanent state that pretends to be a transitory one). The point of being in transition is to get beyond it, to make peace somehow with the end of life so as to embrace more fully what follows. Moreover, for this to be possible, the person remains intact and unaffected by death. The focus remains squarely on the persons who died. In *Lincoln in the Bardo*, the spirits may no longer have bodies, but their minds are intact; they are capable of accessing their memories and understanding what is happening to them as a continuation of whoever they were before. Death may mark a threshold, which they occupy, but once they pass through it, they will remain somehow the same person they have been. In *Elizabeth Costello*, the body seems to remain more or less corporeal, retaining its form in death and able to occupy a world that is as solid as the readers' own. Nothing has changed. Life after death is little different from life before: Costello still eats, sleeps, and presumably goes to the bathroom. She consoles herself, "How beautiful it is, this world, even if it is only a simulacrum! At least there is that to fall back on."[25]

This is not the case with *Human Acts*, which depicts little possibility of getting over a death. The spirits it begins by depicting hover over their deceased bodies, aware of their quick decomposition. Han's novel thus considers the dead as interacting with the political concerns of the living directly (and not indirectly as in Saunders's novel). Indeed, Han's novel repeatedly emphasizes the physicality of the dead body. Even when the soul is separated from it, the soul is aware of the body, including its decay. This attention to the body as part of ongoing physical processes even after death recalls Donna Haraway's argument that humans "are compost, not posthuman; we inhabit the humusities, not the humanities. Philosophically and materially, I am a compostist, not a post-humanist."[26] This awareness of the dead body's physicality, and its continued participation in the physical cycles of the Earth, is notably absent in the other examples I consider—the ghosts in *Lincoln in the Bardo* actively turn away from their dead bodies and refuse to acknowledge them; Elizabeth Costello has no connection to her predeath terrestrial body.

These refusals suggest that while all of these novels respond to familiar ideas about the afterlife, some, like Han's, do not participate in the split between body and mind. Even in death, whatever remains of the mind stays wedded to the decomposing body. Just as important, if not more so, this attention to the body's physicality in both life and death seems part of the overt political concerns of Han's novel, which focuses on the violent suppression of a popular uprising in Gwangju by Chun Doo-Hwan, a brutal dictator who took control of Korea in a military coup in 1980.

The novel, much like Han's better-known *The Vegetarian*, is told from multiple perspectives and revolves around a tragic figure whose tragedy has rippling effects on the other characters they come into contact with. The first two chapters of *Human Acts* center on two friends, both in their third year of middle school in Korea (roughly the ninth grade in the United States). In chapter 1, Dong-ho is looking for Jeong-dae's body; he saw him killed by the soldiers sent to Gwangju to suppress the popular uprising. Dong-ho ends up volunteering at the local hospital, turned into a makeshift morgue, where he is asked to record facts about the arriving bodies and to cover them with cloth. The large number of bodies he has to attend to and the gruesomeness of their condition amplify the violence of the soldiers, who cannot suppress the uprising without maiming and murdering. When grieving relatives arrive, he shows them the remains. The reader discovers only later that Dong-ho was also shot and killed by soldiers returning to take control of the city. Chapter 2 is told from Jeong-dae's perspective, or rather his soul's perspective, as he is now an immaterial being.

The narration is complex as these different story threads are thoroughly interwoven, suggesting how the lives of the novel's characters are connected to each other. The first chapter is written entirely in the second person, with the "you" addressing Jeong-dae specifically. The second chapter is written in the first person, with the narrator, Jeong-dae, also addressing Dong-ho in the second person. This has an eerie lyrical effect, separating the speaker and the spoken to from being associated with specific characters and focusing instead on the telling itself. This unusual narrative effect, which seems more focused on creating a moment than advancing a plot, shouldn't be too surprising, perhaps, since Han began her writing career as a poet and hasn't, it seems, entirely given up the habits associated with poetry, as can be seen in her more recent—and gorgeously written—*The White Book*, which is as much prose poem as memoir. Throughout the novel, and especially in these early chapters, there is a heightened focus on portraying the intensity of the characters' emotional state and their relationship to their bodies.

Jeong-dae's narrative, in chapter 2, begins with a description of the bodies that the soldiers are collecting in an empty courtyard: "Our bodies are piled on top of each other in the shape of the cross."[27] The deliberateness of this image obviously makes reference to Christianity and suggests perhaps at once the question of the holy and the sacred in reference to the bodies of protesters killed by soldiers and the question of Christianity's, and perhaps by extension the West's (and in particular the United States'), role in making sense of the behavior of a murderous authoritarian regime. The Christian iconography also suggests there is ceremony behind the arrangement of the corpses. While their numbers are large, the soldiers responsible for moving them from where they were killed have at least had the decency to make some kind of gesture of respect, as meager as it is, which recognizes that these bodies were once more than mere things.

Whatever solace Jeong-dae's spirit finds in this image is quickly dispelled when new bodies are added to the pile. This time, the bodies bear traces of having been treated first. They are in hospital gowns. Their faces have been cleaned. There are signs of the effort that has been made to save their lives, including "sutures," "poultices," and a "bandage coiled" around the head of one of the bodies, which "gleamed white in the darkness." They are, of course, all dead, and so there isn't much to differentiate them, at least in a way that would matter to the spirits, Jeong-dae reasons, but then again "there was something infinitely noble about how his body still bore the traces of hands that had touched it, a tangible record of having been cared for, been valued, that made me envious and sad." The realization that his own body bears no traces of such care leads him to a "hatred" of his body: "Our bodies, tossed there like lumps of meat. Our filthy, rotting faces, reeking in the sun."[28]

Human Acts thus centers on the treatment of the body after death, especially when the state kills its own residents. As such, I find it difficult to read these descriptions in the context of the United States without thinking about the police's killing of African Americans. I'm thinking in particular of Michael Brown, whose body was allowed to lie on the street for several hours unattended after he was murdered by the police in Ferguson, Missouri, in 2014. The same fate, sadly, happened to George Floyd in Minneapolis, Minnesota, in 2020. The lack of care given to Brown's and Floyd's dead bodies continues to reverberate as much as the killing itself, as in Morgan Parker's deliberately prosaic poem "A Brief History of the Present":

> Which is greater: the amount of minutes
> it takes for requested backup to arrive at the scene of

a twelve-year-old in a park playing with toys, or the
varieties of insects that might make contact with a person
laid in a street over the course of four hours in a summer
evening in St. Louis? How patient must we be?[29]

There are also the thousands of bodies of the dead in New Orleans in the
aftermath of Hurricane Katrina in 2005, many not found for days or weeks.
I'm reminded as well of the body of Tamerlan Tsarnaev, killed during the
massive police hunt for those responsible for the 2013 Boston Marathon
bombing. The original funeral home where his body was sent was besieged
by protests, and it had to be transferred to a mortuary in Worcester. Several
cities in Massachusetts, in a latter-day reenactment of *Antigone*, refused to
allow his body to be buried within their limits. It was finally secretly buried
in Virginia.

My mention of Sophocles's ancient play also reminds me of the extraordinary cycle of poems by the Mexican poet Sara Uribe. Entitled *Antígona
González*, the poems focus on the title character's search for the body of
her lost brother, who has been killed in the midst of the war on drugs in
northern Mexico. The poems are set in the state of Tamaulipas, where the
highest number of missing persons has been reported. The book focuses
its emotional intensity on a specific case, an individual loss—that of the
brother, Tadeo—in much the same way Jeong-dae's spirit focuses attention
on his and Dong-ho's deaths. And as the latter's death in particular echoes
through the rest of *Human Acts*, tracking the ways in which his absence has
profoundly affected the lives of many others both close to and far from him,
Tadeo's death becomes a way of making sense of the enormity of the losses
that have been occurring in Mexico. The speaker is repeatedly told to stop
searching for her brother's body, that if she continues to stir up trouble, she'll
"*fucking end up dead.*"[30] She is also told, "Without a body there's no crime,"
to which she replies:

> I tell them
> Without a body there's no refuge, no peace possible for
> my heart.
>
> For anyone.[31]

Uribe's poems thus toggle back and forth between the specificity of Tadeo's
missing body (and the sister's focus on the right to bury it) and the ways in
which the search for this body is also a search for all the bodies of the dead.
In another poem, the antecedent for the "I" shifts between different people

looking for their relatives, not just a brother but a father, a husband, and a son, until it ends, "I came with the others for the bodies of our people."[32] The term Antigone becomes, then, a generic honorific, a title given to women who insist on the need to bury their dead:

: *I didn't want to be an Antigone*

but it happened to me.[33]

My thinking of these examples reveals my own inability to read about an atrocity that occurred far away and not try to relate it somehow to examples that are closer (tragedies that happened in the United States) or more familiar in a literary way (via a work of ancient Greek literature). But these examples suggest something else as well: how the unattended deceased body has become commonplace, both in the United States and elsewhere. There is, in the intense lyrical style of Han's novel and the way it strips down details to focus on the feelings its characters endure, a self-conscious vying for the universal. That is, while the novel takes place in a specific time and place and narrates an actual historical event, it resembles the experiences of many other people around the world who have no shortage of similar historical events, as Uribe's poems in particular help foreground. The lack of details or extended descriptions of Gwangju in *Human Acts* adds to this focus on experience over specificity. The neglect of a body murdered by agents of the state, mass death, and the disavowal of a politically abject body are part of the everyday experiences of people everywhere, especially in the Global South and among the disenfranchised and racially minoritized. They have become, and continue to be, ordinary. As the final narrator of *Human Acts* observes, "In autumn 1979, when the democratic uprising in the southern cities of Busan and Masan was being suppressed President Park Chung-hee's chief bodyguard Cha Ji-cheol said to him, *The Cambodian government's killed another 2 million of theirs. There's nothing stopping us from doing the same.*"[34]

How do you mourn for all of these lives that have ended sooner than they should have? This is the question Han addresses in her novel, as successive chapters take up the perspective of other characters who have in some intimate way been involved in the Gwangju massacre. There is Eun-sook, who had been an older student responsible for taking care of the dead as they came in; an unnamed narrator who, as an older college student just finished with his mandatory military duty, became a militia leader and was subsequently imprisoned and tortured; a "Miss Lim" who was a textile factory worker and labor organizer involved with the militia; Dong-ho's mother, who was unable to convince her son to come home before the killing began; and a writer, who seems to be Han herself remembering an event that occurred in her hometown, or *gohyang*, when she was nine. The story of each of these characters is told as a flashback, with each subsequent telling taking place years after the previous telling (1985, 1990, 2002, 2010, 2013). The characters mostly lead stunted lives, transfixed by a gaze back at a past event that remains in many ways livelier than the present they inhabit. In this way, the novel shows how the event itself persists, a moment that can't be forgotten and indeed may not have come to an end, even as it haunts and helps shape a fast-modernizing Korea. Like residence time, grass time, and butcher time, as discussed in chapter 6, Han evokes a temporality that isn't defined by linear progression and a rush to get on to the next event.

The novel encourages its readers to redefine what they might mean by an afterlife. It's not just the spirit or soul leaving the body and going elsewhere. It is, rather, what remains after death for the living who cannot for whatever reason forget the dead and as a result are debilitated by mourning. The mourning can last decades, as in *Human Acts*, or longer. As Saidiya Hartman observes, "If slavery persists as an issue in the political life of black America, it is not because of an antiquarian obsession with bygone days or the burden of a too-long memory, but because black lives are still imperiled and devalued by a racial calculus and a political arithmetic that were entrenched centuries ago. This is the afterlife of slavery—skewed life chances, limited access to health and education, premature death, incarceration, and impoverishment."[35] What remains after death for the living can remain for a long time, affecting the experiences of whole groups of people rather than individuals, and making them susceptible to a math that devalues them.

The afterlife is also the life that might have been possible if death hadn't come too soon. In Jeong-dae's case, his spirit conjures memories of his past, happy moments with his sister and the joys of bodily experience, such as the taste of a watermelon or the triumph of doing forty pushups in a row. And this leads to a memory of his life as it might have been led if he had lived: "For the time I would hold a woman in my arms. That first woman who would permit such a liberty, whose face I didn't yet know, how I longed to extend my trembling fingers to the other edge of her heart."[36] The dead are never dead but haunt the living by gesturing toward a life that could have been led otherwise.

This very kind of thinking is invoked by Danez Smith, whose stunning poem "Summer, Somewhere" invites readers to imagine a young Black man murdered by the police as occupying a vibrant afterlife distant from the hazards he faced while alive. The speaker of the poem observes:

i spent my life arguing how i mattered
until it didn't matter.

who knew my haven
would be my coffin?

dead is the safest i've ever been.
i've never been so alive.[37]

For those who survive, like the many characters in *Human Acts*, this last sentiment might lead to a lot of agreement. Death is horrible, but so is living after the death of loved ones and reckoning with the psychic pain their absence leaves behind. This, too, is a form of debilitation, as are the policies enacted by a brutal regime that came to power through death and remains in power through more violence.

LIFE AFTER THE RETREAT FROM THE GLOBAL

The sociologist Bruno Latour has argued that the forceful political movement toward greater and greater government deregulation (which I referred to at the start of this chapter as neoliberalism), soaring inequalities, and a "systemic effort to deny the existence of climate change" are all related phenomena. He writes, "It is as though a significant segment of the ruling class . . . had concluded that the earth no longer had room enough for them and for everyone else."[38] Hence, there's a massive concentration of wealth, the buildup of security forces, the erecting of walls, and a heavy investment in owning integrated media conglomerates that can soothe their audiences by minimizing, ignoring, or mischaracterizing the severity of the myriad, and related, problems they face. The journalist Christian Parenti calls this strategy of adaptation "the armed life boat," or "responding to climate change by arming, excluding, forgetting, repressing, policing, and killing."[39] When he coined the phrase in 2011, he worried this strategy was likely to be adopted. For Latour, writing a few years later in the wake of the 2016 U.S. presidential election, this strategy is no longer a concern for the future. It is a reflection of the present.

If Latour is correct and the world's ruling classes (a term that he prefers over *elites* and that I've adopted in this book) are spearheading a coordinated effort to adapt by practicing an extreme prejudice when making necropolitical calculations, one important function that writers from around the world can perform is to dramatize what such a policy means in terms of what people must endure to live, and in terms of how people are forced to mourn their dead. Han performs this function admirably in *Human Acts*, especially in the way it invites readers to consider how the deaths it depicts are structurally similar to deaths elsewhere. Hence, a kind of intertextuality is made possible between *Human Acts* and Morgan Parker's and Danez Smith's poems and Sara Uribe's *Antígona González*.

Such intertextuality could also be extended to Khaled Khalifa's novel *Death Is Hard Work*, which chronicles the voyage of three siblings—Bolbol, Hussein, and Lamia—who try to honor their father's dying wish by transporting his body from Damascus to a small village in Aleppo during the Syrian Civil War. They run into endless complications, including checkpoints, competing armed factions, and their own long-held grievances against one another. Meanwhile, their father's corpse rots and grows putrid, a nightmare of decaying flesh that reminds the reader of what happens to the body after a person's death. There is no sentimental frame around what happens to this body, nor is there any possibility that the siblings will end the journey better for it. If anything, they are more embittered and estranged from each other, and individually they must reckon with the wreckages of their individual lives, as they have each had to compromise and give up the things they've truly valued in order to get along.

Only their father, whose life the reader glimpses in flashbacks, seems to have found something renewing in the midst of wartime tragedy. Unlike his children, the elderly Abdel Latif found renewed purpose at the start of the civil war. He became involved with the rebels and made himself the caretaker of a graveyard full of men who had fought against the Assad regime and others who had been killed by "the unceasing bombardment": "Whole families were killed, including children and women and old people who couldn't get away. This territory of death became his whole life, and he spent most of his time looking after it."[40] He was, in other words, someone who took the time to walk the dead, as David Bowie put it.

As this was happening, Abdel Latif renewed a romantic relationship with a woman he had loved for most of his life but had not been able to marry. This relationship led him to take care of the graveyard, and as he did, and became more involved with others in the rebellion, he experienced a transformation of the self. This part of the story is told from the perspective of the woman, Nevine: "From the moment she had looked in the void, Abdel Latif also transformed and became like her. He no longer had anything to be frightened of. He was the bravest he had ever been."[41] What had been a life of idle pursuits became defined by activity and purpose: "There wasn't much time left for the man granted inexhaustible energy by the revolution. He suffered from a surfeit of projects, discussed every detail pertaining to the town, joined every committee, swept the streets with young volunteers, filled placards with his beautiful calligraphy for the Friday protests."[42]

Although the characters in the novel believe that the rebellion will eventually be defeated by the government, and although Abdel Latif knows his own time is short and death imminent, this description of this last, brief period of his life offers a vision of a living with death that is not only full of mourning and personal devastation. Instead, it suggests resolve, the formation of new collectivities, a reviving of interests that makes every moment of this existence rich with meaning, and a general buildup of human agency. This part of his life is told from another's perspective, which emphasizes how this activity is part of a larger shared experience.

While far from ideal, Abdel Latif's last days suggest to me a different way of being in the world that is not beholden to a culture of life and the death worlds it creates, nor the debility that exists somewhere in between as a suppression of the will, but rather is what Anna Lowenhaupt Tsing might call a "life without the promise of stability."[43] This is the making up of meaning as you go along, finding purpose where you can, recognizing that there is no grand narrative of which you are part that moves you and everyone around you toward some prescribed goal. "Indeterminacy is not the end of history," Tsing writes, "but the node in which many beginnings lie in wait."[44]

Perhaps with this thought in mind, it's possible to think of the afterlife not as what happens to the human person after death but as what beginnings are made possible when death and debility are acknowledged and allowed into a collectivity's sense of itself. The afterlife might be about living on after the death of others and finding resolve to carry on a common pursuit, regardless of what the outcome might be. If so, such resolve is something everyone will need more of as climate change becomes climate breakdown and even—a possibility that can't be ruled out if the ruling classes continue crafting armed lifeboats—environmental collapse. Even in the worst-case scenarios, this kind of afterlife names a will to go on, to keep fighting, to remain, like Latif, engaged and enlivened with purposeful action. This is the model of shared agency I have been trying to sustain attention to in this book.

CONCLUSION

The Foreign Present—Who Are We to Each Other?

I AM ON MY DAILY WALK with Grace. We walk every day to get some fresh air, to clear our heads, to tire our bodies. If we don't exhaust ourselves physically, we have trouble falling asleep. Even when we do, we still have trouble sleeping, but less. For weeks, as a result of the pandemic, we've been sheltering in place with our two kids, and we expect to shelter in place for many more weeks and months.

On this late spring day, we deviate from our routine by attending a vigil for George Floyd. Many people are around. The air is humid, stifling, especially with a mask on. I am no longer used to crowds and find them menacing. We arrive just in time for a moment of silence. Eight minutes and forty-six seconds. The time a police officer held Floyd's neck down with his knee, killing him, while three other officers stood guard, keeping observers—stunned by the inhumanity they were witnessing—at a distance. All the observers could do was beg for his life.

The crowd recalls this horrific act by kneeling on one knee. Grace and I resist the pull to do likewise. We do not kneel. If observers didn't know the gesture copies the quarterback Colin Kaepernick's getting down on one knee at the start of each football game, for which he has paid a stiff career penalty, they might think the protesters are copying the police officer kneeling. We do not think of this as we stand awkwardly in the crowd, attracting curious looks, but something about the gesture doesn't feel right.

Eight minutes and forty-six seconds feels interminable. The stillness recalls the stillness of the days many of us have been experiencing while remaining at home, which I am already, perversely, missing as the state's economy begins to rev back up—those quiet, seemingly endless days of repose and reflection. It is difficult to sit at home day after day and have no place else to go. It is chilling to think of the people getting sick and dying. The sound of sirens in the greater quiet of the day or evening startles with what it portends. The images of long lines of cars waiting at food banks testifies to the economic hardship the response to the pandemic set in motion. The kids get restless. My youngest especially gets upset about minor setbacks, which is so unlike her usual behavior. She misses being with her friends, she tells us.

But day-to-day, we find a simple rhythm. It takes time and error to find it. There is no rush to get the kids to school or ourselves to work. Hardly any cars are on the streets, and the sound of the birds is loud. Indeed, the birds are louder than I ever remember them being. We spend a lot of time together, and I savor this time, because there never seems to be enough of it. My oldest is already in high school, and our conversations drift more and more to college. In unspoken agreement, we develop a schedule. We eat breakfast together, and then the kids do their schoolwork, and Grace and I our adult work. We reconvene for lunch. In the midafternoon, we retreat into our corners of the apartment and give each other much-needed space until Grace and I feel the need to take a walk. Pull together, separate, pull together again.

We drift apart from the crowd. We are glad the vigil is happening, but on this day it doesn't comfort us or make us feel as if we contribute somehow to solving the problem of police violence and dismantling systemic racism. Grace Lee Boggs's words echo in my ear: "Still, it becomes clearer every day that organizing or joining massive protests and demanding new policies fail to sufficiently address the crisis we face. They may demonstrate that we are on the right side politically, but they are not transformative enough. They do not change the cultural images or the symbols that play such a pivotal role in molding us into who we are."[1]

The most startling moment in Boggs's book *The Next American Revolution: Sustainable Activism for the Twenty-First Century* (co-written with Scott Kurashige) is when she recalls her husband's words about what an American revolution would look like. This is what James Boggs argued: because of this country's unique history and culture, whatever revolution might occur here would need to be unique as well. What would differ? Unlike other revolutions, which have been about giving the masses more, this revolution would require everyone in the United States to make do with less. Grace Lee Boggs expands on her late husband's idea:

> The next American Revolution, at this stage in our history, is not principally about jobs or health insurance or making it possible for more people to realize the American Dream of upward mobility. It is about acknowledging that we Americans have enjoyed middle-class comforts at the expense of other peoples all over the world. It is about living the kind of lives that will not only slow down global warming but also end the galloping inequality both inside this country and between the Global North and the Global South.[2]

What kind of revolution do we speak of that asks those involved to do with less?

Boggs wrote these words when she was almost a hundred years old. She had grown up in Rhode Island, in a small apartment above her parents' Chinese restaurant, and went to Barnard on a scholarship before getting a PhD in philosophy from Bryn Mawr. Because of her race, she could not hope to get a job as a professor, and so she drifted instead into organizing with the African American community and became a fiery political theorist, working alongside figures like C. L. R. James and Raya Dunayevskaya (who was once Leon Trotsky's secretary). She eventually married James Boggs, who had migrated from rural Alabama to Detroit, like many of the Black residents of that city. He worked most of his life on a car assembly line and spent his spare time engaging in political activism and writing political essays. Together, they became important figures in Detroit's Black community, and after her husband's death, Boggs continued to work within this community and sought to find ways to improve its horrendous conditions.

I find Boggs a charismatic figure and her writings inspirational for her lifetime commitment to social change from the bottom up. She never gave up on the idea that the most marginalized could band together and craft forms of shared agency capable of transforming the society they live in. And yet I want to pause with the call to do with less. So many of us have already been forced to make do with less and less over the past several decades, and I wonder if such a call is targeted enough. Some should definitely do with less, but others need more, so much more.

This is not the first vigil or protest we've attended. It won't be the last. We feel stuck in a cycle. The police continue to kill Black, Indigenous, and Latinx people. Millions are incarcerated. The wealth gap is enormous. The

United States is engaged in a forever war against terror. South Asian Americans, as well as people with ancestry in the Middle East and North Africa, at least since 9/11, have been drawn into this phantom war as suspects. The Chinese origins of the coronavirus have made East and Southeast Asian Americans (as well as Latinx individuals mistaken for Asian) the targets of racial harassment and hate crimes. The weather is more unpredictable than ever before. The institutions in this country seem to be failing, one by one, and with them our sense of the everyday becomes more menacing.

As it is, I find it impossible not to imagine the lives our children will lead. The future that seems to be waiting for them is scary and difficult. The ice melts faster than predicted; the oceans acidify; wildlife goes extinct; supplies of food and fresh water are under threat; the wealthy retreat behind walls both literal and figurative; democracies everywhere, including in this country, are in trouble; and the old prejudices endure and, if anything, gain potency. We are in a period of calamitous change, unheralded and unheeded but present nonetheless. Nothing fills me with as much dread as seeing the world through my children's eyes. Will they have to make do with less and less as well? Will whatever remains be enough for them to make do at all?

Maybe Boggs is asking a question rather than offering a solution to her readers. Who are we? If so, I want to add something to this question, prompted by my reflections on the lyric and climate change in this book. Not just, Who are we? but, Who are we *to each other*? This leads to more questions, which I've been wrestling with in the previous pages. What basis for common struggle is there? If we share a society, what kind of society can contain so many differences? What forms of social organization will allow us to survive the calamities that are already here and that still lie ahead? Can we find ways to flourish instead of just survive? Is it possible to imagine, as Adam Trexler puts it with scholarly precision, "the creation of a composite political entity with sufficient agency to redress climate change?"[3]

These questions have never felt more urgent to me as elected officials in the United States cut taxes for the wealthiest, who do not know what to do with all the wealth they already possess, and pay for this continued massive redistribution of resources upward by cutting the flow of capital to other important uses. There is never enough money to maintain and improve critical infrastructure, to make sure the sick get access to needed health care, to educate the young from preschool to college and beyond, and to ensure a spirited debate flourishes in the country's multiple public spheres about how to govern ourselves in a time of increasing peril. Meanwhile, many groups are demonized, including undocumented immigrants, who are rounded up from their homes in aggressive, militaristic style, as well as the asylum seekers at the United States' southwestern border, who are held in concentration camps and whose children, many under five years old, are separated from their guardians.

The very idea of a society faces a legion of problems. These are manifested everywhere, in crumbling roads and depressing cityscapes, in overcrowded prisons, in rural towns struggling with few jobs and an epidemic of opioid addiction, in the lack of affordable health care, in neighbors' faces lined with worry about how they will make ends meet, in the many brilliant graduate students and recent doctorate holders I know who struggle to find a job in the profession they have trained so hard for. If the protests teach me anything, it's an appreciation of how large police department budgets are in every city and municipality in the country. As the effects of global warming worsen, exacerbating the serious problems people already face, a militarized police force is asked to keep populations in line, especially African Americans and other minority communities. Meanwhile, the military is asked to police populations elsewhere, especially in the Middle East, North Africa, and South Asia.

People's lives are hard. This is a stupid, banal statement but a true one nonetheless. And now we have to imagine how much harder these lives will become as we move from one degree Celsius of warming beyond preindustrial levels, roughly where we're at now at the time of this writing, to the two degrees of warming we will most likely experience, with all of its existential implications, before we reach 2050. What lies beyond is, for me, nearly unimaginable. Or maybe it's too imaginable. There seems to be no end of dystopic and apocalyptic narratives ready to speculate about what might lie beyond the approaching thresholds of warming—and as my relative lack of attention to these narratives in this book might suggest, I am tired of them. I don't want only depictions of how bad things can get (they are bad enough already). I also want, desperately at times, depictions of how we can find ways to work together to make our situation better.

The United States is governed by an eighteenth-century constitution designed in part to protect the rights of slave owners. It grants every state two senators, no matter how many people live in each state. It sets up a process for electing presidents—the Electoral College—that grants those living in less populous states more of a say in the outcome. It allows individual states to determine the geographic distribution of their congressional districts, which has long made for funny-shaped districts designed to favor one political party over another. This means that some votes are worth much more than others, and a minority of voters (usually older and whiter than the general electorate) can dictate to the rest of the population, no matter how vocally and passionately the latter might protest, how everyone should be governed.

When the voters are not too divided, this system might seem to reflect the will of the people. When voters are divided, however, as in the present, the system strains for legitimacy. Two of the past four presidents have been selected because they won a plurality of Electoral College votes even though they lost the popular vote. The same minority of voters have thrown their support behind politicians who refuse the science of climate change. These politicians, in turn, embrace extreme denialist positions that make the difficult task of switching energy sources and adapting to the changes that are already underway much more difficult. These well-known facts highlight the ways in which the state has been structured in the United States to favor specific demographics as opposed to others. The divisions are racial, classed, and geographic; above all, they reflect the belief that some lives are worth more than others. I have repeatedly been told that the United States is a republic and not a democracy. I fear this is true.

The state is not, however, the only place in which people can seek to exert pressure on the way they are governed. There is something that might be called civil society, which is less rigid in form and more amenable to persuasion and evidence. I turn to this idea of civil society, as nebulous and difficult to define as it is, in part because it's an informal gathering of people where they can discuss important matters and try to determine for themselves what it means to be part of a larger group. Any one of us is more likely to influence civil society than the state. The latter is calcified and resistant to popular dissent. It will have to change somehow or crumble under the weight of its own illegitimacy, but the crowd we have just been a part of forms in the hope that those involved can exercise a different kind of power. Maybe these protests speak profoundly to the question of who we are to each other. Maybe that represents a civil society trying to pressure the state to become more democratic.

Some of what I have learned from being a professor of Asian American literature, and engaging more broadly in the study of race and ethnicity, can be boiled down to this. Find people you feel a deep affinity with and who you think will do good. Define your interests broadly, so that you leave room for solidarity with the struggles of others. Fight like hell to advance these interests. And don't ever let others speak for you.

These same lessons apply double in the age of climate change we now find ourselves in. I believe wholeheartedly that we need each other and that we need to shore up, or invent, bonds of community that have everywhere become, at this most unfortunate moment, attenuated. Margaret Thatcher is famous for having once said, "Who is society? There is no such thing! There are individual men and women and there are families."[4] This is a monstrous statement, and that is why it has been so often quoted and remembered. It also speaks to an era of incredible migration and population change, of wholesale displacement and disruption of settled ways of living. The very presence of Asian faces like mine in places where we were once, not too long ago, a rarity, and even a curiosity, indexes some of these changes. Maybe it is no coincidence that Thatcher questioned the very idea of a society precisely at the moment when faces like mine began appearing more frequently in crowds from which we were once absent. The more racially diverse a society becomes and the more demands are made that power be shared equitably, the less society might seem like a real thing to those used to being in a majority.

Grace tells me about her frustration as we walk by a river, trying to find the right words. I won't share them here because they aren't mine to share.[5] There is barely any water in the river, mostly a wide muddy bank. It hasn't rained in a long while. We stop to look at a rabbit that's staring, contemplatively, into the distance.

She asks, "What are we doing? What good is any of this?"

I don't know where it comes from or whether it's an appropriate response, but I say, after a long pause, that I'm trying to affect my little circle of influence as much as I can, making it grow and contributing in whatever way I can to making life better for others. I have to believe that others are doing the same. Maybe our circles are near each other, and they help each other grow and refine what we are doing. We're each an island, and together we make archipelagos.

When I say this, I think of Carlos Bulosan, primarily because he was born in the Philippines (an archipelago) and spent his youth there. In *America Is in the Heart*, one character famously says, "This is the greatest responsibility of literature: to find in our struggle that which has a future."[6] Maybe the making of archipelagos is just another way of trying to imagine what this struggle looks like.

The future is tricky, of course, as it always lies ahead of us and can't ever be known with certainty. What we know is the past, and for many of the writers I've been reading, the past is full of pain. Vulnerability and powerlessness and tragedy are a constant theme. Loss and absence are constitutive. Theresa Hak Kyung Cha in *Dictee* meditates on the enduring war between the north and south in Korea, a war that still has no peace treaty despite the formal cessation of military violence more than half a century ago: "Nothing has changed, we are at a standstill. I speak in another tongue now, a second tongue a foreign tongue. All this time we have been away. But nothing has changed. A stand still."[7] Cha chronicles the violence that continues in the mind and the experiences of the people whose country has been torn apart by the machinations of foreign powers. The violence itself must be understood in temporalities of long duration; it seems even for those who've migrated elsewhere and returned for a visit like a "stand still." As Solmaz Sharif observes in her poem "The Master's House":

> To know, for example, that in Farsi the present perfect is called the
> relational past, and is used at times to describe a historic event whose
> effect is still relevant today, transcending the past
> To say, for example, *Shah dictator bude-ast* translates to *The Shah was a
> dictator*, but more literally to *The Shah* is *was a dictator*
> To have a tense of is-was, the residue of it over the clear bulb of your eyes[8]

Cha's "stand still" is the relational past of Farsi, the "is-was" of the present and past that can't be separated from each other.

Similarly, in the poem "Doc—," Cathy Linh Che observes:

> In Vietnam, the landscape
> is aftermath—
> tourist shops, sunbathers,
> packs of motorbikes—
>
> there were still
> bomb craters
>
> and, in them, the grass
> grown in.[9]

At least in this image, where the past continues on in the landscape, there is a marker of time passing. The grass shoots up in the mutilated earth. Nevertheless, psychically, the past remains a part of the present and informs what the speaker of this poem can expect. The psychic costs of this feeling of being stuck, subtly gestured to by the poem's frequent use of em dashes, are heavy because it affects not only what we know of the present but how we can imagine the future. The dashes signal long pauses, gaps in thinking, and even some information being repressed. The very title is interrupted in this way. What follows the "Doc"? The dash can only signal that something has been withheld.

Many poems I read speak to this sense of a difficult past—barely articulable, if at all—that makes the future daunting to contemplate. Fatimah

Asghar's poem "For Peshawar" commemorates the 2014 Taliban massacre of schoolchildren in northwestern Pakistan by asking:

> From the moment our babies are born
> are we meant to lower them into the ground?
> To dress them in white?[10]

Chen Chen's poem "For I Will Do/Undo What Was Done/Undone to Me" makes an ethic out of this inability to imagine a future that's better than now:

> I pledge allegiance to the always
> partial, the always translated, the always never
> of knowing who's walking around, what's being left behind,
> the signs, the cries, the breadcrumbs & the blood.[11]

Franny Choi also calls forth another ethic, this time of vulnerability rather than incompletion, in the poem "& O Bright Star of Disaster, I Have Been Lit." She proclaims:

> I am no god.
> only woodworm, only termite burrowing
> like a light in the flesh.[12]

So many children are born into a world full of premature death; they might not make it past their childhoods. Childhood itself is also so often imagined as a preparation for the future that the child never really gets to exist as a being in the present. So what if we stop thinking so much about what we will become? What if we embrace what we are instead? And what are we if not something lowly, a humble being inextricably entangled in a being we can apprehend only in the most limited and reductive ways? This is an understanding of our humanity that many of us begin with and not something we have to be convinced of.

Choi explores this view of the human further in another poem, "How to Let Go of the World," one of my favorite poems about climate change. The very title is phrased less as a question and more as a guide—a how-to manual for accepting the lowliness of our existence and its brevity and the way loss acts as its condition of possibility. It conjures explicitly the ways in which the specter of the police, whose militarization and expansion over the past several decades have increased wariness of them, especially among Black and other minority peoples, can conjure a visceral feeling of alarm, maybe even terror, before it reveals that what lies beyond this feeling is a much larger, and perhaps not unrelated, threat: "One evening, I turned a corner and panicked at a sudden flash in my rearview, teeth chattering into my highest throat. Every nerve prepared for the acrid drip of cop talk until I realized: it was no cruiser. It was the sky. The sky, shocked with dying."

The poem goes on to record the thoughts of the speaker, whose first lover seems to have committed suicide and who watches a documentary about climate change, making her ponder the subject more and more as she goes about her daily living. Everything reminds her of dying reefs, of dying skies, of dying in general. By the end, she embraces the dying and all the things she doesn't have. The final stanza is so extraordinary, I want to reproduce it in full here:

> In lieu of proximity to firefighters; in lieu of the ability to speak the airless language of ghosts; or to reverse the logic of molecules; or to force Exxon to call the hurricane by its rightful name; or to convince my friends not to launch themselves from the rooftops of every false promise made by every rotten idol; in lieu of all I can't do or undo; I hold. The faces of the trees in my hands. I miss them. And miss and miss them. Until I fly out of grief's arms, and the sky. Catches me in its thousand orange hands. It catches me, and I stay there. Suspended against the unrelenting orange. I stay there splayed, and dying. And shocking the siren sky.[13]

A few key images stand out for me: "I hold," with its pronounced subject and active verb, conjures for me an assertion of human agency; "catches," which is the response of the sky itself, and perhaps of the atmosphere and the climate, refigures what has been something threatening throughout the poem into something reassuring; and "I stay" feels like a promise not to give up despite what is here and what might be coming.

Nothing about this passage is easy or even necessarily comforting. It doesn't try to inspire the reader or cheerlead action. Instead, it encourages engagement with the difficulty of the moment we're in. It asks us to treat the present as something we have to work hard to make sense of. Our feelings of concern or anxiety or even terror are not something to apologize for, or feel ashamed about, or pretend don't exist. They are understandable responses to a present that is full of reasons to feel these difficult emotions. As hard as it is to stay with them, they nevertheless can signal that we have not turned away from the problems associated with climate change or our obligation to face these problems as head-on as we can muster. These emotions speak that we are still here and that we, too, refuse to give up. We hold. We are caught. We stay.

In many ways, we are in the middle of the story. What this means is that whatever might seem inevitable about our present to those living several decades in the future just doesn't seem inevitable to us now. I really do believe that any-thing can happen, and one of the things holding us back from engaging with the many challenges associated with climate change *and* racism is the limita-tions of our own imagination. We just can't imagine how bad things can get (maybe our worst-case scenarios aren't bad enough?), and we can't convince ourselves that we can make better worlds—and not just better worlds, but stupendously, wildly, deliriously better worlds. It's intense to try to open up the horizons of our imagination in this way, to see the range of what's possi-ble as occupying such extremes. It's so much safer, and easier, to assume some middle ground, and to live on with an impoverished imagination.

I understand our duty, as members of a society, as a responsibility to hew to the more difficult path and insist on occupying a present of terrifying pos-sibilities for what the future holds for us. Our worst-case scenarios need to be more terrifying and our best-case scenarios more utopic, and we shouldn't think there is some safe middle of greatest likelihood. Anything is possible. A lot of radically different pathways radiate from the present with equal plausibility.

In order to imagine such possibilities, we also need to think about how race affects whatever responses there may be to the environmental challenges facing all of us. And we must also think hard about the ways in which the worsening effects of climate change will exacerbate present-day racisms with potentially cascading political consequences. In short, there is no way—no way—to imagine the kind of best-case scenarios surrounding climate change that we need to imagine into being without also imagining greater racial equal-ity and justice.

These thoughts beg the question of what terrifies us more: the worst-case scenarios or the idea of making the world better? The latter, after all, will re-quire more of us while the former only needs us to continue on as we are.

These aren't the thoughts that are on my mind as Grace and I make our way home (I came to them slowly and over a much longer period of time), but some fragments of the poems I had just referenced must surely pulse in my mind, adding something to the swing of our steps. We are silent now, in the comfortable way that long togetherness allows, walking up some resi-dential streets that bend and curve, every yard heavy with flowers and the air heavy with moisture. This path leads us back out to the main street. Just as we cross it, the vigil has caught up to us. It has turned into a march, and the leaders are many yards away. Because we are uphill from them, we can see a lot of the crowd moving toward us on a wide, straight boulevard. There is one young person, African American, with a bullhorn, in the front, but even without it I think I could still hear her voice, as loud and impassioned as it is, as she leads the people in a familiar chant. She seems tireless.

We pause to take in the enormity of the crowd. It stretches to the horizon. And then we wait respectfully as it moves past us.[14] The parade of people marches on and on. Their chants are loud. They are mostly young, although there are some who are our age and older. They seem diverse for our town but similar to the many people around the country and the world who walk alongside them. White and Black, but some Asians mixed in. I can't tell if there are other racial groups; I assume they're there. Most are wearing masks. Many are in black, as if in mourning. There is no end to the parade. It's not clear where they are going or when they will stop marching.

ACKNOWLEDGMENTS

LeiLani Nishime probably doesn't know it, but she played a major role in the writing of this book. For years, I had wanted to write about climate change and literature from a race and ethnic studies perspective. The book seemed necessary and urgent, and yet I was stalled. I kept dragging my feet and feeling doubtful about my ability to give shape to my ideas. I even wrote a different book! I was still trying to find my way into the subject when LeiLani came along and asked me to contribute to a volume she was co-editing with Kim Hester Williams. LeiLani was patient, encouraging, and, well, persistent, in all the right amounts, and eventually succeeded in eroding whatever was preventing me from writing about the subject.

The essay I wrote for her was the first articulation of what I call in this book *climate lyricism*, and some of it has found its way into these pages, albeit greatly transformed. Just before the publication of their edited collection, LeiLani and Kim invited me to participate in a conference on race and ecology at the University of Washington, and this event gave me further occasion to develop these ideas alongside some very brilliant people. For their many encouragements, I thank both LeiLani and Kim heartily—and LeiLani especially.

At the University of Washington conference, I tried out a piece that I was working on for the Smithsonian Asian Pacific American Center, which had invited me to take part in its first-ever Asian American Literature Festival. I thank Lawrence-Minh Buí Davis for the invitation to participate in this festival, and for the opportunity to develop my thinking on climate change and literature further. The piece I wrote for this event eventually appeared in the *Massachusetts Review*, where I benefited from Emily Wojcik's careful editing. I also thank Patty Chu for her eloquent response to my talk, which has since become available on the Smithsonian Asian Pacific American Center website.

I want to thank several other people who gave me more opportunities to test the ideas in this book. These were all important occasions for me, as they remind me of the community I write with and for. Early on, during my stalled phase, Kathy Knapp invited me to share some preliminary thoughts about ruin and photography at the University of Connecticut. I don't know if the talk was any good, and I ended up abandoning that essay, but it got me flowing in the right direction—and I greatly appreciated all the encouragement I received from a warm and receptive audience. Sarah Wald, who is a groundbreaking scholar in the burgeoning study of Asian American literature and the environment, included me in a thought-provoking panel at the ASLE conference in Detroit alongside the so, so smart Julie Minich, Priscilla Ybarra, and Jina Kim. J. D. Schnepf and David Alworth included me in a roundtable discussion on the novel and the environment at the Mahindra Humanities Center, which prompted me to develop some early thoughts about Richard Powers's *The Overstory*. My chapter on climate fiction probably wouldn't exist if not for that occasion. Takeo Rivera, Joseph Revek, and Theo Davis invited me to present part of the introduction of this book at their seminar, also at the Mahindra, and Josh Williams gave me a rigorous response. This event got me to think very hard about why attention matters to me so much. Floyd Cheung and Richard Millington asked me to speak to a class at Smith College, where I was able to test out my ideas further with a group of very smart undergraduates (some of the toughest interlocutors I faced). Corey Byrnes of the Comparative Literary Studies Program at Northwestern hosted me for a virtual talk that gave me more confidence in the final form my introduction had taken.

There are a lot of other people I want to thank. Rajini Srikanth has been a coeditor of many projects on Asian American literature and a much-valued intellectual collaborator for many decades. She even coedited the volume in which my very first piece of scholarly writing appeared in print. Rajini has always modeled for me what it means to do engaged intellectual work. Jim Lee has long been a close friend and colleague, and I am grateful for his steadfast intellectual provocations. Pat Chu has also been another close friend and intellectual provocateur, who never ceases to keep me on my toes. Viet Nguyen and I had an invigorating conversation just as I was sitting down to write the first draft of this book, and it gave me courage to say the things I wanted to say. Joe Jeon read through a draft of one of the chapters and steered me away from making some egregious errors. Anna Kornbluh read the introduction and offered important substantive feedback.

I also want to give a shout out to the following people for their intellectual companionship, thought-provoking conversations, and all-around inspirational selves: Patricia Stuelke, Ignacio Sánchez Prado, Lee Konstantinou, Andrew Hoberek, Anita Mannur, Cathy Schlund-Vials, Michelle Chihara, Leif Sorenson, Sheila Liming, Sheri Harrison, Sangeeta Ray, Angela Allan, Aimee Bahng, Heather Houser, Jeff Santa Ana, Yogita Goyal, and Gordon Hutner.

I want to say an extra-special thank you to Grace Sunghae Kim for her constant companionship and love. I feel so grateful to share my life with her, and to share in the wonder of watching our children Yohan and Yuri mature into such admirable human beings.

I've been incredibly fortunate to work with Courtney Berger, whose expert and steady editorial supervision has guided all three of my books into print, including this one. I am deeply grateful to her and to everyone else I've been lucky enough to work with at Duke University Press—including Sandra Korn, who readied the book for production; Lisa Lawley, the project editor; and Kimberly Miller, the copyeditor. I am also grateful to the two anonymous readers, whose rigorous input forced me to revise my manuscript substantially and state more explicitly the intervention I am offering. And I want to make sure to thank Sarah Osment, who created the index. All the mistakes in this book are my own.

Parts of chapter 1 and chapter 2 appeared—in an earlier form—under the title "The Artful Things of Climate Change," in LeiLani Nishime and Kim D. Hester Williams's edited volume *Racial Ecologies* (University of Washington Press, 2018), and the epilogue borrows from "Asian American Literature in the Twenty-First Century," published in the *Massachusetts Review* 59, no. 4 (December 2018): 770–73. In chapter 3, I used a couple of paragraphs from a short piece I wrote for the *Washington Post*, "What Venice and Its Floods Taught Me about Responding to Climate Change" (November 14, 2019).

As I was waiting to hear back from Duke University Press about the fate of this book, one of my oldest and closest friends, James A. Wu, passed away from a heart attack as he was delivering the mail. He and I have known each other since the start of graduate school and were roommates for several years. We helped each other through many difficult times over many decades, such as when he left graduate school and struggled for years to figure out what to do with the rest of his life—and when he kept me company one Christmas holiday in New York City, when I was feeling especially down, and watched all of the television adaptation of *Dune* with me in a marathon exercise in escapism. James had an infectious laugh, an encyclopedic knowledge of novels, films, and comic books, and was all around one of the most unique people it's been my privilege to know. He found great meaning working as a mail carrier and was very angry about the inhumane austerity the federal government has inflicted on this vital public service. I wonder if he'd still be alive if the post office weren't so caught up in a regime of ever-greater efficiency and work speedups. James is dearly missed.

I also want to add that I learned about James's death while I was visiting my parents in the midst of the pandemic. My mother has advanced dementia (she was later diagnosed as having both Parkinson's and Alzheimer's), and on that occasion she was going through a very difficult time. Her condition has stabilized somewhat; she has regained a lot of physical mobility, thanks to my father's tireless care and some very powerful drugs, but her mental faculties continue to decline as I write these words. Being with her is like being with someone who is in a perpetual dream state, within which she gets continually more lost.

I share these deeply personal details about my life because, as I grow older, I am more keenly aware of my own fragility as a living being. I think not only about my own mortality but about that of other close friends, in addition to James, who have passed away when they still had so much to look forward to: the brilliant scholar Yoonmee Chang, for example, and Sonya Lee (who died decades ago but whose presence still remains fresh in my mind). I also think about those who, through circumstance—and carelessness on my part—I've lost touch with. And I think of the many whom I don't know but whose struggles and deaths nevertheless weigh heavily on my mind. Loss always has a context, and the grief I experience is shared by so many, many others.

In the introduction, I speak of subjects who are constituted by loss, and I often find myself thinking about what it means to let loss into the very ways in which we define ourselves. What if absence is the very stuff that makes us who we are?

INTRODUCTION

1 See the documentary *American Revolutionary: The Evolution of Grace Lee Boggs*,
   directed by Grace Lee (2013), in which Boggs makes this point emphatically
   during one of her interviews. Boggs contributes to a similar point in J. Boggs
   et al., *Conversations in Maine*, 306. They write, "A philosophy is not some sort of
   abstraction that one discovers like a crocodile as one is going up the Nile. It is the
   culmination of experiences and thoughts about those experiences." For more about
   Boggs herself and the extraordinary life she led, see G. Boggs, *Living for Change*;
   and G. Boggs and Kurashige, *Next American Revolution*.
2 H. Nguyen, *Red Juice*, 101.
3 Hong, *Minor Feelings*, 103.
4 Hong, *Minor Feelings*, 196–97.
5 Ngai, *Our Aesthetic Categories*, 18.
6 Kolbert, *Field Notes from a Catastrophe*, 2–3.
7 An interesting companion to Kolbert's book is Richard Primark's *Walden Warming: Climate Change Comes to Thoreau's Woods*, in which the author, after doing
   fieldwork in Borneo, comes home to the Boston area, where he is employed and
   grew up, to look for signals of climate change and finds them in the detailed notes
   Henry David Thoreau left behind in his notebooks.
8 Chuh, *Difference Aesthetics Makes*, 3.
9 Kapadia, *Insurgent Aesthetics*, 10.
10 For more discussion of "conviviality," see Gilroy, *Postcolonial Melancholia*, 121–52.
11 Sze, *Environmental Justice*, 77.
12 M. Chen, *Animacies*, 234.
13 Saranillio, *Unsustainable Empire*, 21.
14 Chuh, *Difference Aesthetics Makes*, 3–4.
15 Bahng, *Migrant Futures*, 170.
16 Nishime and Williams, "Introduction," 4.

17 Harney and Moten, *Undercommons*, 28.

18 Halberstam, "Wild Beyond," 4.

19 Kaba, *We Do This 'Til We Free Us*, 3.

20 Song, "New Materialism," 52, 53. In that article I used the term *new materialism* in the singular because I thought of it as being highly organized around a response to the cultural turn, but I have since decided—following the lead of others—that the response moves in many different directions and is therefore so heterogeneous that it is more accurate to use the plural.

21 Coole and Frost, "Introducing the New Materialisms," 3.

22 See Haraway, *Staying with the Trouble*; Latour, "Networks, Societies, Spheres"; Bennett, *Vibrant Matter*; Morton, *Hyperobjects*; and Alaimo, *Exposed*.

23 Ghosh, *Great Derangement*, 3.

24 There has been a lot of interest in the Little Ice Age in recent years. See, for instance, Mann, *1493*, 38–47. In Ghosh's novel, a speaker at a conference Deen attends focuses on the Little Ice Age and its destructive consequences. See Ghosh, *Gun Island*, 134.

25 Ghosh, *Gun Island*, 237.

26 Ghosh, *Gun Island*, 237.

27 Thoreau, *Walden*, 96.

28 It's not entirely accurate to say that the scholars I've named so far would agree with my summary of new-materialist ways of thinking as expressed by Cinta, for several of them maintain deep skepticism that such a risveglio is even possible, while others are not at all concerned with epistemology, which I'm using here to refer to the question of how one knows what one knows. Indeed, as a group, they seem more interested in ontology, or the focus on being. As Ian Baucom explains, "While the questions the interdisciplinary humanities have been asking have been fundamentally epistemological or representational, the questions the life sciences are now forcing are fundamentally ontological, questions of the nature of being, questions above all, of the nature of *human being* as a particular form of life among other forms of life." Baucom, "Human Shore," 6. Also, see Sonya Posmentier's response to this point when she insists "that black diasporic writers have been theorizing the 'nature of being' for some time." Posmentier, *Cultivation and Catastrophe*, 266. Nevertheless, implicit in these arguments is the sense that a proper way to perceive the world exists. They favor an onto-epistemology that requires a shrinking of the human's role in it and an understanding of the human as deeply imbricated in its stitching rather than as somehow self-woven and apart.

29 Houser, *Ecosickness*, 18.

30 Giraud, *What Comes after Entanglement?*, 2.

31 Houser, *Ecosickness*, 18.

32 Kornbluh, *Order of Forms*, 2.

33 Powers, *Overstory*, 454.

34 Powers, *Overstory*, 460.

35 Powers, *Overstory*, 466.

36 Kornbluh, *Order of Forms*, 156.

37 O'Hara, "Having a Coke with You," in *Collected Poems*, 360. See Glavey, "Having a Coke with You." This article helped me to think more concretely about my use of the second person and its connection to the lyric—particularly, the way the lyric lends itself to a desire to share with others the extraordinary aesthetic objects I've come across.

CHAPTER ONE. WHAT IS DENIAL?

Parts of this chapter appeared under the title "The Artful Things of Climate Change," in LeiLani Nishime and Kim D. Hester Williams's edited volume *Racial Ecologies* (University of Washington Press, 2018).

1 Ishiguro, *Never Let Me Go*, 13.
2 Ishiguro, *Never Let Me Go*, 287.
3 For instance, 2010 witnessed the publication of Naomi Oreskes and Timothy Conway's *Merchants of Doubt: How a Handful of Scientists Obscured the Truth on Issues from Tobacco Smoking to Global Warming*, a landmark study that focused attention on the deliberate corporate-funded spread of falsehoods about climate change that built on past misinformation campaigns.
4 Cohen, *States of Denial*, 7.
5 Cohen, *States of Denial*, 7.
6 Ishiguro, *Never Let Me Go*, 175; emphasis in original.
7 I'm describing the news report about the 2018 Hurricane Michael published in the *New York Times*. Richard Fausset, Patricia Mazzaei, and Alan Blinder, "Storm Charges North, Leaving Destruction in Florida," *New York Times*, October 10, 2018, https://www.nytimes.com/2018/10/10/us/hurricane-michael-live-updates -florida.html.
8 Ishiguro, *Never Let Me Go*, 81.
9 Cohen, *States of Denial*, 8.
10 Jacquelyn Ardam, "*Never Let Me Go* and the Human Condition," *Avidly*, October 9, 2017, http://avidly.lareviewofbooks.org/2017/10/09/never-let-me-go-and -the-human-condition/.
11 Ardam, "*Never Let Me Go*."
12 For more discussion of allegory, see Teskey, *Allegory and Violence*; and Quilligan, *Language of Allegory*. I am also drawing directly from my own writing about allegory in Song, *Children of 1965*, 152–78.
13 Ishiguro, *Never Let Me Go*, 40.
14 Norgaard, *Living in Denial*, 12. Also see chapter 3, where Norgaard systematically critiques attention deficit explanations for inaction and explains why she prefers sociological approaches that emphasize an informal but powerful organization of emotions.
15 Norgaard, *Living in Denial*, 12, 4.
16 Norgaard, *Living in Denial*, 93.
17 Cohen, *States of Denial*, 24; emphasis in the original.
18 Sturken, "Absent Images of Memory," 692. Sturken ends this essay with a discussion of the extraordinary film *Bad Day at Black Rock*, directed by John Sturgess

(1955), which focuses on a visit by a white veteran (played by Spencer Tracy) to a small western town in search of the father of a Japanese American soldier who died saving his life. He finds only hostility and eventually the truth: the father had been murdered by the townsfolk for the land he had been renting, where he had somehow made water flow. While explicitly a film about the legacies of mass incarceration and anti-Japanese sentiments during wartime in the United States, the film features an all-white cast.

19 Simpson, *Absent Presence*, 3.

20 Saranillio, *Unsustainable Empire*, 134.

21 T. Yamamoto, *Masking Selves, Making Subjects*, 103. Also, see Sone, *Nisei Daughter*; and H. Yamamoto, *Seventeen Syllables*.

22 Cole, *Open City*, 235.

23 Cole, *Open City*, 59.

24 Cole, *Open City*, 223.

25 Sohn, *Racial Asymmetries*, 138.

26 The criticism about the novel centers primarily on its critique of cosmopolitanism. See, for instance, Vermeulen, "Flights of Memory"; and Hallemeier, "Literary Cosmopolitanism." See also James Wood, "The Arrival of Enigmas: Teju Cole's Prismatic Début Novel *Open City*," *New Yorker*, February 29, 2011, https://www .newyorker.com/magazine/2011/02/28/the-arrival-of-enigmas. Cole describes Wood's review of his novel as crucial to its wide circulation and attention (personal communication, February 21, 2013). Notably, none of this criticism addresses the novel's references to climate change or its careful attention to the weather.

27 Cole, *Open City*, 67.

28 Cole, *Open City*, 245.

29 Cole, *Open City*, 28.

30 Hansen, Sato, and Reudy, "Perception of Climate Change," E2415.

31 Cole, *Open City*, 28.

32 Hansen, Sato, and Reudy, "Perception of Climate Change," E2415.

33 Cole, *Open City*, 28.

34 Cole, *Open City*, 28.

35 Chun, "On Hypo-real Models," 681. Aaron Hanlon makes a similar point in a *Washington Post* article, which generated a great deal of controversy, when he writes, "Scientism is the untenable extension of scientific authority into realms of knowledge that lie outside the scope of what science can justifiably determine." See Aaron Hanlon, "How Blind Reverence for Science Obscures Real Problems," *Washington Post*, January 28, 2019, https://www.washingtonpost.com/outlook /2019/01/28/how-blind-reverence-science-obscures-real-problems.

36 U.S. Global Change Research Program, *Impacts, Risks, and Adaptations*, 41.

37 Jason Plautz, "Watch James Inhofe Throw a Snowball on the Senate Floor," *National Journal*, February 26, 2015, http://www.nationaljournal.com/energy/watch -jim-inhofe-throw-a-snowball-on-the-senate-floor-20150226.

38 Cole, *Open City*, 198.

39 Cole, *Open City*, 149–50.

40 Cole, *Open City*, 258.

41 Cole, *Open City*, 259.

42 Chun, "On Hypo-real Models," 679.

43 Ishiguro, *Never Let Me Go*, 77.

44 Mao, *Oculus*, 9–10.

CHAPTER TWO. WHY REVIVE THE LYRIC?

Parts of this chapter appeared under the title "The Artful Things of Climate Change," in LeiLani Nishime and Kim D. Hester Williams's edited volume *Racial Ecologies* (University of Washington Press, 2018).

1 Chu, *Do Metaphors Dream*, 13–14.

2 Chu, *Do Metaphors Dream*, 14.

3 Chu, *Do Metaphors Dream*, 14. Examples of science-fictional poetry include Margaret Rhee's *Love, Robot*, Franny Choi's *Soft Science*, and Brenda Shaughnessy's *The Octopus Museum*. Interestingly, all three of these examples are by Asian American women.

4 W. Hunter, *Forms of the World*, 52.

5 V. Jackson, "Who Reads Poetry?," 183.

6 V. Jackson and Prins, "General Introduction," 7.

7 Kaveh Akbar, Twitter @KavehAkbar, March 17, 2019, https://twitter.com/KavehAkbar/status/1107479721669849088. Account, along with the tweet, since deleted.

8 H. Nguyen, *Red Juice*, 101.

9 Epstein, *Attention Equals Life*, 183.

10 Ronda, *Remainders*, 6.

11 Posmentier, *Cultivation and Catastrophe*, 4.

12 Park, *Apparitions of Asia*, 130.

13 Rankine, *Don't Let Me Be Lonely*; and Rankine, *Citizen*.

14 White, *Lyric Shame*, 7.

15 Adam Kirsch, "Over Easy," *New Republic*, October 29, 2001, https://newrepublic.com/article/92146/billy-collins-review-over-easy. Epstein quotes Kirsch, equating this phrase with the lyrical. See Epstein, *Attention Equals Life*, 2.

16 Johnson, *Idea of Lyric*, 72–73.

17 Lerner, *Hatred of Poetry*, 38, 39.

18 Lerner, *Hatred of Poetry*, 42.

19 Edward Clifford, "(Not Quite) 20 Questions for Ilya Kaminsky," *Massachusetts Review*, May 21, 2018, https://www.massreview.org/node/6577.

20 Javadizadeh, "Atlantic Ocean," 477.

21 Lerner, *Hatred of Poetry*, 67.

22 Rankine, *Citizen*, 18.

23 Lerner, *Hatred of Poetry*, 68.

24 See especially Sue et al., "Racial Microaggressions in Everyday Life."

25 For further discussion about the cultural significance of the cute as an aesthetic category, see Ngai, *Our Aesthetic Categories*.

26 Rankine, *Citizen*,154.

27 Sharpe, *In the Wake*, 104.

28 Kate Marshall, "The Readers of the Future Have Become Shitty Literary Critics,"
    b20: The Online Community of the *Boundary 2* Editorial Collective, February 26,
    2018, https://www.boundary2.org/2018/02/kate-marshall-the-readers-of-the
    -future-have-become-shitty-literary-critics/.

29 Bennett, *Influx and Efflux*, 116.

30 Bennett, *Influx and Efflux*, 21.

31 Chakrabarty, "Postcolonial Studies," 14.

32 Lowe, *Intimacies of Four Continents*, 3.

33 Yusoff, *Billion Black Anthropocenes*, 67–68.

34 Ray, *Ecological Other*, 184.

35 Wynter, "Unsettling the Coloniality," 262, 329.

36 Weheliye, *Habeas Viscus*, 2. He is also skeptical about the "lexicon of resistance and
    agency." As he explains on the same page as the quotation in the text: "As modes
    of analyzing and imagining the practices of the oppressed in the face of extreme
    violence—although this is also applicable more broadly—resistance and agency as-
    sume full, self-present, and coherent subjects working against something or some-
    one." In many ways, Weheliye's yoking of agency with resistance reminds me how
    much my own investment in agency stems from the emphasis on resistance that
    scholars like Stuart Hall, Raymond Williams, and others working within a broadly
    defined cultural studies field once championed. While these scholars could often
    overfind resistance in every text they happened to be examining, I share with them
    a broad commitment to dramatic and beneficial social change through collective
    action.

37 Z. Jackson, *Becoming Human*, 21.

38 See Berlant, "Big Man." Berlant expanded the idea of "genre flailing" in a subse-
    quent publication. See Berlant, "Genre Flailing."

39 Patricia Stuelke, "Horror and the Arts of Feminist Assembly," *Post45: Contempo-
    raries*, April 4, 2019, https://post45.org/2019/04/horror-and-the-arts-of-feminist
    -assembly/.

40 Rankine, *Citizen*, 156.

41 Craig Santos Perez, "Love Poems in the Time of Climate Change," *New Republic*,
    March 3, 2017, https://newrepublic.com/article/140282/love-poems-time-climate
    -change.

42 Culler, *Theory of the Lyric*, 4. Caroline Levine works in a similar vein when she
    associates forms with institutions and then argues that institutions exist in hetero-
    geneous temporalities that resist discrete periodization. See Levine, *Forms*, 60.

43 Ali, *Veiled Suite*. See also D. Ward, "Space of Poetry."

44 Culler, *Theory of the Lyric*, 89.

45 Culler, *Theory of the Lyric*, 89.

46 Culler, *Theory of the Lyric*, 242.

47 Bishop, "Roosters," 36.

48 O'Hara, *Collected Poems*, 306.

49 Parker, *There Are More Beautiful Things*, 15.

50 Haraway, *Staying with the Trouble*, 1.

51 Culler, *Theory of the Lyric*, 287–88.

52 C. Perez, *Habitat Threshold*, 26.

53 Edelman, *No Future*, 3.

54 C. Perez, *Habitat Threshold*, 11.

55 Houser, *Ecosickness*, 11.

56 Ian Frazier, "The Toll: Sandy and the Future," *New Yorker*, February 11 and 18, 2013, https://www.newyorker.com/magazine/2013/02/11/the-toll.

57 Ishiguro, *Never Let Me Go*, 287–88.

58 Pollan, *Omnivore's Dilemma*, 37, 56.

CHAPTER THREE. WHY STAY WITH BAD FEELINGS?

Parts of this chapter borrow from a short piece written for the *Washington Post*: "What Venice and Its Floods Taught Me about Responding to Climate Change" (November 14, 2019).

1 I think, for the most part, I was right that I would not have been heartily welcomed in poetry circles. They have been and continue to be dominated by white authors and white audiences at readings. For more discussion of these racial dynamics, see Juliana Spahr and Stephanie Young, "The Program Era and the Mainly White Room," *Los Angeles Review of Books*, September 15, 2015, https://lareviewofbooks.org/article/the-program-era-and-the-mainly-white-room/.

2 Stevens, *Collected Poems and Poetry*, 306; and Culler, *Theory of the Lyric*, 184.

3 See Mann, *1493*, 53. For a discussion on race and discourses of invasive species, see Cardozo and Subramaniam, "Assembling Asian/American Naturecultures."

4 Kaminsky, *Deaf Republic*, 71.

5 Kaminsky, *Deaf Republic*, 40.

6 Kaminsky, *Deaf Republic*, 33.

7 Kaminsky, *Deaf Republic*, 43.

8 Kaminsky, *Deaf Republic*, 47.

9 Kaminsky, *Deaf Republic*, 55.

10 M. Chen, *Animacies*, 29.

11 M. Chen, *Animacies*, 30.

12 Kaminsky, "Notes," *Deaf Republic*, n.p.

13 Kaminsky, *Deaf Republic*, 3.

14 Kaminsky, *Deaf Republic*, 75.

15 Kaminsky, *Deaf Republic*, 76.

16 Associated Press of Milan, "Three Quarters of Venice Flooded by Exceptional High Tide," *Guardian*, October 29, 2018, https://www.theguardian.com/world/2018/oct/29/venice-experiences-worst-flooding-since-2008.

17 See the video at @WeDontHaveTime, "Life goes on in Venice. Even at high water. But, for how long?," Twitter, October 30, 2018, 12:56 a.m., https://twitter.com/WeDontHaveTime0/status/1057149157423661056.

18　This account of the flooding in Venice borrows from a piece I wrote elsewhere. See Min Hyoung Song, "What Venice and Its Floods Taught Me about Responding to Climate Change," *Washington Post*, November 14, 2019, https://www-washingtonpost-com.proxy.bc.edu/outlook/2019/11/14/what-venice-its-floods-taught-me-about-responding-climate-change/.

19　Seymour, *Bad Environmentalism*, 14, 17.

20　Pico, *IRL*, 34.

21　Pico, *IRL*, 38.

22　Pico, *IRL*, 38.

23　Lefebvre, *Critique of the Everyday*, 118.

24　Rancière, *Politics of Aesthetics*, 12.

25　Stewart, "Afterword," 339, 340.

26　Ju Yon Kim, *Racial Mundane*, 33.

27　Ahmed, *Promise of Happiness*, 87.

28　Seymour, *Bad Environmentalism*, 230.

29　Rush, *Rising*, 5.

30　Rush, *Rising*, 6.

CHAPTER FOUR. HOW SHOULD I LIVE?

1　For instance, even when voters signaled how important the topic was to them during the 2019–20 presidential primaries, the Democratic National Convention refused to sponsor a debate devoted to the topic, and it was rarely asked about in the many debates the convention did sponsor—and in at least one was not mentioned even once. The topic figured more largely during the presidential debates, but it's not clear at the time of writing if it will continue to remain prominent in future debates or if any tangible policies will emerge.

2　See *Godzilla: King of the Monsters*, directed by Michael Dougherty, and *A Star Is Born*, directed by Bradley Cooper.

3　LeMenager, *Living Oil*, 6.

4　Wynes and Nicholas, "Climate Mitigation Gap."

5　See David Wallace-Wells, "The Uninhabitable Planet," *New York Magazine*, July 10, 2017, http://nymag.com/intelligencer/2017/07/climate-change-earth-too-hot-for-humans.html. This article preceded the full-length book that Wallace-Wells eventually published with the same title, which I quote from in this chapter and later in the book.

6　Ray, *Field Guide to Climate Anxiety*, 86.

7　Quoted in Rich, *Losing Earth*, 130.

8　Rich, *Losing Earth*, 181.

9　Wallace-Wells, *Uninhabitable Earth*, 149.

10　Tsing et al., *Arts of Living*, G1.

11　Robinson, *Forty Signs of Rain*, 268.

12　Aronoff et al., *Planet to Win*, 3.

13　Marez, *Farm Worker Futurism*, 11.

14 Fisher, *Capitalist Realism*, 2. Also see La Berge and Shonkwiler, *Reading Capitalist Realism*; and Kornbluh, "Climate Realism."

15 Epstein, *Attention Equals Life*, 30.

16 See, for example, Claire Parker, "Swedish Climate Activist Greta Thunberg Is Sailing to America amid a Storm of Online Attacks," *Washington Post*, August 15, 2019, https://www.washingtonpost.com/world/2019/08/15/swedish-climate-activist -greta-thunberg-is-sailing-america-amid-storm-criticism/.

17 See the website No Fly Climate Sci, accessed August 31, 2019, https:// noflyclimatesci.org/.

18 Both were doctoral students in the English Department at Stony Brook University, attending the 2017 annual meeting of the Association for the Study of Literature and the Environment. Names mentioned here with permission.

19 Epstein, *Attention Equals Life*, 155.

20 Benjamin, *Arcades Project*, 422.

21 Puar, *Right to Maim*, 12.

22 Clifton, "Won't You Celebrate with Me." I thank my colleague Rhonda Fredericks for sharing this poem with me.

23 Bennett, *Vibrant Matter*, 122.

CHAPTER FIVE. WHAT'S WRONG WITH NARRATIVE?

1 Rodge Glass, "Global Warming: The Rise of Cli-Fi," *Guardian*, May 31, 2013, https://www.theguardian.com/books/2013/may/31/global-warning-rise-cli-fi.

2 Houser, *Infowhelm*, 15.

3 Powers, *Overstory*, 31.

4 Powers, *Overstory*, 16.

5 Forster, *Aspects of the Novel*, 86.

6 Powers, *Overstory*, 18.

7 Powers, *Overstory*, 113.

8 Wallace-Wells, *Uninhabitable Planet*, 149.

9 Ghosh, *Great Derangement*, 24.

10 Katie Dowd, "California Wildfire Smoke Has Now Made It All the Way to New York City," *SF Gate*, November 28, 2018, https://www.sfgate.com/california -wildfires/article/camp-fire-smoke-noaa-maps-nyc-texas-paradise-13408526.php. Also see Sanderson and Fisher, "Fiery Wake-Up Call."

11 Nixon, *Slow Violence*, 6.

12 Alaimo, *Exposed*, 3.

13 Singh, *Unthinking Mastery*, 10.

14 Tsing, *Mushroom at the End of the World*, 20.

15 Shotwell, *Against Purity*, 4.

16 Streeby, *Imagining the Future*, 5.

17 Houser, *Infowhelm*, 7.

18 Adam Trexler also offers a robust affirmation of climate fiction as a form that "can convey cultural narratives, create detailed speculation, incorporate diverse

points of views, and hold a multitude of things, from species to machines, places to weather systems." Trexler, *Anthropocene Fictions*, 27. In addition, see Mehnert, *Climate Change Fictions*, which similarly argues that climate fiction offers crucial insights to a discussion of climate change dominated by the natural sciences; Johns-Putra, *Climate Change*, which approaches the topic of climate fiction in a discussion with liberalism and narratives that focus on reproduction; Menely and Taylor, *Anthropocene Reading*, for thoughtful readings of literary texts that focus on different aspects of climate change that cut across literary periods; J. Pérez and Aycock, *Climate and Literature*, which collects essays that cut across even larger swaths of literary periods and work with different language traditions, especially Spanish; and Marshall, "What Are the Novels," for a discussion of the use of the Anthropocene to characterize recent novels that focus on climate change and related environmental issues. Also, some preliminary empirical studies suggest that reading climate fiction can have an impact on readers' perception of climate change. See Schneider-Mayerson, "Influence of Climate Fiction."

19 Houser, *Infowhelm*, 104.

20 Houser, *Infowhelm*, 127.

21 Dimaline, *Marrow Thieves*, 89.

22 Lowe, *Intimacies of Four Continents*, 41.

23 Ybarra, *Writing the Good Life*, 7.

24 V. Nguyen, *Nothing Ever Dies*, 4.

25 Jemisin, *Stone Sky*, 334.

26 Robinson, *New York 2140*, 604.

27 Sudbanthad, *Bangkok Wakes to Rain*, 273.

28 For a general audience, one of the earliest and still compelling articles on ocean acidification is Elizabeth Kolbert's "The Darkening Sea," *New Yorker*, November 12, 2006, https://www.newyorker.com/magazine/2006/11/20/the-darkening-sea.

29 Alaimo, *Exposed*, 168.

30 Chiang, *Lifecycle of Software Objects*, 99.

31 VanderMeer, *Acceptance*, 338.

32 Walker, *Age of Miracles*, 269.

33 Powers, *Overstory*, 97.

34 Fagan, *Sunlight Pilgrims*, 272.

35 Offill, *Weather*, 30–31.

36 Offill, *Weather*, 203.

37 Ozeki, *Tale for the Time Being*, 60.

38 Shotwell, *Against Purity*, 113.

39 Robinson, *New York 2140*, 259.

40 Watkins, *Gold Fame Citrus*, 195.

41 See Song, *Children of 1965*, 179–96.

42 Yamashita, *Through the Arc*, 100.

43 Powers, *Overstory*, 454.

44 Powers, *Overstory*, 18.

45 Powers, *Overstory*, 466.

46 Powers, *Overstory*, 264.

47 Lukács, *Theory of the Novel*, 29.

48 Weisman, *World without Us*, 273. The book Weisman wrote next advocates for even stricter population control. See Weisman, *Countdown*.

CHAPTER SIX. WHERE ARE WE NOW?

1 Pam Thurschwell, "I Don't Think We Know We Are in This Song," *Los Angeles Review of Books*, January 20, 2016, https://lareviewofbooks.org/article/i-dont-think-we-know-we-are-in-this-song/.

2 Ramazani, *Poetry and Its Others*, 184.

3 Ramazani, *Poetry and Its Others*, 281.

4 Morton, *Hyperobjects*, 12. Morton is adamant that the term *climate change* should not replace *global warming*. See Morton, *Hyperobjects*, 7–9. I find the distinction unhelpful, especially as both terms serve specific uses: *climate change* names a phenomenon that is occurring as a result of anthropogenic *global warming*.

5 Clark, *Ecocriticism on the Edge*, 74.

6 Chakrabarty, "Climate of History," 197.

7 Dimock, "*Gilgamesh's* Planetary Turns," 131.

8 Woods, "Epistemic Things," 62.

9 Woods, "Epistemic Things," 63.

10 Woods, "Epistemic Things," 65.

11 Keller, *Recomposing Ecopoetics*, 53.

12 Roberson, *To See the Earth*, 128.

13 Nezhukumatathil, *Oceanic*, 22.

14 Farrier, *Anthropocene Poetics*, 16.

15 Mazzucchelli, *Asterios Polyp*, n.p.

16 Sharpe, *In the Wake*, 40.

17 Sharpe, *In the Wake*, 41.

18 Philip, *Zong!*, 194.

19 Philip, *Zong!*, 197.

20 Philip, *Zong!*, 199.

21 Philip, *Zong!*, 37.

22 Philip, *Zong!*, 173.

23 Posmentier, *Cultivation and Catastrophe*, 223.

24 Long Soldier, *Whereas*, 5.

25 Long Soldier, *Whereas*, 53.

26 L.-Y. Lee, *City in Which I Love You*, 86.

27 Pinsky, *Sounds of Poetry*, 3.

28 Attridge, *Poetic Rhythm*, 9; Culler, *Theory of the Lyric*, 153.

29 Attridge, *Poetic Rhythm*, 54–55.

30 Bowie and Mercury, "Under Pressure."

31 Attridge, *Poetic Rhythm*, 6, 9.

32 Ronda, *Remainders*, 1.

33 Wallace-Wells, *Uninhabitable Earth*, 4.

34 Bowie, *Next Day*.

35 Hungerford, "On the Period," 410. Also, see Hyde and Wasserman, "Contemporary."

36 Fukuyama, "End of History?"

37 See Jodi Kim, *Ends of Empire*.

38 For discussion of this concept of democratic substitutability, see Honig, *Antigone Interrupted*, 102.

CHAPTER SEVEN. THE SCALE OF THE EVERYDAY, PART I

1 Harris, "Charles David Keeling," 7868.

2 Gore, *Inconvenient Truth*, at 14:50.

3 Harris, "Charles David Keeling," 7868.

4 Weart, *Discovery of Global Warming*, 22.

5 See Pollan, *Omnivore's Dilemma*, 41–47; and Smil, *Enriching the Earth*.

6 Saranillio, *Unsustainable Empire*, 203. Also, see Doug Herman, "The Heart of the Hawaiian People's Arguments against the Telescope on Mauna Kea," *Smithsonian Magazine*, April 23, 2015, https://www.smithsonianmag.com/smithsonian -institution/heart-hawaiian-people-arguments-arguments-against-telescope -mauna-kea-180955057/.

7 Ronda, *Remainders*, 1.

8 Ngai, *Our Aesthetic Categories*, 97.

9 O'Hara, *Lunch Poems*, 1.

10 O'Hara, *Lunch Poems*, 15.

11 O'Hara, *Lunch Poems*, 30–31.

12 O'Hara, *Lunch Poems*, 31.

13 O'Hara, *Lunch Poems*, 58.

14 Bernes, *Work of Art*, 56.

15 Ngai, *Our Aesthetic Categories*, 3.

16 Ngai, *Our Aesthetic Categories*, 87.

17 O'Hara, *Lunch Poems*, 27.

18 O'Hara, *Lunch Poems*, 51.

19 O'Hara, *Lunch Poems*, 52.

20 Ngai, *Our Aesthetic Categories*, 183.

21 Ngai, *Our Aesthetic Categories*, 188.

22 Ngai, *Our Aesthetic Categories*, 196.

23 Thoreau, *Walden*, 99.

24 Epstein, *Attention Equals Life*, 161.

25 Mayer, *Midwinter Day*, 26.

26 Mayer, *Midwinter Day*, 29.

27 Mayer, *Midwinter Day*, 114–15.

28 Mayer, *Midwinter Day*, 116.

29 Mayer, *Midwinter Day*, 106.

30 Mayer, *Midwinter Day*, 118.
31 Mayer, *Midwinter Day*, 118.

CHAPTER EIGHT. THE SCALE OF THE EVERYDAY, PART 2

1 Burning a gallon of gasoline emits about five pounds of carbon dioxide. Figure cited in Kolbert, *Field Notes from a Catastrophe*, 133.
2 Margaret Ronda and Lindsay Turner, "Introduction: Poetry's Social Forms," *Post45: Contemporaries*, April 22, 2019, https://post45.org/2019/04/introduction-poetrys-social-forms/.
3 Limón, *Carrying*, 12.
4 Limón, *Carrying*, 12.
5 Elizabeth Bruenig, "Why Bother to Bear Children in a World Wracked by Climate Change?," *Washington Post*, October 12, 2018, https://www.washingtonpost.com/opinions/why-bother-to-bear-children-in-a-world-racked-by-climate-change/2018/10/12/bda4bf82-cd8a-11e8-a360-85875bacob1f_story.html.
6 Maggie Astor, "No Children because of Climate Change? Some People Are Considering It," *New York Times*, February 5, 2018, https://www.nytimes.com/2018/02/05/climate/climate-change-children.html.
7 Overall, *Why Have Children?*, 191.
8 Limón, *Carrying*, 13.
9 Limón, *Carrying*, 13.
10 Limón, *Carrying*, 49.
11 See Kolbert, *Sixth Extinction*.
12 Limón, *Carrying*, 70.
13 Limón, *Carrying*, 73.
14 Limón, *Carrying*, 77.
15 Limón, *Carrying*, 87.
16 Limón, *Bright Dead Things*, 82.
17 Limón, *Carrying*, 60.
18 Monica Youn, "Study of Two Figures (Pasiphaë/Sado)," *Poetry Foundation*, February 2019, https://www.poetryfoundation.org/poetrymagazine/poems/148962/study-of-two-figures-pasipha-sado.
19 Wang, *Thinking Its Presence*, 22.
20 Wang, *Thinking Its Presence*, 23.
21 Cathy Park Hong, "Delusions of Whiteness in the Avant-Garde," *Arcade: Literature, the Humanities, and the World*, November 2014, https://arcade.stanford.edu/content/delusions-whiteness-avant-garde. The essay originally appeared in the *Lana Turner Journal* in November 2014 but has since been taken down.
22 Rachel Greenwald Smith, "Fuck the Avant-Garde," *Post45: Contemporaries*, April 22, 2019, https://post45.org/2019/05/fuck-the-avant-garde/.
23 Yusoff, *Billion Black Anthropocenes*, xiii.
24 Pico discussed this in a joint podcast interview with the poet Morgan Parker. LARB AV, "Brooklyn's Loss Is LA's Gain: Morgan Parker and Tommy Pico," *Los*

Angeles Review of Books, April 5, 2019, https://lareviewofbooks.org/av/brooklyns
-loss-las-gain-morgan-parker-tommy-pico/.

25 Pico, *Nature Poem*, 1.

26 Pico, *Nature Poem*, 2.

27 Pico, *Nature Poem*, 50.

28 Pico, *Nature Poem*, 54.

29 Pico, *Nature Poem*, 56.

30 Pico, *Nature Poem*, 74.

31 Molly McHugh, "The Instagram Obsession with Flowers Is Killing Them," *Ringer*,
May 1, 2019, https://www.theringer.com/tech/2019/5/1/18524074/instagram
-obsession-with-flowers-is-killing-them.

32 Pico, *Nature Poem*, 67.

33 Arundhati Roy, "Literature Provides Shelter. That's Why We Need It," *Guardian*, May 13, 2019, https://www.theguardian.com/commentisfree/2019/may/13
/arundhati-roy-literature-shelter-pen-america.

34 Pico, *Nature Poem*, 40.

35 Kapadia, *Insurgent Aesthetics*, 8.

36 DOD *Dictionary of Military and Associated Terms*, updated January 2021. https://
www.jcs.mil/Portals/36/Documents/Doctrine/pubs/dictionary.pdf

37 Sharif, *Look*, 95.

38 Sharif, *Look*, 10.

39 Sharif, *Look*, 11.

40 Sharif, *Look*, 39.

41 Sharif, *Look*, 47.

42 Sharif, *Look*, 67.

43 Schnepf, "Domestic Aerial Photography," 284.

44 Ngai, *Our Aesthetic Categories*.

45 Sharif, *Look*, 93.

CHAPTER NINE. THE GLOBAL NOVEL IMAGINES THE AFTERLIFE

1 Wallace-Wells, *Uninhabitable Earth*, 4.

2 For discussion about how the very idea of the Anthropocene depends on thinking
with deep time, and especially a deep future, see Marshall, "What Are the Novels."

3 Harvey, *Brief History of Neoliberalism*, 1.

4 Tsing, *Mushroom at the End of the World*, 110.

5 Brouillette, "Post-colonial Authorship Revisited," 90.

6 Nasia Anam, "Introduction: Forms of the Global Anglophone," *Post45: Contemporaries*, February 22, 2019, https://post45.org/2019/02/introduction-forms-of-the
-global-anglophone/.

7 Brouillette, "Post-colonial Authorship Revisited," 82.

8 Roy Scranton, "Learning How to Die in the Anthropocene," *New York Times*, November 10, 2013, https://opinionator.blogs.nytimes.com/2013/11/10/learning-how
-to-die-in-the-anthropocene/. Scranton elaborated on these ideas in a short book,

Learning to Die in the Anthropocene: Reflections on the End of Civilization, and in a collection of essays titled *We're Doomed. Now What? Essays on War and Climate*.

9 Purdy, *After Nature*, 5.
10 Scranton, *We're Doomed*, 334.
11 Foucault, *History of Sexuality*, 138.
12 Mbembe, "Necropolitics," 39–40.
13 Singh, *Unthinking Mastery*, 10.
14 Cacho, *Social Death*, 99.
15 Puar, *Right to Maim*, 137.
16 Puar, *Right to Maim*, 148.
17 Saunders, *Lincoln in the Bardo*, 8–9.
18 Saunders, *Lincoln in the Bardo*, 203.
19 Saunders, *Lincoln in the Bardo*, 232.
20 Coetzee, *Elizabeth Costello*, 209.
21 Coetzee, *Elizabeth Costello*, 224–25.
22 Coetzee, *Elizabeth Costello*, 202–3.
23 Coetzee, *Elizabeth Costello*, 204.
24 Coetzee, *Elizabeth Costello*, 225.
25 Coetzee, *Elizabeth Costello*, 215.
26 Haraway, *Staying with the Trouble*, 97.
27 Han, *Human Acts*, 49.
28 Han, *Human Acts*, 56.
29 Parker, *Magical Negro*, 41.
30 Uribe, *Antígona González*, 33.
31 Uribe, *Antígona González*, 29.
32 Uribe, *Antígona González*, 103.
33 Uribe, *Antígona González*, 11.
34 Han, *Human Acts*, 203.
35 Hartman, *Lose Your Mother*, 6.
36 Han, *Human Acts*, 59.
37 Smith, *Don't Call Us Dead*, 16.
38 Latour, *Down to Earth*, 1.
39 Parenti, *Tropic of Chaos*, 11.
40 Khalifa, *Death Is Hard Work*, 149.
41 Khalifa, *Death Is Hard Work*, 149.
42 Khalifa, *Death Is Hard Work*, 150.
43 Tsing, *Mushroom at the End of the World*, 2.
44 Tsing, *Mushroom at the End of the World*, 254.

CONCLUSION

Parts of this conclusion borrow from "Asian American Literature in the Twenty-First Century," published in the *Massachusetts Review* 59, no. 4 (December 2018): 770–73.

1 G. Boggs and Kurashige, *Next American Revolution*, 36.

2 G. Boggs and Kurashige, *Next American Revolution*, 72.

3 Trexler, *Anthropocene Fictions*, 122.

4 Quoted in Hoberek, *Considering Watchmen*, 133–34. Hoberek points out that this statement highlights the ways in which economic deregulation occurred alongside the idealizing of families (and in particular heterosexual marriage) and law and order. These moves sought to demonize other ways of thinking about community or collectivity.

5 Grace is an accomplished scholar and psychologist, and her published words are easy to find. See, for instance, G. Kim and Shah, "When Perceptions Are Fragile."

6 Bulosan, *America Is in the Heart*, 188.

7 Cha, *Dictee*, 80.

8 Solmaz Sharif, "The Master's House," *Poetry Foundation*, April 2018, https://www.poetryfoundation.org/poetrymagazine/poems/146216/the-masters -house.

9 Che, *Split*, 44.

10 Asghar, *If They Come*, 3.

11 C. Chen, *When I Grow Up*, 61.

12 Choi, *Soft Science*, 33.

13 Franny Choi, "How to Let Go of the World," PEN Poetry Series, PEN America, October 3, 2019, https://pen.org/how-to-let-go-of-the-world/.

14 This last paragraph is inspired by the end of Jeff Chang's *Can't Stop Won't Stop: A History of the Hip-Hop Generation*, which describes a similar scene of popular protest in Los Angeles. Chang writes, "When they arrived in front of the State Building, these daughters and sons of the revolution—to whom so much had been given, from whom so much had been stolen—stopped and turned to face the offices above" (465).

BIBLIOGRAPHY

Ahmed, Sara. *The Promise of Happiness*. Durham, NC: Duke University Press, 2010.

Alaimo, Stacy. *Exposed: Environmental Politics and Pleasures in Posthuman Times*. Minneapolis: University of Minnesota Press, 2016.

Ali, Agha Shahid. *The Veiled Suite: The Collected Poems*. New York: Norton, 2009.

Aronoff, Kate, Alyssa Battistoni, Daniel Aldana Cohen, and Thea Riofrancos. *A Planet to Win: Why We Need a Green New Deal*. New York: Verso, 2019.

Asghar, Fatimah. *If They Come for Us*. New York: One World, 2018.

Attridge, Derek. *Poetic Rhythm: An Introduction*. Cambridge: Cambridge University Press, 1995.

Bahng, Aimee. *Migrant Futures: Decolonizing Speculation in Financial Times*. Durham, NC: Duke University Press, 2018.

Baucom, Ian. "The Human Shore: Postcolonial Studies in an Age of Natural Science." *History of the Present* 2, no. 1 (Spring 2012): 1–23.

Benjamin, Walter. *The Arcades Project*. Translated by Howard Eiland and Kevin McLaughlin. Cambridge, MA: Harvard University Press, 1999.

Bennett, Jane. *Influx and Efflux: Writing Up with Walt Whitman*. Durham, NC: Duke University Press, 2020.

Bennett, Jane. *Vibrant Matter: A Political Ecology of Things*. Durham, NC: Duke University Press, 2010.

Berlant, Lauren. "Big Man." *Social Text Online*, January 19, 2017. https://socialtextjournal.org/big-man/.

Berlant, Lauren. "Genre Flailing." *Capacious: Journal for Emerging Affect Inquiry* 1, no. 2 (2018): 156–62.

Bernes, Jasper. *The Work of Art in the Age of Deindustrialization*. Stanford, CA: Stanford University Press, 2017.

Bishop, Elizabeth. "Roosters." In *The Complete Poems, 1927–1979*, 35–39. New York: Farrar, Straus and Giroux, 1983. Available at https://www.poetryfoundation.org/poems/48289/roosters.

Boeke, Kees. *Cosmic View: The Universe in 40 Jumps*. New York: John Day, 1957.

Boggs, Grace Lee. *Living for Change: An Autobiography*. Minneapolis: University of Minnesota Press, 1998.

Boggs, Grace Lee, and Scott Kurashige. *The Next American Revolution: Sustainable Activism for the Twenty-First Century*. Berkeley: University of California Press, 2012.

Boggs, James, Grace Lee Boggs, Lyman Paine, and Freddy Paine. *Conversations in Maine*. 2nd ed. Minneapolis: University of Minnesota Press, 2018.

Bowie, David. *Next Day*. London: ISO Records, 2013.

Bowie, David, and Freddie Mercury. "Under Pressure." In Queen, *Hot Space*. London: EMI Records 1981.

Brouillette, Sarah. "Post-colonial Authorship Revisited." In *Bourdieu and Postcolonial Studies*, edited by Raphael Dalleo, 80–101. Liverpool: Liverpool University Press, 2016.

Bulosan, Carlos. *America Is in the Heart*. 1946. Seattle: University of Washington Press, 2015.

Cacho, Lisa Marie. *Social Death: Racialized Rightlessness and the Criminalization of the Unprotected*. New York: New York University Press, 2012.

Cardozo, Karen, and Banu Subramaniam. "Assembling Asian/American Naturecultures: Orientalism and Invited Invasions." *Journal of Asian American Studies* 16, no. 1 (February 2013): 1–23.

Cha, Theresa Hak Kyung. *Dictee*. San Francisco: Tanam Press, 1982.

Chakrabarty, Dipesh. "The Climate of History: Four Theses." *Critical Inquiry* 35, no. 2 (Winter 2009): 197–222.

Chakrabarty, Dipesh. "Postcolonial Studies and the Challenge of Climate Change." *New Literary History* 43, no. 1 (Winter 2012): 1–18.

Chang, Jeff. *Can't Stop Won't Stop: A History of the Hip-Hop Generation*. New York: St. Martin's Press, 2005.

Che, Cathy Linh. *Split*. Farmington, ME: Alice James Books, 2014.

Chen, Chen. *When I Grow Up I Want to Be a List of Further Possibilities*. Rochester, NY: BOA Editions, 2017.

Chen, Mel. *Animacies: Biopolitics, Racial Mattering, and Queer Affect*. Durham, NC: Duke University Press, 2012.

Chiang, Ted. *The Lifecycle of Software Objects*. Burton, MI: Subterranean Press, 2010.

Choi, Franny. *Soft Science*. Farmington, ME: Alice James Books, 2019.

Chu, Seo-Young. *Do Metaphors Dream of Literal Sleep? A Science-Fictional Theory of Representation*. Cambridge, MA: Harvard University Press, 2010.

Chuh, Kandice. *The Difference Aesthetics Makes: On the Humanities "After Man."* Durham, NC: Duke University Press, 2019.

Chun, Wendy Hui Kyong. "On Hypo-real Models or Global Climate Change: A Challenge for the Humanities." *Critical Inquiry* 41, no. 3 (Spring 2015): 675–703.

Clark, Timothy. *Ecocriticism on the Edge: The Anthropocene as a Threshold Concept*. London: Bloomsbury, 2015.

Clifton, Lucille. "Won't You Celebrate with Me." In *Book of Light*. Port Townsend, WA: Copper Canyon, 1993. 25–28. Available at https://www.poetryfoundation.org/poems/50974/wont-you-celebrate-with-me.

Coetzee, J. M. *Elizabeth Costello*. New York: Penguin, 2003.

Cohen, Stanley. *States of Denial: Knowing about Atrocities and Suffering*. Cambridge, UK: Polity, 2001.

Cole, Teju. *Open City*. New York: Random House, 2011.

Coole, Diana, and Samantha Frost. "Introducing the New Materialisms." In *New Materialisms: Ontology, Agency, and Politics*, edited by Diana Coole and Samantha Frost, 1–43. Durham, NC: Duke University Press, 2010.

Cooper, Bradley, dir. *A Star Is Born*. Los Angeles: Warner Brothers, 2018.

Culler, Jonathan. *Theory of the Lyric*. Cambridge, MA: Harvard University Press, 2015.

Dimaline, Cherie. *The Marrow Thieves*. Toronto: DCB, 2017.

Dimock, Wai Chee. "*Gilgamesh's* Planetary Turns." In *The Planetary Turn: Relationality and Geoaesthetics in the Twenty-First Century*, edited by Amy Elias and Christian Moraru, 125–42. Evanston, IL: Northwestern University Press, 2015.

Dougherty, Michael, dir. *Godzilla: King of the Monsters*. Los Angeles: Warner Brothers, 2019.

Eames, Charles, and Ray Eames, dirs. *Powers of Ten*. Los Angeles: IBM and Offices of Charles and Ray Eames, 1977.

Edelman, Lee. *No Future: Queer Future and the Death Drive*. Durham, NC: Duke University Press, 2004.

El Akkad, Omar. *American War*. New York: Knopf, 2017.

Epstein, Andrew. *Attention Equals Life: The Pursuit of the Everyday in Contemporary Poetry and Culture*. New York: Oxford University Press, 2016.

Fagan, Jenni. *The Sunlight Pilgrims*. London: Hogarth, 2016.

Farrier, David. *Anthropocene Poetics: Deep Time, Sacrifice Zones, and Extinction*. Minneapolis: University of Minnesota Press, 2019.

Fisher, Mark. *Capitalist Realism: Is There No Alternative?* London: Zero Books, 2009.

Forster, E. M. *Aspects of the Novel*. New York: Harcourt, 1927.

Foucault, Michel. *The History of Sexuality*. Vol. 1, *An Introduction*. Translated by Robert Hurley. New York: Vintage, 1990.

Fukuyama, Francis. "The End of History?" *National Interest* 16 (Summer 1989): 3–18.

Ghosh, Amitav. *The Great Derangement: Climate Change and the Unthinkable*. Chicago: University of Chicago Press, 2016.

Ghosh, Amitav. *Gun Island*. New York: Farrar, Straus and Giroux, 2019.

Gilroy, Paul. *Postcolonial Melancholia*. New York: Columbia University Press, 2005.

Giraud, Eva Haifa. *What Comes after Entanglement? Activism, Anthropocentrism, and an Ethics of Exclusion*. Durham, NC: Duke University Press, 2019.

Glavey, Brain. "Having a Coke with You Is Even More Fun than Ideology Critique." *PMLA* 134, no. 5 (October 2019): 996–1011.

Gore, Al. *An Inconvenient Truth*. Los Angeles: Paramount, 2006.

Halberstam, Jack. "The Wild Beyond: With and for the Undercommons." In Harney and Moten, *The Undercommons*, 2–13.

Hallemeier, Katherine. "Literary Cosmopolitanism in Teju Cole's *Every Day Is for the Thief* and *Open City*." *Ariel: A Review of International English Literature* 44, nos. 2–3 (April–July 2013): 239–50.

Han Kang. *Human Acts*. Translated by Deborah Smith. London: Hogarth, 2016.

Han Kang. *The White Book*. Translated by Deborah Smith. London: Hogarth, 2016.

Han Kang. *The Vegetarian*. Translated by Deborah Smith. London: Hogarth, 2015.

Hansen, James, Makiko Sato, and Reto Reudy. "Perception of Climate Change." *Proceedings of the National Academy of Sciences* 109, no. 37 (September 2012): E2415–E2423. http://www.pnas.org/cgi/doi/10.1073/pnas.1205276109.

Haraway, Donna. *Staying with the Trouble: Making Kin in the Chthulucene*. Durham, NC: Duke University Press, 2016.

Harney, Stefano, and Fred Moten. *The Undercommons: Fugitive Planning and Black Study*. New York: Minor Compositions, 2013.

Harris, Daniel. "Charles David Keeling and the Story of Atmospheric CO_2 Measurements." *Analytical Chemistry* 82, no. 19 (October 2010): 7865–70.

Hartman, Saidiya. *Lose Your Mother: A Journey Along the Atlantic Slave Route*. New York: Farrar, Straus and Giroux, 2007.

Harvey, David. *A Brief History of Neoliberalism*. London: Oxford University Press, 2005.

Hoberek, Andrew. *Considering the Watchmen: Poetics, Property, and Politics*. New Brunswick, NJ: Rutgers University Press, 2014.

Hong, Cathy Park. *Minor Feelings: An Asian American Reckoning*. New York: One World, 2020.

Honig, Bonnie. *Antigone Interrupted*. Cambridge: Cambridge University Press, 2013.

Houser, Heather. *Ecosickness in Contemporary U.S. Fiction: Environment and Affect*. New York: Columbia University Press, 2014.

Houser, Heather. *Infowhelm: Environmental Art and Literature in an Age of Data*. New York: Columbia University Press, 2020.

Hungerford, Amy. "On the Period Formerly Known as Contemporary." *American Literary History* 20, no. 1–2 (Spring–Summer 2008): 410–19.

Hunter, Megan. *The End We Start From*. New York: Grove, 2017.

Hunter, Walt. *Forms of the World: Contemporary Poetry and the Making of Globalization*. New York: Fordham University Press, 2019.

Hyde, Emily, and Sarah Wasserman. "The Contemporary." *Literature Compass* 14, no. 9 (September 2017): e12411.

Intergovernmental Panel on Climate Change (IPCC). *Fifth Assessment Report* (AR5), 2015. https://.ipcc.ch/report/ar5/syr.

Ishiguro, Kazuo. *Never Let Me Go*. New York: Vintage, 2005.

Jackson, Virginia. "Who Reads Poetry?" *PMLA* 123, no. 1 (January 2008): 181–87.

Jackson, Virginia, and Yopie Prins, eds. "General Introduction." In *The Lyric Theory Reader: A Critical Introduction*. Baltimore: Johns Hopkins University Press, 2014. 1–16.

Jackson, Zakiyyah Iman. *Becoming Human: Matter and Meaning in an Antiblack World*. New York: New York University Press, 2020.

Javadizadeh, Kamran. "The Atlantic Ocean Breaking on Our Heads: Claudia Rankine, Robert Lowell, and the Whiteness of the Lyric Subject." *PMLA* 134, no. 3 (May 2019): 475–90.

Jemisin, N. K. *The Stone Sky*. New York: Orbit Books, 2017.

Johnson, W. R. *The Idea of Lyric: Lyric Modes in Ancient and Modern Poetry*. Berkeley: University of California Press, 1982.

Johns-Putra, Adeline. *Climate Change and the Contemporary Novel*. Cambridge: Cambridge University Press, 2019.

Kaba, Mariame. *We Do This 'Til We Free Us*. Chicago: Haymarket Books, 2021.

Kaminsky, Ilya. *Deaf Republic*. Minneapolis: Graywolf, 2019.

Kapadia, Ronak. *Insurgent Aesthetics: Security and the Queer Life of the Forever War*. Durham, NC: Duke University Press, 2019.

Keller, Lynn. *Recomposing Ecopoetics: North American Poetry of the Self-Conscious Anthropocene*. Charlottesville: University of Virginia Press, 2017.

Khalifa, Khaled. *Death Is Hard Work*. Translated by Leri Price. New York: Farrar, Straus and Giroux, 2016.

Kim, Grace S., and Tanvi Shah. "When Perceptions Are Fragile but Also Enduring: An Asian American Reflection on COVID-19." *Journal of Humanistic Psychology* 60, no. 5 (September 2020): 1–7.

Kim, Jodi. *Ends of Empire: Asian American Critique and the Cold War*. Minneapolis: University of Minnesota Press, 2010.

Kim, Ju Yon. *Racial Mundane: Asian American Performance and the Embodied Everyday*. New York: New York University Press, 2015.

Kolbert, Elizabeth. *Field Notes from a Catastrophe: Man, Nature, and Climate Change*. New York: Bloomsbury, 2006.

Kolbert, Elizabeth. *The Sixth Extinction: An Unnatural History*. New York: Picador, 2014.

Kornbluh, Anna. "Climate Realism, Capitalist and Otherwise." *Mediations* 33, nos. 1–2 (Fall 2019–Spring 2020): 99–118.

Kornbluh, Anna. *The Order of Forms: Realism, Formalism, and Social Space*. Chicago: University of Chicago Press, 2019.

La Berge, Leigh Clare, and Alison Shonkwiler, eds. *Reading Capitalist Realism*. Iowa City: University of Iowa Press, 2014.

Latour, Bruno. *Down to Earth: Politics in the New Climate Regime*. London: Polity, 2018.

Latour, Bruno. "Networks, Societies, Spheres: Reflections of an Actor-Network Theorist." *International Journal of Communication* 5 (2011): 796–810.

Lee, Grace, dir. *American Revolutionary: The Evolution of Grace Lee Boggs*. Los Angeles: LeeLee Films, 2013.

Lee, Li-Young. *The City in Which I Love You*. Rochester, NY: BOA Editions, 1990.

Lefebvre, Henri. *The Critique of the Everyday*. Vol. 1. Translated by John Moore. London: Verso, 1991.

LeMenager, Stephanie. *Living Oil: Petroleum Culture in the American Century*. Oxford: Oxford University Press, 2014.

Lerner, Ben. *The Hatred of Poetry*. New York: Farrar, Straus and Giroux, 2016.

Levine, Caroline. *Forms: Whole, Rhythm, Hierarchy, Network*. Princeton, NJ: Princeton University Press, 2015.

Limón, Ada. *Bright Dead Things*. Minneapolis: Milkweed Editions, 2015.

Limón, Ada. *The Carrying*. Minneapolis: Milkweed Editions, 2018.

Long Soldier, Layli. *Whereas*. Minneapolis: Graywolf, 2017.

Lowe, Lisa. *The Intimacies of Four Continents*. Durham, NC: Duke University Press, 2015.

Lukács, Georg. *The Theory of the Novel*. Translated by Anna Bostock. Cambridge, MA: MIT Press, 1996.

Mann, Charles C. *1493: Uncovering the New World Columbus Created*. New York: Vintage, 2011.

Mao, Sally Wen. *Oculus*. Minneapolis: Graywolf, 2019.

Marez, Curtis. *Farm Worker Futurism: Speculative Technologies of Resistance*. Minneapolis: University of Minnesota Press, 2016.

Marshall, Kate. "What Are the Novels of the Anthropocene? American Fiction in Geological Time." *American Literary History* 27, no. 3 (Fall 2015): 523–38.

Mayer, Bernadette. *Midwinter Day*. New York: New Directions, 1982.

Mazzucchelli, David. *Asterios Polyp*. New York: Pantheon Books, 2009.

Mbembe, Achille. "Necropolitics." Translated by Libby Meintjes. *Public Culture* 15, no. 1 (Winter 2003): 11–40.

McClellan, George B. *The Civil War Papers of George B. McClellan: Selected Correspondences, 1860–1865*. Edited by Stephen Sears. New York: Ticknor and Fields, 1989.

Mehnert, Antonia. *Climate Change Fictions: Representations of Global Warming in American Literature*. New York: Palgrave Macmillan, 2016.

Menely, Tobias, and Jesse Oak Taylor, eds. *Anthropocene Reading: Literary History in Geological Times*. University Park: Pennsylvania State University Press, 2017.

Morton, Timothy. *Hyperobjects: Philosophy and Ecology after the End of the World*. Minneapolis: University of Minnesota Press, 2013.

Nevins, Allan. *The Emergence of Lincoln, Volume II: Prologue to the Civil War, 1859–1861*. New York: Charles Scribner's Sons, 1950.

Nezhukumatathil, Aimee. *Oceanic*. Port Townsend, WA: Copper Canyon, 2018.

Ngai, Sianne. *Our Aesthetic Categories: Zany, Cute, Interesting*. Cambridge, MA: Harvard University Press, 2012.

Nguyen, Hoa. *Red Juice: Poems, 1998–2008*. Seattle: Wave, 2014.

Nguyen, Viet Thanh. *Nothing Ever Dies: Vietnam and the Memory of War*. Cambridge, MA: Harvard University Press, 2016.

Nishime, LeiLani, and Kim D. Hester Williams. "Introduction: Why Racial Ecologies?" In *Racial Ecologies*, edited by LeiLani Nishime and Kim D. Hester Williams, 3–18. Seattle: University of Washington Press, 2018.

Nixon, Rob. *Slow Violence and the Environmentalism of the Poor*. Cambridge, MA: Harvard University Press, 2011.

Norgaard, Kari. *Living in Denial: Climate Change, Emotions, and Everyday Life*. Cambridge, MA: MIT Press, 2011.

Offill, Jenny. *Weather*. New York: Knopf, 2020.

O'Hara, Frank. *The Collected Poems of Frank O'Hara*. Edited by Donald Allen. Berkeley: University of California Press, 1995.

O'Hara, Frank. *Lunch Poems.* San Francisco: City Lights Books, 1964.

Oreskes, Naomi, and Timothy Conway. *Merchants of Doubt: How a Handful of Scientists Obscured the Truth on Issues from Tobacco Smoke to Global Warming.* New York: Bloomsbury, 2011.

Overall, Christine. *Why Have Children? The Ethical Debate.* Cambridge, MA: MIT Press, 2012.

Ozeki, Ruth. *A Tale for the Time Being.* New York: Viking, 2013.

Parenti, Christian. *The Tropic of Chaos: Climate Change and the New Geography of Violence.* New York: Nation Books/Perseus, 2011.

Park, Josephine. *Apparitions of Asia: Modernist Form and Asian American Poetics.* New York: Oxford University Press, 2008.

Parker, Morgan. *Magical Negro.* Portland, OR: Tin House, 2019.

Parker, Morgan. *There Are More Beautiful Things than Beyoncé.* Portland, OR: Tin House, 2017.

Perez, Craig Santos. *Habitat Threshold.* Oakland, CA: Omnidawn, 2020.

Pérez, Jane, and Wendell Aycock. *Climate and Literature: Reflections of Environment.* Lubbock: Texas Tech University Press, 1995.

Philip, M. NourbeSe. *Zong!* Middletown, CT: Wesleyan University Press, 2008.

Pico, Tommy. *Feed.* Portland, OR: Tin House, 2019.

Pico, Tommy. *IRL.* Minneapolis: Birds, 2016.

Pico, Tommy. *Junk.* Portland, OR: Tin House, 2018.

Pico, Tommy. *Nature Poem.* Portland, OR: Tin House, 2017.

Pinsky, Robert. *The Sounds of Poetry: A Brief Guide.* New York: Farrar, Straus and Giroux, 1998.

Pollan, Michael. *The Omnivore's Dilemma: A Natural History of Four Meals.* New York: Penguin, 2006.

Posmentier, Sonya. *Cultivation and Catastrophe: The Lyric Ecology of Modern Black Literature.* Baltimore: Johns Hopkins University Press, 2017.

Powers, Richard. *The Overstory.* New York: Norton, 2018.

Primark, Richard. *Walden Warming: Climate Change Comes to Thoreau's Woods.* Chicago: University of Chicago Press, 2016.

Puar, Jasbir. *The Right to Maim: Debility, Capacity, Disability.* Durham, NC: Duke University Press, 2017.

Purdy, Jedediah. *After Nature: A Politics of the Anthropocene.* Cambridge, MA: Harvard University Press, 2015.

Quilligan, Maureen. *The Language of Allegory: Defining the Genre.* Ithaca, NY: Cornell University Press, 1979.

Ramazani, Jahan. *Poetry and Its Others: News, Prayer, Song, and the Dialogues of Genres.* Chicago: University of Chicago Press, 2014.

Rancière, Jacques. *The Politics of Aesthetics: The Distribution of the Sensible.* Translated by Gabriel Rockhill. London: Continuum, 2004.

Rankine, Claudia. *Citizen: An American Lyric.* Minneapolis: Graywolf, 2014.

Rankine, Claudia. *Don't Let Me Be Lonely: An American Lyric.* Minneapolis: Graywolf, 2004.

Ray, Sarah Jaquette. *The Ecological Other: Environmental Exclusion in American Culture*. Tucson: University of Arizona Press, 2013.

Ray, Sarah Jaquette. *A Field Guide to Climate Anxiety: How to Keep Your Cool on a Warming Planet*. Berkeley: University of California Press, 2020.

Rhee, Margaret. *Love, Robot*. Brooklyn, NY: operating system print, 2017.

Rich, Nathaniel. *Losing Earth: A Recent History*. New York: Farrar, Straus and Giroux, 2019.

Roberson, Ed. *To See the Earth before the End of the World*. Middletown, CT: Wesleyan University Press, 2010.

Robinson, Kim Stanley. *Forty Signs of Rain*. New York: Bantam, 2004.

Robinson, Kim Stanley. *New York 2140*. New York: Orbit, 2017.

Ronda, Margaret. *Remainders: American Poetry at Nature's End*. Stanford, CA: Stanford University Press, 2018.

Rush, Elizabeth. *Rising: Dispatches from the New American Shore*. Minneapolis: Milkweed Editions, 2018.

Sandburg, Carl. *Abraham Lincoln: The War Years III*. New York: Charles Scribner's Sons, 1946.

Sanderson, Benjamin, and Rosie Fisher. "A Fiery Wake-Up Call for Climate Science." *Nature Climate Change* 10 (March 2020): 175–77.

Saranillio, Dean Itsuji. *Unsustainable Empire: Alternative Histories of Hawai'i Statehood*. Durham, NC: Duke University Press, 2018.

Saunders, George. *Lincoln in the Bardo*. New York: Random House, 2017.

Schneider-Mayerson, Matthew. "The Influence of Climate Fiction: An Empirical Survey of Readers." *Environmental Humanities* 10, no. 2 (November 2018): 473–500.

Schnepf, J. D. "Domestic Aerial Photography in the Era of Drone Warfare." *Modern Fiction Studies* 63, no. 2 (Summer 2017): 270–87.

Scranton, Roy. *Learning to Die in the Anthropocene: Reflections on the End of Civilization*. San Francisco: City Lights, 2015.

Scranton, Roy. *We're Doomed. Now What? Essays on War and Climate*. New York: Soho, 2018.

Seymour, Nicole. *Bad Environmentalism: Irony and Irreverence in the Ecological Age*. Minneapolis: University of Minnesota Press, 2018.

Sharif, Solmaz. *Look*. Minneapolis: Graywolf, 2016.

Sharpe, Christina. *In the Wake: On Blackness and Being*. Durham, NC: Duke University Press, 2016.

Shaughnessy, Brenda. *The Octopus Museum*. New York: Knopf, 2019.

Shotwell, Alexis. *Against Purity: Living Ethically in Compromised Times*. Minneapolis: University of Minnesota Press, 2012.

Simpson, Caroline Chung. *An Absent Presence: Japanese Americans in Postwar American Culture, 1945–1960*. Durham, NC: Duke University Press, 2002.

Singh, Julietta. *Unthinking Mastery: Dehumanism and Decolonial Entanglements*. Durham, NC: Duke University Press, 2018.

Smil, Vaclav. *Enriching the Earth: Fritz Haber, Carl Bosch, and the Transformation of World Food Production*. Cambridge, MA: MIT Press, 2001.

Smith, Danez. *Don't Call Us Dead.* Minneapolis: Graywolf, 2017.

Sohn, Stephen. *Racial Asymmetries: Asian American Fictional Worlds.* New York: New York University Press, 2014.

Sone, Monica. *Nisei Daughter.* 1953. Seattle: University of Washington Press, 1979.

Song, Min Hyoung. *The Children of 1965: On Writing, and Not Writing, as an Asian American.* Durham, NC: Duke University Press, 2013.

Song, Min Hyoung. "The New Materialism and Neoliberalism." In *Neoliberalism and Contemporary Literary Culture,* edited by Mitchum Huehls and Rachel Greenwald Smith, 52–69. Baltimore: Johns Hopkins University Press, 2017.

Stevens, Wallace. *Collected Poems and Poetry.* New York: Library of America, 1997.

Stewart, Kathleen. "Afterword: Worldling Refrains." In *The Affect Reader,* edited by Melissa Gregg and Gregory Seigworth, 339–53. Durham, NC: Duke University Press, 2010.

Streeby, Shelley. *Imagining the Future of Climate Change: World-Making through Science Fiction and Activism.* Berkeley: University of California Press, 2018.

Sturgess, John, dir. *Bad Day at Black Rock.* Los Angeles: MGM, 1955.

Sturken, Marita. "Absent Images of Memory: Remembering and Reenacting the Japanese Internment." *Positions* 5, no. 3 (Winter 1997): 687–707.

Sudbanthad, Pitchaya. *Bangkok Wakes to Rain.* New York: Riverhead Books, 2019.

Sue, Derald Wing, Christina M. Capodilupo, Gina C. Torino, Jennifer M. Bucceri, Aisha M. B. Holder, Kevin L. Nadal, and Marta Esquilin. "Racial Microaggressions in Everyday Life: Implications for Clinical Practice." *American Psychologist* 62, no. 4 (May–June 2007): 271–86.

Szasz, Eva, dir. *Cosmic Zoom.* Ottawa: National Film Board of Canada, 1968.

Sze, Julie. *Environmental Justice in a Moment of Danger.* Berkeley: University of California Press, 2002.

Tagg, Larry. *The Unpopular Mr. Lincoln: The Story of America's Most Reviled President.* New York: Savas Beatie, 2009.

Teskey, George. *Allegory and Violence.* Ithaca, NY: Cornell University Press, 1996.

Thoreau, Henry David. *Walden.* Edited by Jeffrey S. Cramer. New Haven, CT: Yale University Press, 2006.

Trexler, Adam. *Anthropocene Fictions: The Novel in a Time of Climate Change.* Charlottesville: University of Virginia Press, 2015.

Tsing, Anna Lowenhaupt. *The Mushroom at the End of the World: On the Possibility of Life in Capitalist Ruins.* Princeton, NJ: Princeton University Press, 2015.

Tsing, Anna Lowenhaupt, Heather Anne Swanson, Elaine Gan, and Nils Budandt, eds. *Arts of Living on a Damaged Planet: Ghosts and Monsters of the Anthropocene.* Minneapolis: University of Minnesota Press, 2017.

Uribe, Sara. *Antígona González.* Translated by John Pleucker. Los Angeles: Les Figues, 2016.

U.S. Global Change Research Program. *Impacts, Risks, and Adaptations in the United States: Fourth National Climate Assessment.* Vol. 2. Washington, DC: U.S. Global Change Research Program, 2018.

VanderMeer, Jeff. *Acceptance.* New York: Farrar, Straus and Giroux, 2014.

Vermeulen, Pieter. "Flights of Memory: Teju Cole's *Open City* and the Limits of Aesthetic Cosmopolitanism." *Journal of Modern Literature* 37, no. 1 (Fall 2013): 40–57.

Walker, Karen Thompson. *The Age of Miracles*. New York: Random House, 2012.

Wallace-Wells, David. *The Uninhabitable Earth: Life after Warming*. New York: Tim Duggan Books, 2019.

Wang, Dorothy. *Thinking Its Presence: Form, Race, and Subjectivity in Contemporary Asian American Poetry*. Stanford, CA: Stanford University Press, 2014.

Ward, David. "The Space of Poetry: Inhabiting Form in the Ghazal." *University of Toronto Quarterly* 82, no. 1 (Winter 2013): 62–71.

Ward, Jesmyn. *Salvage the Bones*. New York: Bloomsbury, 2011.

Watkins, Claire Vaye. *Gold Fame Citrus*. New York: Riverhead Books, 2015.

Weart, Spencer. *The Discovery of Global Warming*. Cambridge, MA: Harvard University Press, 2003.

Weheliye, Alexander. *Habeas Viscus: Racializing Assemblages, Biopolitics, and Black Feminist Theories of the Human*. Durham, NC: Duke University Press, 2014.

Weisman, Alan. *Countdown: Our Last, Best Hope for a Future on Earth*. New York: Little, Brown, 2013.

Weisman, Alan. *The World without Us*. New York: Picador, 2008.

White, Gillian. *Lyric Shame: The "Lyric" Subject of Contemporary American Poetry*. Cambridge, MA: Harvard University Press, 2014.

Woods, Derek. "Epistemic Things in Charles and Ray Eames's *Powers of Ten*." In *Scale in Literature and Culture*, edited by Michael Tavel Clarke and David Wittenberg, 61–92. Basingstoke, UK: Palgrave Macmillan, 2017.

Wynes, Seth, and Kimberly Nicholas. "The Climate Mitigation Gap: Education and Government Recommendations Miss the Most Effective Individual Actions." *Environmental Research Letters* 12 (July 2017). https://iopscience.iop.org/article/10.1088/1748-9326/aa7541/pdf.

Wynter, Sylvia. "Unsettling the Coloniality of Being/Power/Truth/Freedom: Towards the Human, after Man, Its Overrepresentation—an Argument." *CR: The New Centennial Review* 3, no. 3 (Fall 2003): 257–337.

Yamamoto, Hisaye. *Seventeen Syllables and Other Stories*. New Brunswick, NJ: Rutgers University Press, 2001.

Yamamoto, Traise. *Masking Selves, Making Subjects: Japanese American Women, Identity, and the Body*. Berkeley: University of California Press, 1999.

Yamashita, Karen Tei. *Through the Arc of the Rain Forest*. Minneapolis: Coffee House, 1990.

Ybarra, Priscilla Solis. *Writing the Good Life: Mexican American Literature and the Environment*. Tucson: University of Arizona Press, 2016.

Yusoff, Kathryn. *A Billion Black Anthropocenes or None*. Minneapolis: University of Minnesota Press, 2018.

INDEX